Social Conflicts and Collective Identities

Social Conflicts and Collective Identities

Edited by
Patrick G. Coy and Lynne M. Woehrle

Associate Editors
Bruce W. Dayton, Timothy Hedeen,
Michael W. Hovey, and Anna Snyder

ROWMAN & LITTLEFIELD PUBLISHERS, INC.
Lanham • Boulder • New York • Oxford

ROWMAN & LITTLEFIELD PUBLISHERS, INC.

Published in the United States of America
by Rowman & Littlefield Publishers, Inc.
4720 Boston Way, Lanham, Maryland 20706
http://www.rowmanlittlefield.com

12 Hid's Copse Road, Cumnor Hill, Oxford OX2 9JJ, England

British Library Cataloguing in Publication Information Available

Library of Congress Cataloging-in-Publication Data

Social conflicts and collective identities / edited by Patrick G. Coy and Lynne M. Woehrle.
    p. cm.
  Includes bibliographical references and index.
  ISBN 0-7425-0050-0 (alk. paper) — ISBN 0-7425-0051-9 (pbk. : alk. paper)
    1. Social conflict—Case studies. 2. Group identity—Case studies. I. Coy, Patrick G.
  II. Woehrle, Lynne M., 1965-

HM1121 .S63 2000
303.6—dc21

                                                00-031108

Printed in the United States of America

♾™ The paper used in this publication meets the minimum requirements of American
National Standard for Information Sciences—Permanence of Paper for Printed Library
Materials, ANSI/NISO Z39.48-1992.

Dedicated to Dr. Louis Kriesberg
for all the lessons taught,
dissertations read,
and young scholars you taught how to fly.
Your contributions to
peacemaking are beyond measure.
Thank you.

Contents

Part Two: Constructing Identities and Resolving Conflicts

Chapter One

Introduction

Collective Identities and the Development of Conflict Analysis

Lynne M. Woehrle and Patrick G. Coy

Conflicts are potentially constructive and destructive social phenomenon. Because of their complexities most conflicts are marked by a combination of constructive and destructive effects, located somewhere along a continuum. Social scientists study conflict at many levels, including interpersonal interactions, group competition, and wars between states. Whether viewed as positive or negative, conflict is generally seen as an expected and functional outcome in a social system. Where there are human beings organized in social structures, there will be conflict.[1]

Conflict has too often been labeled as a negative social function due to its perceived destructive and chaotic nature. For Parsonian theorists in particular, conflict was thought to be the state of societies which do not function properly. It was seen as a social dysfunction to be avoided in achieving a harmonious society. And in Elton Mayo's school of industrial sociology, avoiding conflict was characteristic of a healthy society since conflict was viewed as a disease.[2] Typically, various societal structures were used to reduce conflict, introduce strict systems of norms and expectations, limit individual creativity and communication, strive for homogeneity and severely punish social deviance.[3]

The construction of conflict as negative and to be avoided broke with some earlier conflict theorists who saw conflict as a necessary function of social and political change. In sociology, for example, members of the Chicago school argued that conflict was an integral part of addressing social inequalities. Marx built his social analysis around the necessary and potentially positive aspects of conflict between socio-economic classes. In political science, wars (a type of conflict) were often regarded as important components in the process of state-building and the development of a national identity.

Lewis Coser challenged theorists to inspect what roles conflict plays in society by building on George Simmel's argument that conflict is part of social organization and the socialization process:

> No group can be entirely harmonious, for it would then be devoid of process and structure. Groups require disharmony as well as harmony, dissociation as well as association; and conflicts within them are by no means altogether disruptive factors. . . . On the contrary, both "positive" and "negative" factors build group relations.[4]

Simmel thus argued that conflict is not the absence of social order (that would be indifference or isolation), but rather a different kind of social order.[5] It is this idea of conflicts as potentially positive and creative that undergirds contemporary conflict theory and which partly inspires contemporary analysis of conflict resolution processes.

Conflict is not simple competition. While competition often happens impersonally, parties in conflict recognize their respective goals as incompatible. It is generally agreed that conflict requires some form of social organization. But not all social systems produce conflict in every circumstance. Conflict will not emerge in every situation of human interaction; rather a complex set of factors must be present for overt conflict to emerge. Without those factors conflicts may either be nonexistent or latent. Differences may co-exist rather harmoniously.[6]

Generally speaking, conflicts occur when parties perceive that they have incompatible goals and that the difference matters. Louis Kriesberg has identified four specific conditions that must be minimally satisfied for social conflicts to emerge.[7] First, the parties must have developed a sense of themselves as entities separate from one another. Second, one or more of the parties must have a grievance. Third, one or more of the parties must develop goals to change the other party in order to reduce the grievance. Fourth, the aggrieved party must believe that they can be successful in changing the other party. This approach is highly interactionist; people are rarely caught unawares and just "find" themselves embroiled in conflict. Rather, people create conflict as part of their search for meaning, as part of their definition of themselves and of the groups to which they belong, and to achieve what they need to survive and develop. Conflict is thus part of the construction of our social reality.[8]

Differences in culture (values and beliefs), power inequalities, resource distribution, a lack of communication and a sense of collective identity all contribute to the emergence of conflict. Moreover, the history of individual or group relations (i.e., previous conflicts or reasons for a loss of trust) can significantly influence the emergence and later escalation of conflict situations. In short, the social context must be ripe for conflicts to emerge. Above all, there must be an understanding that the goals or needs are not only different but are viewed as incompatible or in opposition, and there must be a social system that supports or encourages conflict.

In this volume, conflict dynamics are regarded as social interactions that can be analyzed and understood, providing insights into social conflict in general as well as into specific conflicts. The authors portray conflicts as actions or reactions to identifiable causes and process dynamics. These case studies analytically map the ways in which conflicts emerge, escalate and de-escalate, thus contributing to the change process. The chapters also remind us that in any conflict situation there is the potential for relatively constructive or destructive social and political change. What matters is not preventing conflicts but understanding them so they may be conducted or organized in ways that make positive contributions to the social systems and the people involved.

This book develops a base of data regarding the social processes that underlie a wide spectrum of conflict situations, paying particular attention to the processes of collective identity formation. The conflicts analyzed here range from the interpersonal to the international, and they occur within (*intra*) groups and between (*inter*) groups. Conflicts are manifest as salient group identities shift, split, and come into competition with each other. The contributors to this book treat identities as part of a critical process of social construction, largely developed through social interactions within a group as well as between groups. Groups play the role of encouraging and sometimes enforcing these social identity attachments that individuals form. The contributors identify and analyze the inner workings of collective identity processes as they relate to and support the emergence, escalation and de-escalation of conflicts.

Collective Identity

If, as Kriesberg suggests, groups must have a sense of themselves as a group in order to engage in a conflict, then conflict analysis requires understanding the means by which a collective identity is formed.[9] To create collective identity there must be a synthesis of commonalties, and members need to notice how much more they are like the other members of the group than they are like people in a different group. Sean Byrne's chapter in this book on the development of nationalism among Protestant Irish children reveals that socialization is a key process in the development of this sense of "we-ness." Collective identity formation processes are also important determinants in nation-state power politics, as the chapters by Ross Klein and Nora Femenia both demonstrate.

Klein's comparative analyses of the Cod Wars (Iceland and the United Kingdom) and the Tuna Wars (Ecuador, Peru, and the United States) clearly suggests that the work of collective identity formation is more easily accomplished by smaller states/groups. This can be attributed to a combination of factors: that in smaller groups it is easier to build a sense of homogeneity, and that the smaller group is often weaker and more embattled, thus producing a deeper sense of allegiance among its membership. This analysis is echoed in Christine Wagner's chapter on the conflict waged by community groups for control over their city's annual Memorial Day parade. Wagner shows that the perception of being disenfranchised or excluded also serves to create strong group identification. Moreover, Wagner's chapter further suggests that this holds true even in the face of clear intra-group differences. Brian Polkinghorn's study of the Environmental Protection Agency's negotiated rulemaking (reg-neg) process also highlights how important it often is for groups in a social conflict to maintain a strong collective identity throughout the conflict process. However, much more significant for the field of conflict analysis are Polkinghorn's findings that the reg-neg conflict management process seems to encourage one party (industry) to assure the collective identity of its adversary (environmental activists) so that industry representatives can focus on negotiating in only one direction and on fewer issues. This is perceived as preferable to facing a splintered and therefore less predictable opposition party or parties. Thus it becomes clear that the relative strength of a party's collective identity, and the manner in which that identity is constructed and maintained, helps shape how conflicts and their resolutions are likely to develop.

Social conflicts are framed by their disputants in particular ways to achieve specific goals. Once disputing parties have engaged in aggressive behavior, their cause is often endowed with added significance, including symbolic meaning, in an attempt to garner more commitment to it.[10] This dynamic is perceptively analyzed in Wagner's participant observation-based research, which demonstrates that identities were re-prioritized and symbolic meanings proliferated as veterans groups, peace organizations, and women's groups each contested access to the community's Memorial Day parade.

Both Femenia's chapter on the Falklands/Malvinas conflict and Klein's comparative analyses of the Cod Wars and the Tuna Wars demonstrate that states will not only appeal to but also intentionally manipulate collective identities to garner support among their domestic constituencies. A common approach, and one amply in evidence in the chapters presented here, is for governments to frame a dispute as an issue of national sovereignty or, at an even more basic level, as an issue of national honor. Doing so tends to undercut both domestic and international bases of opposition to the government's conflict escalation behaviors. Opposition is undercut on the domestic side by virtue of the fact that a particularly strong motivator of individual action is the desire to successfully claim, nurture, and defend a prized collective identity: that of "loyal member" or "patriotic citizen."

The undercutting of individual opposition to group policies or actions is frequently accomplished through both implicit and explicit pressures to conform socially and to at least go along with if not actively agree with the group's official stance or party line regarding the conflict situation. For it remains true that embracing a collective identity brings with it certain obligations to the individual members of the collectivity, including attitudes, values, and even behavioral norms. Frequently, one of those norms is clear support for the group in its conflicted interactions with other groups. This dynamic of appealing to collective identity concerns in order to mobilize constituent support for a group's actions is not exclusive to states. It also occurs among religious communities, civic groups, and social movement organizations, as the chapters by Verna Cavey on the Quakers, Celia Cook-Huffman on an urban church, and Christine Wagner on community groups and social movements each demonstrate in different ways.

Appeals to and manipulation of identity concerns are not used only to mobilize existing constituencies; they are also employed to broaden a constituency and to bring in outsiders and bystanders who then may become active in the group's cause. Richard Kendrick's participant observation study of two peace movement organizations shows that movement interests are often constructed and framed in particular ways in order to build bridges to the individual identities of potential members. For example, collective identity can be constructed around invitations to support community events or actions that reinforce a sense of common values. In this way, others may be mobilized to participate in issues and campaigns that are designed to effect social change. This is reflected as well in Wagner's study of the Memorial Day parade conflict, where the initial grievance is the realization by some community members that they were not invited to participate in the parade. Only later, as a war veterans' group protested the peace group's participation, did the conflict develop a zero-sum, competitive nature. Thus the more tightly bounded a system is believed to be, the more likely groups will perceive their goals as incompatible.[11]

As Cook-Huffman's urban church study reveals, however, the fabrication of a collective identity may come at a high price for those members whose salient identities are forced to shift to meet group norms. Thus, collective identity is actually a process of negotiation where a more narrow definition of the group is constructed out of its diverse membership. Both Cook-Huffman and Wagner suggest that sub-groups (such as women), whose concerns may vary slightly given their social situation, are expected to cooperate in minimizing intra-group conflicts in the interest of unifying the larger group effort. This is one important reason why the resolution of a primary conflict often results in the emergence of secondary conflicts that contribute to the splintering of once-cohesive groups.

For example, Cavey's study of the Quaker Separation of 1827 shows that conflicts sometimes emerge as sub-groups increase in strength and it becomes increasingly difficult to maintain a larger unified collective identity definition. As she suggests, shifts in the socio-historical context may make it difficult for group leadership to continue to construct an inclusive ideology and to quell dissension within the group. The symbolic and behavioral signifiers of group membership—and the meaning of that membership—may become contested. Even then, however, it is possible for once-unified groups to fragment and to use opposing sub-groups to create a sense of "we" and "they," thereby strengthening the independent identity of that sub-group.

Resource Issues in Identity-Based Conflicts

Most conflicts emerge and are waged for multiple, often interlocking reasons. As Klein's analysis of the Cod and Tuna Wars and Femenia's study of the Malvinas/Falklands War each indicate, it is seldom easy and frequently impossible to untangle the resource-based issues from the identity-based concerns that drive disputant behavior. Moreover, Cook-Huffman's study reveals that an identity such as "woman" or "pastor" may significantly affect the very definitions of what the material resource issues are for the group and for the individuals in3volved. While conflicts that are primarily identity-based typically include material resource issues as well, concerns related to collective identity definition or preservation are not easily perceived in conflicts that are presumed to be resource-based. Whether identity concerns are salient or not depends on a number of factors. For example, some conflict research reveals that the longer a conflict goes unresolved the more likely identity-related issues will emerge, since the conflict becomes part of disputant self-understanding and part of how they are viewed by other parties. Allowed to proceed unchecked, this dynamic is a significant contributor to identity-based conflicts becoming intractable.[12]

For example, although the Cod Wars were originally about Iceland's control of offshore cod resources, Klein's analysis shows that over time identity issues having to do with honor, pride, and national sovereignty also came to the fore. Although identity concerns may not always be as explicit and overt as concerns over material resources tend to be, they are often more powerful influences on conflict behavior because their currents run so deep in both the individual and the national grouping. This was especially true for the smaller state of Iceland, and to a lesser extent for Britain as well. The Cod Wars between Iceland and the United Kingdom occurred four times between 1952 and 1976. The first dragged on for four years, while the second manifestation lasted for three years. The final two conflicts were each of one year's duration. A group's self-awareness and collective identity is both formed and transformed through the course of a conflict, usually in an interactionist manner vis-à-vis the adversary.[13] This appears especially important for the disputing party with fewer material resources, which will often use its underdog status as a prod to mobilization and a means of collective identity transformation. Thus the small and poorer states of Iceland, Peru, Ecuador and Argentina analyzed in various chapters of this book each actively transformed their sense of self and the presentation of their national identity in conflicts with larger, richer and more powerful adversaries.

Group Differentiation and Enemy-Imaging

Groups are always in the process of reifying their collective identity and boundaries, but this is especially critical when faced by an external threat. One might think of difference and similarity as two sides of a coin. While difference within groups is seen as a problem for collective identity formation, recognizing external difference can assist in highlighting internal similarity, thereby strengthening group cohesiveness and the ability to act in a unified manner. Theorists refer to this as the formation of "in-group" and "out-group" designations.

Conflicts where identity issues are important engage disputants on deep psychocultural levels. Conflict theorists such as John Burton, who work primarily out of the human needs tradition, emphasize that identity needs are fundamental and for the most part non-negotiable. However, Kriesberg's research has emphasized the multiple identities that each disputant brings into a conflict situation and the shifting significances associated with each one.[14] At different times particular identities will be more and others less salient; in other words, some are more amenable to negotiation while others are less so. The meanings and the importance of these multiple identities are "negotiated" in social conflict; this book demonstrates that the character of that negotiation process tells us much about the character of the conflict. For example, when this negotiation process is reciprocal and relatively uncoercive it is also positive and mutually beneficial for both parties. In those circumstances, the conflict can then be characterized as constructive. However, when the parties' identity needs are actively denigrated, dismissed as illegitimate, or violently suppressed, the conflict has become destructive. Multiple examples of the latter process, drawn from a range of social conflict situations, are analyzed in the chapters by Wagner, Cook-Huffman and Gina Petonito.

Individual members of a group involved in conflict are rarely able to avoid this identity-negotiation process. Yet the individual may easily perceive this process as a threat to their sense of self and to their feelings of belonging to the group, creating insecurity for the individual members of a collective. Faced with the crisis of a conflict that threatens their sense of self, disputants will often cling to their group membership more tightly than usual. They may cultivate an even closer relationship between their individual identity and the collective identity that is closest to them and most meaningful to them.[15] This narrowing of identity definition intensifies their estrangement from the other parties in the dispute and helps images of the enemy "Other" to more easily emerge and take hold. These complex yet relatively common dynamics are delineated and analyzed in Byrne's chapter on Protestant school children in Northern Ireland. Byrne shows that the British queen became an important political and religious symbol for the Protestant school children, providing a sense of secure identity for them as they matured in a context of protracted conflict.

Ethno-nationalism serves as an instructive example of the group differentiation processes that can produce either a positive or a negative effect.[16] Positive effects include individual integration into a group and its mobilization, the stimulation and survival value of a diverse human species, and the encouragement of popular participation in governance. However, the potential negatives are also grippingly familiar. They include ethnocentrism, xenophobia, discrimination, torture, and at its worst, brutal violence such as genocide. Thus difference is used to manufacture a sense of external threat. This can heighten internal unity, quell intra-group conflicts and prepare a collectivity to engage in a conflict with another group. But it can also revitalize a sense of collective identity, such as ethnic identity in the face of socio-cultural pressure to assimilate to dominant norms.

Femenia's treatment of the Malvinas/Falklands War and Petonito's analysis of the internment of Japanese-Americans during World War II develop a fuller understanding of the complex dynamics of enemy-imaging in identity conflicts. Enemy-imaging uses stereotypes to denigrate members of the identified outgroup while aggrandizing the goodness and superiority of the members of the ingroup. Enemy-imaging effectively pushes conflicts into a spiral of escalation evidenced by a deterioration of the relationship of groups in the exchange. As evidenced by Petonito's study, it is far too easy during the heightened emotions that come with conflicts such as war to convince otherwise congenial groups that they are, in fact, a threat to each other. Thus Petonito shows that the normative "we" of the "white American" was formed on the basis of yet another construction: that of the "yellow and inscrutable Japanese-American other." Here we see that the techniques of dehumanization are critical to rationalizing acts deemed necessary for "national security." Usually such actions are justified as a struggle for justice or as a defense against the real or constructed aggression of an adversary. Examples include unwarranted declarations of war (Femenia, this volume), the internment of productive U.S. citizens of Japanese descent during World War II (Petonito, this volume), and the widespread bombing of the "enemy other," including civilians during the Persian Gulf War.[17]

Polkinghorn's chapter on the process of negotiating environmental regulations also explores an adversarial environment that is built on a perception of competing interests. Stereotyping and negative labeling of the adversary are often critical in the definition of a conflict as unsolvable. As his study points out, at times labels are applied to establish or undermine the credibility of participants. These stereotyping processes are used by adversaries to determine who is legitimately welcome at the negotiating table. As many of the chapters in this book suggest, adversaries often believe that they are more likely to achieve a favorable outcome in a conflict if they can convince their own constituency to ignore the genuine human needs of the constructed "other." One way of doing that is to frame the dispute in ways that make it easier to refuse to recognize a group as a legitimate party to the dispute.

The creation of the in-group is intricately linked to the identification of an out-group; there cannot be one without the presence of the other. When social harmony exists and resources or ideologies are not in contention, out-groups are regarded with a benign sense of matter-of-factness. People realize—even with thankfulness at times—that not everyone can or will belong to the same group. However, in times of conflict, the simultaneous existence of sameness within groups and differences between groups are each exploited to garner leverage for achieving dominance. Once a party's essential legitimacy is threatened and these escalatory dynamics are put in motion, they become entrenched and difficult to overcome. This is one reason why conflicts that engage identity concerns may become intractable.

Collective Identity in Conflict Escalation

Collective identity can function in both positive and negative ways in the processes of group differentiation discussed above. An especially instructive example of this is provided in Femenia's provocative analysis of the Malvinas/Falkland Islands war. Here the collective identity definition processes of the respective domestic populations were manipulated and "displaced" by both the British and the Argentine governments.

Femenia shows, for example, that much of the public discourse in Argentina about the status of the islands was linked to the population's need to work through and heal the deep emotional wounds occasioned by years of repressive military dictatorship and widespread use of the "disappearance" tactic. Thousands of disappearances, coupled with the long-running denial of fundamental human rights and liberties, created a gaping hole in the Argentine national psyche. What it meant to be Argentinean could no longer be taken for granted and became deeply contested; the citizen's sense of belonging to a larger national whole changed significantly and in ways over which the individual citizen had little control or influence. The Malvinas/Falklands dispute then took on symbolic meanings that were tied to these collective identity needs.

Playing on the pain that the disappearances had caused, the military junta constructed the islands dispute as a venture to find and bring home the "missing" islands. Being reunited with the Malvinas at least meant that it felt good to be Argentinean again. A sense of security returned, even if the disappeared fellow citizens did not. A similar process occurred in Britain, where the national angst over the 1956 loss of the Suez Canal had come to symbolize the end of the British Empire. Argentina's invasion of the Falklands was promptly linked to the collective identity redefinition that the Suez Crisis had earlier forced upon Great Britain, freighting the Falkland's invasion with great symbolic meaning.

The escalation of conflict by intentionally embracing collective identity does not always lead to violent and/or destructive conflict. As Wagner and Kendrick show in their respective chapters, nonviolent social change can emerge from identity-based conflicts. In Wagner's study, a social movement organization (SMO) actually provoked a conflict in the community over the annual Memorial Day parade and celebration. In order to do this, diverse members and groups within the community had to be brought together under a shared identity of being excluded from participating in the parade. The salience of this shared identity was actively nurtured and the conflict was brought to public attention and intentionally escalated in order to achieve a shift in the status quo. The SMOs studied by Kendrick, on the other hand, were operating in a period of social movement abeyance. In order to maintain their movement and raise awareness of critical social issues, they created projects that were designed to appeal to the identity needs of potential members. Thus this collection demonstrates that individual's identities can be expanded and shaped to provoke and escalate a conflict process, and that this may be ultimately negative or positive, with violent or nonviolent consequences.

Collective Identity in Conflict Resolution

The shifting saliences of particular identities and the constructed nature of collective identities shape the emergence and escalation of conflicts. Yet it is also true that these same processes open space for the de-escalation and the resolution of conflicts. The chapters in this book provide insight not only into conflict emergence, but also into the potential for conflict to create much-needed social change and for conflicts to be constructively resolved. Resolutions are defined in diverse and elastic ways by our authors. They include the dissolution of the pri-

mary group into sub-groups (Cavey), the prevalence of subordinate group independence (Klein), the downplaying of identity differences between groups
(Polkinghorn), the reification of national self-esteem (Femenia), the subordina-
tion of some interests in the pursuit of others deemed to be more important
(Cook-Huffman), and the redefinition of individual identity and organizational
identities (Wagner).

In some cases these resolutions require time and patience. Indeed, Cavey's
chapter on the Quaker Separation suggests that there are stages of resolution in
social conflicts. One of these may simply be to agree to disagree. The Quaker
experience suggests as well that historical shifts in collective identity not only
produce conflict but also can create new levels of harmony, or even re-
unification. In other cases, such as in the environmental disputes reviewed in
Polkinghorn's chapter, the ethno-religious dispute explored by Byrne, and the
community conflict analyzed by Wagner, the key to building a systematic approach to conflict resolution is found in the demystifying of stereotypes and labels. While conflict can emerge via group differentiation, it can also be resolved
by highlighting the many ways in which difference is based on compatible interests rather than on competing positions. In the field of conflict resolution practice, this is commonly called creating a "win-win" outcome.

Overview of Individual Chapters

We now turn to a short descriptive profile of each of the chapters in the order in
which they appear. In chapter two, Gina Petonito investigates how attitudes concerning race and enemies were constructed and used by opinion-makers and
politicians in the United States to categorize Japanese-Americans as "problem
people" during World War II. This categorization was then used to justify massive violations of their human rights through forced internment. Petonito urges
that race be understood as a "constructed category, not an objective fact" as she
examines the complicated process of how Japanese-Americans came to be seen
as "condemnation-worthy."

Petonito's data are drawn from her incisive document analysis of two
governmental sources (*Hearings before the Select Committee Investigating
National Defense Migration*, and *Papers of the U.S. Commission on Wartime
Relocation and Internment of Civilians*) and two newspaper sources (articles and
letters to the editor appearing in the *San Francisco Chronicle* and *Sacramento
Bee*). This combination of sources allows her to show how "everyday racism"
became official policy. Petonito demonstrates that the widespread perception of
the United States as a "white country" lent support to the refusal to see German-
Americans and Italian-Americans as the Other, even though the United States
was also at war with their countries of origin. Petonito distills from her sources
the two dominant constructs that Japanese-Americans were forced to contend
with: the Japanese-as-nationality racial construct, and the Japanese-as-skin-color
racial construct. These racialized people-categories, according to Petonito, led to
a generalized support of the status quo and internment, rather than to a critique

of government policies. This study is especially timely, as it not only provides valuable insights into the social and political dynamics of identity constructions but also helps explain similar contemporary situations in which whole peoples are marginalized and targeted, sometimes to the point of near-extermination.

Nora Femenia's case study in chapter three explores how national self-image and the need for national self-esteem—or normative/affective factors—played a decisive part in the 1982 war between Argentina and Great Britain over the Falklands/Malvinas islands. She suggests that a disputant like Argentina may dehumanize an enemy in an effort to stir constituent support of war, while also needing the enemy to define/reflect the disputant's self-definition and recognition. Femenia analyzes the respective self-images of the Argentine and British societies as they were expressed—in a patterned, action-reaction way— through the course of the seventy-four-day-long war. More important, she demonstrates how the perceived images affected the decisions of policy-makers. In doing so, Femenia challenges the widely accepted realist view that nations make foreign policy decisions in a rational, unemotional manner based on national interest. Rather, this case study points to the importance of emotions and affect in foreign policy decision-making, and the need for greater attention to these factors in efforts aimed at the resolution of international conflicts.

In chapter four, Ross Klein furthers the analysis of the roles and functions of collective identity concerns in international relations. This chapter focuses on two twentieth-century disputes over fishing rights, the Cod Wars and the Tuna Wars, and analyzes the ways in which militarily and economically weaker states (Iceland, Peru, Ecuador) successfully confronted more powerful states (Great Britain and the United States). Klein critiques the conventional notion that power is the most important variable in predicting the outcome of international conflicts. Among his findings are that perceived threats to sovereignty, import/export and investment dependencies, and public relations campaigns can all serve to offset the impact of more-traditional power disparities. Klein offers a number of provocative insights that may stimulate debate as to the "big power" of weaker parties in conflicts at the international, national, and communal levels. He also highlights the potential negative impacts on the image and identity of big power states that may opt to use military force or other bullying tactics against smaller, weaker states, and the ways smaller states may exploit this to reduce the likelihood of being attacked by the stronger state. Klein shows that smaller, more homogeneous states may have an easier time using collective identity as a domestic mobilizing factor in support of foreign policy choices.

In chapter five, a case study examining the attitudes of Protestant schoolchildren in Northern Ireland regarding the British queen and prime minister, Sean Byrne details the formation and relevance of ethnoreligious and national identity among children living in situations of violent political conflict. Analyzing interview data he collected at a Protestant grammar school and at an integrated (i.e., Protestant and Catholic) school in Belfast, Byrne emphasizes the need to examine the cognitive and evaluative components of children's political images in order to understand their ideological schemas or world views—views which in many cases are carried well into adulthood. This study examines the degree to which the safety and openness of integrated schooling—which allows children to explore religious and political differences while retaining ethno-religious identity and political attachments—make a difference in the political attitudes of school children.

Taken collectively, the findings presented in part one of the book suggest that conflict resolution practitioners and scholars should further analyze the formation of identity in opposition to the constructed Other as a critical component of the conflict process. Implicit in the recommendations of each of these studies is the urgent need to develop methods to deconstruct the images of "problem people" or enemies, while at the same time creating alternative and less-costly avenues for the positive identity formation processes in which all individuals and collectivities must engage.

Part two begins with Celia Cook-Huffman's participant observation study of conflicts in a small community-oriented urban church. Collective identity operates in conflicts on a number of different levels. Offering a gender analysis of a church-based conflict, Cook-Huffman shows that social identities, such as "women," function both as fixed constructs and as shifting, dynamic products of the social interactions within and between groups. While her contemporary church-based group valued cooperative interactions, the various and often competing conceptions of salient social identities resulted in conflicts on both the inter-group and intra-group level. Cook-Huffman's complex analysis applies the insights of social identity theory to analyze and identify how social identities, operating as fluid categories, become both a source of conflict and a product of conflict.

Verna Cavey's contribution in chapter seven offers a second study of conflict in a religious milieu, examining an intra-group conflict within a religious group that also values cooperative relations. The Religious Society of Friends (Quakers) has a well-deserved reputation for being peaceable—which is not the same as being conflict-free. An intense internal conflict ultimately rooted in competing conceptions of Quaker identity divided the American Quaker community and eventually brought about schism and the "Separation of 1827." Although initially rooted in a religious debate over the relative emphasis on mystical vs. scriptural approaches to Quaker life, Cavey's historiographical methods reveal that the religious conflict was deeply intertwined with social and economic issues, including class, language, kinship groupings, and approaches to modernization and industrialization. Cavey contextualizes the conflict by analyzing how socioeconomic factors created threats to Quaker identity. These identity threats in turn encouraged conflict emergence and escalation. Her research is especially instructive because she analyzes why a social group that had institutionalized conflict resolution mechanisms as an important dimension of its collective identity failed to adequately employ them precisely when they were most needed.

Chapter eight by Brian Polkinghorn is based on a study of twelve cases of regulatory negotiation (reg-neg) among representatives of the Environmental Protective Agency (EPA), industry, and environmental organizations. He examines the roles that collective identity and negative labeling play in determining the method and the outcome of EPA's reg-neg process. Polkinghorn shows quite effectively how out-group stereotyping is used to keep some adversaries from sitting at the negotiation table and to delegitimate the participation of others already there. Contrary to common opinion, Polkinghorn's findings reveal that it is not just industry representatives who use this tactic, to try to exclude mainstream environmental organizations. He also highlights instances where representatives of the mainstream environmental organizations do the same, effectively excluding members of the more marginalized environmental justice movement from the EPA's reg-neg process. Thus, collective identity processes may disenfranchise those parties who attempt to widen and complicate the definition of group membership.

The book's last two chapters move us squarely into the increasingly busy intersection of collective identity and social movement organizations. Research in new social movements has recently focused on the central and multifunctional roles that identity politics take on in today's contemporary movements. The chapters by Christine Wagner and Richard Kendrick contribute to and extend that trend.

An ongoing conflict over the meaning and control of a mid-sized city's annual Memorial Day parade provides an especially rich and instructive context for Wagner's research. Much like Cook-Huffman's chapter, Wagner's multi-year participant observation study also identifies "women" as a salient collective identity construct in the conflict between a war veterans' group and a peace group over the latter's participation in the Memorial Day parade. Wagner uncovers and deftly explores the differing conceptions of the salience of gender by the various parties in the conflict. Her analysis shows that the meaning of this conflict and most conflicts is fluid, and that the conflict process itself can change how the parties define what the conflict is about at any stage in the dispute. The meanings of other identity-based social constructions such as "Memorial Day," "patriotism," "veteran," "gay and lesbian," and "peace people" are also shown to be sites of public contest as this community conflict develops and is eventually resolved over a number of years.

One of the most established tenets in the social movements literature has to do with mobilization processes. It has been repeatedly shown that movement participants are most often recruited along established lines of already-shared action. In other words, friends recruit acquaintances, work colleagues recruit co-workers, and church members recruit fellow parishioners to social movements. This primary model of recruitment relies on shared identities and activities and the interpersonal trust they produce. These are strong urgings, and they usually translate into effective recruitment methods, unless a social movement is contracting and its primary issues are losing salience in the public arena. Kendrick's participant observation research explores the recruitment efforts of two social movement organizations in just such a position. No longer able to rely on the shared interaction and identity networks, local chapters of SANE/FREEZE and Physicians for Social Responsibility fashioned specific projects to serve as recruitment tools. These projects were intended to highlight positive connections between the organizations' interests and individual identities. Kendrick locates these identity convergence tactics in the literature on frame alignment and frame bridging processes. He finds, however, that the identity convergence that did occur between potential members and the social movement organization occurred at relatively abstract levels that had low mobilizing potential.

As a whole, the chapters in part two clearly demonstrate that an adequate understanding of social conflict dynamics requires extensive attention to collective identity processes. Identity alliances operate within groups and between groups, sometimes strengthening group participation, at other times leading to fragmentation. Moreover, shifting identities are integral to the emergence of conflict within and between groups.

Conclusion

Our contributors focus some of their efforts on conflict analysis, which is always the first step to developing viable systems of conflict resolution. In conflict analysis, as in ethics and medicine, an accurate description is a vital prerequisite to an adequate prescription. Each study discovers and fits into place another piece of the conflict resolution puzzle, whose design is ultimately revealed in the interlocked nature of collective identity formation with the processes of conflict emergence, escalation and resolution. We want to highlight, however, that much of the research included here speaks to the potential for collective identity to be used to resolve conflicts in constructive ways. The clarity by which social boundaries and collective identities are drawn and enforced has implications for the potential likelihood of a conflict's resolution.[18] The idea that salient identities can be shifted to open space for the resolution of conflicts deserves further theoretical attention and more case histories such as those found in this volume. Moving or blurring social boundaries then may hold some promise for creating a shift in seemingly intractable conflicts. Because groups will fight hard to protect collective identities, some reactions will be more constructive than others. As these chapters demonstrate, shifting identities through negotiation, breaking down assumptions about the "Other," and searching for bases to form new, inclusive identities may each contribute to the resolution of identity-based conflicts.

Notes

1. The authors contributed equally to this chapter, as they did to the overall editing and production of the book.

2. Lewis Coser, *The Functions of Social Conflict* (New York: Free Press, 1956), 23-24.

3. Jeffrey Rubin, Dean Pruitt and Sung Hee Kim, *Social Conflict: Escalation, Stalemate, and Settlement* (New York: McGraw-Hill, 1994).

4. Coser, *Functions of Social Conflict*, 31.

5. Randall Collins, *Theoretical Sociology* (San Diego: Harcourt, Brace and Jovanovich, 1988), 118.

6. Louis Kriesberg, *Social Conflicts* (Englewood Cliffs: Prentice-Hall, 1982).

7. Louis Kriesberg, *Constructive Conflicts: From Escalation to Resolution* (Lanham, Md.: Rowman & Littlefield, 1998), 31.

8. John Paul Lederach, *Preparing for Peace* (Syracuse, N.Y.: Syracuse University Press, 1996), 9.

9. Kriesberg, *Constructive Conflicts*, 31.

10. Kriesberg, *Social Conflicts*, 166.

11. Kriesberg, *Constructive Conflicts*, 342.

12. On the emergence of identity concerns over time in conflicts, see Jay Rothman, *Resolving Identity-Based Conflicts* (San Francisco: Jossey-Bass, 1997), 11. On intractability and collective identity issues in conflicts, see Terrell A. Northrup, "The Dynamic of Identity in Personal and Social Conflict," in *Intractable Conflicts and Their Transformation*, ed. Louis Kriesberg, Terrell A. Northrup and Stuart A. Thorson (Syracuse, N.Y.: Syracuse University Press, 1989).

13. Kriesberg, *Constructive Conflicts*, 69-66.

14. See for example John Burton, *Conflict Resolution and Provention* (New York: St. Martins, 1990); and Kriesberg, *Constructive Conflicts*.

15. John Paul Lederach, *Building Peace: Sustainable Reconciliation in Divided Societies* (Washington, D.C.: United States Institute of Peace, 1997), 13.

16. Louis Kriesberg, "Ethnicity, Nationalism, and Violent Conflict in the 1990s," *The Peace Studies Bulletin* 2 (Winter 1992-93): 24-28.

17. On this point and on the functions of collective identity among peace movement organizations who opposed the war in the Persian Gulf, see Patrick G. Coy and Lynne M. Woehrle, "Constructing Identity and Oppositional Knowledge: The Framing Practices of Peace Movement Organizations during the Persian Gulf War," *Sociological Spectrum* 16 (July-September 1996): 287-327.

18. Kriesberg, *Constructive Conflicts*, 12-14.

Part One

Constructing the Other and Creating Conflicts

Chapter Two

Racial Discourse and Enemy Construction

Justifying the Internment "Solution" to the "Japanese Problem" during World War II

Gina Petonito

All conflicts have situations where one group casts the other as enemy. In so doing, the contentious parties draw from available cultural resources to construct the other as a villainous foe. One cache of enemy images is found within the cultural storehouses of racial constructs. Here, social actors can select from a variety of racial notions to draw racial boundaries[1] around peoples. Once distinguished, the constructed group can be transformed into an enemy. This paper will explore this process, centering upon the ways Anglo-American people typified the Japanese as "enemy" during World War II. Although there were voices asserting the loyalty of the American Japanese, I will not focus upon them here. This paper aims to show how people "do everyday racism,"[2] by drawing from racial constructs available in common discourse to create enemies. It will demonstrate how racial constructions became part of an interlocking network of claims regarding the nature and threat of the imputed enemy, and how a racialized category of human beings was designated as a social problem.

To explore these processes, this project aligns its analysis with the social problems constructionist approach.[3] Unlike objectivist approaches which seek to identify causal factors for "actual" problematic conditions, constructionist analysts posit that social problems are what actors "claim" they are. Hence they focus upon the ways claimants use rhetorical and persuasive strategies[4] to define problems, bring them to public attention and derive "solutions" from these definitions. This analysis will examine how Anglo-American claimants[5] constructed all Japanese, both U.S. born (*Nisei*) or alien (*Issei*) as enemy, arguing that their continued freedom constituted a threat to national security. Calling their concern the "Japanese problem," this paper will describe internment proponents' efforts to persuade all those who claimed that Japanese loyalty could be determined with individual loyalty assessment programs that the American Japanese must be treated as a group.

A concept central to this analysis is what Loseke terms "people-categories."[6] This idea is based upon some claimants' propensity to construct problems as "types of people," who reside within particular moral universes of "sympathy-worthiness" or "condemnation-worthiness." For example, victims constitute a people-category which elicits a sympathetic response and claimants construct "solutions" designed to help them overcome their victimization. The category "victimizer" is readily condemned, and solutions range from remediation to annihilation. The enemy construction realm is replete with people-categories worthy of condemnation, and this paper will show how claimants create such groups.

Constructing Enemies

This project is part of a small but growing number of studies using insights from the social constructionist paradigm to examine the enemy construction process. These analyses focus on the ways powerful people utilize culturally available constructs to vilify the "Other." These works show how such notions form the rhetorical groundwork for justifying social policies that range from ostracism to genocide.

Using the Holocaust as a case study, Blain's analysis shows how Hitler's use of hyperbole helped unite a populace to purge the "enemy" Jew from the German community.[7] Berger demonstrated how claims-making regarding the "Jewish problem" followed a "natural history" as people formulated claims and accompanying solutions, eventually leading to the "final solution."[8] Both authors discuss how powerful people drew from racial "stocks of knowledge" to inform their categorization project—so that the vilification of the enemy seemed reasonable to the common people. Both authors show how Nazism drew from available cultural resources to fashion a Jewish "collective representation"[9] that embodied all that was profane, and how the construct was placed in opposition to the Christian German. Claimants treated Jew as a "master status,"[10] selectively ignoring individual variation within the category and endeavoring to convince people that all Jews, not just a select few, constituted a problem. Treating people as "all alike" is akin to treating them as a singular object, as opposed to unique individuals. It is then one short logical step from referring to human beings as hordes or masses in need of extermination.

While Blain and Berger have explored the constructionist paradigm's usefulness in understanding the ways Jewish people were typified as enemy during World War II, this paper will examine how it can apply to the Japanese internment case. While the construction of Jews as "problem people" resulted in the horrifying genocide of the Nazi Holocaust, internment proponents' efforts to align their plan with the tenets of the American way of life with its stress on democracy, fair play, and the securing of individual rights led them to distance their plan from a fascist one.[11] Thus, they never seriously considered annihilating the American Japanese, nor advanced any final solution. However, the construction of problem people across cases carries similar implications. Focusing upon the imputed actions of individuals allows people to sidestep any structural critique. Thus, claimants' rhetorical project helped maintain the status quo, leaving an unjust, racist social structure largely unexamined.

The Japanese Internment Case

During World War II, 110,000 Japanese—alien and citizen, men and women, young and old—were forcibly exiled from their West Coast homes and placed in one of ten camps in seven states. In the ensuing years, many observers have concluded that the internment plan was an unjust, racist policy.[12] While I concur, my analysis moves in a direction different from my predecessors.

One way to distinguish my work from other internment scholars is to consider the notion of warrant. Arguing that internment of American Japanese was without justification, most scholars note that throughout the post-Pearl Harbor period there was no report of sabotage or spying on the part of any Japanese. My focus on the social construction of people-categories as enemies renders this concern with objective conditions immaterial. Whether or not American Japanese engaged in enemy tactics is irrelevant. What is important is how World War II-era claimants dealt with such information and how it fit into their justification scheme. For them, detecting action would be a difficult, if not impossible task, for the work of enemies during wartime is necessarily covert. What claimants argue they must do is identify categories of "potential deviants,"[13] or groups of people which they argue most *probably* contain the true enemies. One way to accomplish this categorization is to demonstrate how the group of "potential enemies" is racially distinct from the larger population.

A second way my work is distinct from other internment scholars is that I see race as a constructed category, not an objective fact. For the most part, internment scholars treat race as an immutable concept and suggest that one only needs a more "enlightened" attitude towards different races to prevent policies like Japanese internment from developing. As a result they tend to apply the racial meanings and typifications of the historical period in which they are writing onto an earlier one.[14] For example, Irons calls World War II-era claimants "amateur anthropologists" when they related a widely held, vernacular view that individual Japanese were indistinguishable to the average Caucasian.[15] Applying constructs from a successive historical period onto an earlier one fails to recognize that claimants employ strategies for publicly presenting their arguments, so that they appear credible to the hearer. Hence, modern-day enemy construction claims will draw from racial discourses they can fashion into the most potent argument, so that "racist talk" (discussions of difference that justify discrimination against people) can appear to the listener as innocuous "racial talk" (everyday conversations about difference). To see how racial talk gives rise to racist policy, one must look at the ways people typify race in everyday life, bracketing one's own racial constructs, in the process.

My analysis treats race as a social accomplishment,[16] where "objective" racial "facts" matter only if social actors see them as such. Race occurs when people infuse meaning into human variation to create categories of human beings. This idea forms the underlying premise of my analysis—that Anglo-American claimants *constructed* the American Japanese as a specific race, thus distinguishing them from other "loyal Americans." This assumption places my work within the burgeoning field of race and ethnic constructionism, which studies the interplay between collective self-presentation and societal labeling.[17] My analysis centers on the process and significance of racial labeling, similar to other works which investigate racial transformation in the political arena.[18] I bracket modern-day assumptions regarding race and attempt to understand the ways World War II-era claimants publicly discussed race, seeking to uncover the ways racial claims are incorporated into the enemy construction process.

Letting others determine what the *real* reasons for internment were, I strive to understand how World War II-era claimants justified the internment plan. Thus, I do not treat internment as an objective social problem, seeking to discover its causes separate from official justifications. Rather, I treat the justifications as *constitutive* of the social problem. *Claimants'* reasons for internment and the accompanying racial constructs become the analytic focus.

Data Sources

In order to attain a variety of claims, I drew data from three data sites concentrating upon the period from December 7, 1941, the day Pearl Harbor was bombed, to March 31, 1942, the day before formal internment proceedings began. The first was the *Hearings before the Select Committee Investigating National Defense Migration*, commonly known as the Tolan Committee Hearings. The hearings provided a public forum for a variety of viewpoints. The second source was *Papers of the United States Commission on Wartime Relocation and Internment of Civilians,* hereafter referred to as *Papers*. These documents contain materials written by government officials and citizens in the form of memoranda, letters and reports. This site provides opportunities to trace government officials' efforts to develop internment policy. The third data source is West Coast newspapers: the *Sacramento Bee* and the *San Francisco Chronicle,* hereafter referred as the *Bee* and *Chronicle*. The *Bee* is a paper of the McClatchy chain known for its virulent anti-Japanese stance, while the *Chronicle* espoused a more moderate position,[19] so I was able to sample different postures with respect to the internment issue. Although the nation of Japan bombed Pearl Harbor on December 7, 1941, Hawaiian Japanese were never interned on a large scale. So, I selected the *Honolulu Star Bulletin* (hereafter referred as *Bulletin*) to search for further contrasts. I reviewed all articles dealing with internment— news, analyses, editorials and letters to the editor. Driven by theoretical sampling concerns,[20] I also collected articles that either explicitly or implicitly discussed race, even if not directly related to internment.

Focusing on vernacular racial constructs in everyday discourse, I will examine how people of the World War II era generally constructed race. Then I will demonstrate how they selectively chose from among these constructs to assert

that Japanese and Japanese-American liberty constituted a singular problem, requiring an internment solution. Please note that the terms I use to refer to racial
groups I have derived from the polite vernacular of the time. For example, I will
use Negro instead of the modern term, African-American. The terms the claimants use to refer to racial groups are their own.

Racial Discourse

Claims-making does not occur in a vacuum. Within ideological and social
realms, certain ideas emerge and become the reality of the time. Claimants' selection and use of constructs are bounded by existing discourses. Facts or truths,
as they exist within the discourse, exert a subtle tyranny over claimants' construction of their social problem.[21] This section will describe the historical back-
drop which framed people's racial claims-making, describing the ways people
constructed racial notions in everyday discourse.

Racial Constructs of the Early 1940s

Use of racial constructs in the 1940s differed from the manner in which they
are used in the 1990s. In the period preceding World War II and on through the
1960s (and in some cases until now), race was viewed as an objective fact. First
arising from anthropological concerns with human taxonomy, the idea took hold
in popular discourse.[22] Racial differences were discussed as real; and one group
was entirely distinct from the other. For example, *Pacific Fisherman* editor
Miller Freeman called for ending Japanese immigration to the United States in
1908: "The *Pacific Fisherman* harbors no enmity toward the Japanese. They are
a wonderfully bright people, frugal and industrious. But—they are Orientals. We
are Caucasians. Oil and water will not mix."[23]
While the essential nature of race was undisputed, there existed several ways
claimants could express that fact during the World War II period. One mode of
discussing race was a scientific one which posited race as a "fact" that biologically distinguished people. For example, the "rational scientific theory of Japanese origins" argued that their "Malaysian and Mongoloid" ancestors displaced
the "hairy Ainu aborigines" from the islands.[24] However, vernacular racial constructs dominated claims regarding the "Japanese problem." While the concept
of race may have originated in scientific discourse, by 1941 racial talk was
framed in terms of what everybody knew. What precisely constituted race was
not always stated, as claimants frequently slipped in and out of two interlinking
notions: race as skin color, and race as nationality. *Chronicle* letter writer Elsie
Bianchi defended the Italians by using the two racial constructs in her appeal: "I
do insist that we should be very careful of the Japs, as they are treacherous. And
anyway they belong to a race entirely different from white people. We should be
very careful of all aliens, but please consider the children born and raised here
and that know nothing of Europe and call us Americans please! I could write

and explain things all day, but what is the use, some people are ignorant."[25] To her, the "Japs," a nationality group, belong to a "race entirely different from white people," a skin color category. Today's race and ethnic scholars would recognize the race-as-nationality construct as *ethnicity* and the race-as-skin-color construct as *race*. However, World War II-era claimants did not employ the term *ethnicity*, since it did not come into common usage until the 1960s.[26] They spoke of nationality distinctions in racial terms, and they placed these groupings into the larger skin color categories.

The most inclusive construction of race-as-skin-color was the dichotomy "white" and "dark." As Bianchi suggested, the "white" race consisted of European nationality members, as well as the transplanted Europeans—the Americans. The "dark" race contained everyone else. An Associated Press piece printed in the *Bee*, which expressed concern over the effects of Japanese propaganda upon the American Negroes, utilized this dichotomy: "They [the Negroes] are hearing they would be 'better off if Japan won the war,' because the Japanese, too, are a dark people oppressed by the white race."[27] Many claimants more finely distinguished the dark race into yellow, black and red.[28] In my analysis, claimants generally referred to "black" people as Negroes and never discussed their nationalities. "Red" people were the American Indians, and "yellow" people consisted of all Asian nationalities including the Chinese, Filipino, Japanese and Korean peoples.

Skin color and nationality were ways to divide people into various races. So much a feature of common-sense discourse were they that claimants liberally ascribed both physical and non-physical characteristics to both racial categories, freely using such typifications to make sense of human nature. Various physical attributes were said to directly arise from race. A Japanese-American referred to himself as having "oriental features";[29] a Hawaiian was described as a "tall, powerfully built true descendent of the old Hawaiian warrior";[30] and Chinese and Japanese were said to "look alike."[31] Non-physical characteristics also were constructed as the result of race. Negroes were "by disposition happy, kind and friendly" people who "like[d] white people";[32] Italians were "home loving people bound by close family ties"[33] or "uneducated village-minded people";[34] and Hawaiians were "disinclined to hard labor."[35] In some cases, claimants suggested that physical characteristics caused non-physical ones. For example, a *Chronicle* editorial referred to the Japanese's alleged superiority at sexing chickens, gardening and growing strawberries and claimed that Japanese workers' "short legs and induration to hard and monotonous toil adapt them to work not agreeable to Americans."[36]

America as a White Country

The America of World War II was a white country. So firmly rooted in common sense discourse, this notion was almost imperceptible, revealed through a subtle use of such pronouns as "we," "our," "them" and "us." This pronoun use occurred in all the sites from which I drew data. In all cases, white claimants presented their arguments assuming the hearer was white. For example, *Chronicle* columnist Chester Rowell positioned himself as white writing for a white readership: "*We* are fighting against Germans and Italians of *our* own race, and with Chinese and Filipinos of other races."[37] Similarly, college student Hildur Coon employed this pronoun use, implying that she and her audience, the Tolan Committee members, were of European descent. Speaking on behalf of fellow Japanese students, she noted, "Then, also, it has been said that many of *them* have gone abroad to Japan. Many of *us* have returned to the home of *our* ancestors in Norway, England and France."[38]

In using these pronouns, white claimants underscored the normative nature of whiteness. For these claimants to self-consciously present themselves as white would be belaboring the obvious. That they and their audience were white was accepted as a matter of course.[39] Non-white claimants frequently identified themselves as such, thus qualifying their claims for the white audience: "Being an American Negro . . ."[40] or "I am a Filipino owing allegiance to the United States of America."[41] White claimants also participated in this rhetoric, frequently pointing out non-white claimants to their white audience. For example, the *Bee* reported news from a *Post-Dispatch* article: "The newspaper reports responsible Negro readers are alarmed at the spread of subversive doctrines among *their* people."[42] Note how the article did not merely state "responsible readers," but qualified the noun with the adjective "Negro." Similarly, a group of Nisei witnesses was designated as a "Japanese-American panel" in proceedings of the Tolan Committee Hearings.[43]

Within this discourse, white racial members could comfortably sit in the category of "we," rarely, if ever, challenged by others. Non-white racial members' participation in public claims-making arenas confined them to the role of "other." Expected to identify themselves as non-white, they reaffirmed America's status as a white country. Never did non-white racial members object to the construction of "we," calling for their inclusion in the collective definition of America. Rather, they remained in their marginal position in American public discourse, silently supporting the racial status quo.

With whiteness constructed as normative, non-white people became "them." As such, they were seen as different "types of people," thus laying the groundwork for the development of people-categories. As merely non-white people-categories, they were morally neutral. However, they could become sympathy- or condemnation-worthy, depending upon the nature of constructed circumstances. During World War II, these circumstances revolved around non-white peoples' placement into loyal or disloyal groups.

Racial Loyalties

During the World War II era, claimants considered the task of identifying the loyal as a vital one. Specifically, they questioned the loyalty of "enemy aliens"—Germans, Italian and Japanese nationals residing in the United States. With America at war with the countries of their birth, claimants feared that spying, sabotage and fifth column activity would undermine national security. Congressman John Tolan spoke for many: "The great problem. . . is simply this: that one person could do a lot of damage."[44] Thus, the continued liberty of enemy aliens constituted a social problem. Newspaper coverage chronicled efforts to contain the threat. Numerous articles wrote of government efforts to round up suspicious aliens[45] or of alien compliance with laws designed to curtail their activity.[46] Meanwhile, behind the scenes, government officials debated the merits of a variety of plans to prevent spying, sabotage and other fifth column activity.[47]

Claimants' typifications of racial loyalty led them to argue that American Japanese were the most menacing of the enemy aliens.[48] For people of the World War II-era, loyalty was but one of the many non-physical traits ascribed to race, and racial groups maintained loyalty to their own race. Racial loyalty was considered to be inherent, incapable of being severed, even with migration to another country:

> I think that the alien Japanese would have much greater difficulty in throwing off any inherent loyalty to his own country than a Japanese who has been born and raised in this country. I believe that if I were an American white man born in Japan I would have a natural predilection for the white race. I don't think it is a matter of criticism, I think it is just a matter of nature and I think it is very natural that a Japanese born in this country, even though born and raised here, should have somewhat of a predilection for the Japanese race. Many of them are fine, high type people that would not let anything interfere with their loyalty to the country to which they belong; but there are probably some that would let it interfere.[49]

Note the underlying assumptions at work here. Even though the Nisei were U.S. citizens, they nevertheless possessed a "natural" loyalty to their own racial country—Japan.[50] Although in this country, they were not fully *of* this country, since common sense maintained that America was a white country.

As part of common knowledge, the notion that white people were loyal Americans was never specifically articulated. Rather, white claimants rhetorically aligned their claims with those who were indisputably loyal. For example, Tolan Hearings witness Dr. J. F. Steiner, a sociologist from the University of Washington, employed the subtle discourse of pronouns: "As to the second-generation Germans, *we* don't doubt their loyalty."[51] His use of "we" went unchallenged by the committee, suggesting their acceptance of *his* implicit claim of loyalty. The certainty some white claimants had that they would be treated as loyal is evidenced in letters to military personnel alerting them of enemy aliens' "suspicious" activities. For example, T. A. Hunter, identifying himself as a war veteran, wrote a letter to Lt. Surfass, in charge of U.S. Army Ordnance. Noting that Japanese farmers were near a military construction site which his "electrical experience" told him was "an anti-aircraft unit," he said: "Several groups of Japs working in the adjoining fields were all eyes and ears, as they stopped work," to watch the activity.[52] Of course, he was also watching the military installation and revealed extensive knowledge about its operations, but never did he indicate *his* loyalty would be suspect. Rather, he was constructing the disloyalty of *them*—the Japs.

Having one's claim regarded as legitimate was a privilege accorded to white claimants. It meant that they could shape the tenor of the claims-making activity. If non-white claimants ventured forward with their assertions, they were compelled by convention to self-identify as such, thus facilitating white claimants' ability to place them within an "othered" people-category. Moreover, white claimants could treat their claims as those emanating from a type of person, who is different from "us," thus rendering them deviant.

Racial Claims

Claimants accomplished the distinction between enemy alien groups by employing both the race-as-nationality and race-as-skin-color constructs. To argue that the Japanese should be treated as a special category of enemy alien, claimants used the race-as-skin-color concept. However, as *Chronicle* columnist Rowell indicated, "our" friends included the Chinese and Koreans, who were also of the yellow race.[53] Therefore, concurrent rhetorics also existed which distanced America's yellow friends from its yellow enemies.

The following sections will detail how these rhetorical strategies were devised. Discussed first will be how claimants distanced the Japanese race from the yellow race that included Chinese, Filipinos and Koreans—America's allies. I will also discuss how these rhetorical strategies differed in Hawaii, where the Japanese were never interned on a large scale. Presented second will be how claimants distinguished the yellow enemies (Japanese and Japanese-Americans) from the white enemy aliens (Germans and Italians).

Distinguishing the Japanese from Other "Yellow" Nationalities

Numerous claimants worried about their inability to physically distinguish the Japanese from their yellow racial counterparts—the Chinese, Filipinos and Koreans. However, some claimants argued that important distinctions lurked beneath the skin. As *Chronicle* letter writer Eve Pollard Davis contends: "It is important just now that *we* Americans quickly learn that there are differences between the Chinese and Japanese Orientals. I have so often heard my friends say: '*They* all look alike to me!' *They* don't all look alike and are very unlike, in every respect . . . . The Chinese are *our* friends as *we* are theirs."[54] Here Davis uses the race as nationality construction, to distance the Japanese from other yellow groups by demonstrating that these people were deserving of *our* friendship. Friends, these claimants maintained, shared commonalties with *us*. Thus, they participated in re-creating racial others to stress similarity over difference. Accompanying these constructions were oppositional rhetorics typifying the Japanese as enemy.

One frequently used convention was a discussion of the ways *our* yellow friends embraced American ideologies such as democracy. To illustrate, consider *Chronicle* letter writer D. Burlingame's claims: "The Japs, Chinese and Koreans all belong to the yellow race. Yet *we* are fighting only the Japs. The Chinese and Koreans are standing shoulder to shoulder with *us*. Why? Because *they*, too, are fighting for democracy, freedom and liberty."[55] Use of this rhetoric served to identify *us* as much as it did our friends. Here *we* are positioned as fighting for what was right, in opposition to the non-democratic, totalitarian enemy—Japan.

As constructed, yellow allies shared not only similar principles but also similar animosities towards Japan. Claimants argued that these antipathies resulted from Japanese actions during their Asian imperialist campaigns prior to the Pearl Harbor attack. Thus, any inherent racial loyalties members of other yellow nations had toward the Japanese were severed due their firsthand experience of atrocities. This *Chronicle* editorial exemplifies this point:

> It is characteristic psychological blindness to other people's points of view for the Japanese to imagine that they can appeal to Filipinos on racial grounds, after having outraged their deepest sentiments on every other ground. The way to make people friendly is not to praise their complexions, but to treat them decently. This, neither Nazis nor Japanese have learned.[56]

As a group also victimized by the Japanese, claimants transformed America's yellow friends into people-categories worthy of sympathy and distinct from *our* common yellow enemy—Japan. Thus, many claimants moved for a more precise naming of the Japanese as a national race. For example, *Chronicle* letter writer Mrs. F. Wing claimed that she "winced" every time she heard "the word 'yellow' used derisively" and expressed satisfaction that the newspaper was "discouraging" its "misuse."[57] Note, however, that she does not object to the *use* of the word, but only its *misuse*, thus accepting the race-as-skin-color construct as a proper way of discussing difference.

The above-quoted *Chronicle* editorial also implied that the Japanese were closer to the Nazis, members of a different race, than to the Filipinos, further distancing them from other yellow national groups. This type of claim employed a rhetoric of binary opposites, which Ivie notes usually involves a rhetoric of "contrasting references to the adversary's coercive, irrational and aggressive attempts to subjugate a freedom-loving, rational, and pacific victim."[58] Operating within a discourse that regarded race as the source of character, claimants could logically ascribe such sinister traits onto the Japanese-as-nationality racial group, transforming them into condemnation-worthy people-categories. For example, one *Bee* letter writer referred readers to a recent Pearl Buck novel, which related a Japanese assault of a Chinese city: "The mere fact a Japanese happens to be born in this country does not mean he possesses in any lesser degree the diabolical traits recalled in this book. In conclusion, may I say that if *we* were to give the Chinese all the sympathy *they* deserve in the long struggle with the now common enemy, *we* would not have any sympathy left to waste on the Japanese."[59] As this passage demonstrates, claimants espousing these ideas maintained that all Japanese, whether American- or foreign-born possessed these diabolical traits. This argument persisted whether the claimant employed the Japanese-as-nationality racial category or the Japanese-as-skin-color one, as will be discussed later. The writer's reference to the sympathy that *we* were wasting on the Japanese was a subtle critique of those arguing against Japanese evacuation or internment. Given the fiendish nature of the people-category, any other plan would be foolhardy at best, she suggested.

This transformation of yellow friends so that they appeared similar to the whites further demonstrates race's socially constructed nature. Although World War II-era claimants may have argued that race was an immutable biological fact, they transformed it into a mutable one when the need arose. Even within a single time frame, racial rhetoric varies. While people on the U.S. mainland were rhetorically distancing the Japanese from other yellow people, Hawaiian claimants were doing the opposite.

Curtis Munson wrote in a report discussing the enemy alien problem in the Hawaiian Islands that "there has been absolutely no bad feelings between the Japanese and Chinese in the Islands due to the Japanese-Chinese war." This observation is ostensibly due to Hawaii's unique nature as a racial "melting pot": "In a word, Hawaii is more a melting pot because there are more brown skins to melt—Japanese, Hawaiian, Chinese and Filipino."[60] This rhetoric also appeared in the *Bulletin*, where claimants urged all of the island's diverse racial groups to unite in fighting the war. Chamber of Commerce president Leslie H. Hicks best exemplified this view. After remarking that in Hawaii one finds "all races living in harmony under the American flag," he implored: "This is war and *we* accept the orders of *our* president and military leaders, but that does not mean that *we* civilians can sidestep *our* responsibility to exert *our* efforts to preserve Hawaii's racial unity and to use every man, regardless of race or color, in the economic scheme of things. *We* must not let go to pot all that *we* have built up here in Hawaii during the past few generations. This is *our* challenge."[61] Munson and Hicks's claims suggest several points of note. Munson's assertion that all "brown races" are "melting" presumes a process of assimilation as Americans. Similarly, Hicks implies that every Hawaiian's primary allegiance is to the United States, when he said *we* must accept the orders of *our* president and military leaders. Given the common-sense notion that America was a white country, the racial unity both are discussing means accepting white as normative. Thus, racial harmony can be achieved when all races are transformed into the norm.

As in the mainland rhetoric, non-white racial claimants in Hawaii identified themselves as such. Unlike their mainland Asian counterparts, they did not distance themselves from the Japanese but accepted the rhetoric of racial unity. At times, they openly supported the Hawaiian Japanese,[62] a gesture I never saw in any of the mainland data sources. Whether or not racial harmony was really a fact of Hawaiian life cannot be determined from these data nor is it a goal of this analysis, but these findings underscore several points regarding enemy-construction. Although the Japanese in Hawaii originated from the same nation as those on the West Coast, they were not vilified. Rather, their status as Hawaiians rendered them like everybody else. As such, claimants presented them not as condemnation-worthy people-categories, but as fellow Hawaiians working towards racial harmony and clearly supporting America's war effort.

Although the Japanese and Japanese-Americans were not interned on a mass scale in Hawaii, I do not suggest that there is a causal connection between a certain kind of racial rhetoric and internment. This is a topic for another paper and a different analytic focus. However, the racial discourse in Hawaii did stress the need to preserve racial unity, which an internment plan would surely disrupt.

Distinguishing Japanese from Germans and Italians

With America considered a white country and white racial members holding "natural" allegiance to it, distinguishing between white German and Italian enemy aliens and yellow Japanese enemy aliens was a logical extension of this racial discourse. Rowell, the *Chronicle* columnist, wrote of this distinction: "What complicates the Japanese part of the problem still more is that the Japanese are a race as well as a nation, and that the race part is hereditary. Therefore there is the impulse among some of *our* people to group native citizens of Japanese ancestry with their parents, and both with Japan, in a way which nobody would do in the case of Germans or Italians."[63]

Although Rowell was critical of this stance, numerous claimants asserted that the American Japanese groups would most *probably* contain the disloyal due to their natural racial affinity for Japan. On the other hand, white enemy alien groups would most *probably* contain loyal individuals due to their inherent loyalty to white America. This notion was frequently expressed as a matter of course, as did Congressman Tolan: "You know you have Italians over there in your districts who are just as loyal as any citizens."[64] Thus, claimants could conveniently apply the race-as-skin-color construct to re-construct the German and Italian enemy alien problem as one of individual loyalty assessment—to discover the few anomalies within the group. However, claimants maintained that the Japanese enemy alien problem was complicated by the racial loyalties involved, with the issue termed the "Japanese problem" so as to encompass both enemy aliens and their citizen children.

Claimants disagreed over the Japanese problem's true nature. For some, loyal Japanese existed, but their distinct racial traits made loyalty detection among them difficult. Other claimants maintained that no loyal individuals existed among the Issei or Nisei groups. They were, as a category, disloyal to the core. The catch phrase "A Jap's a Jap" embodied these two ideas. At one level, it indicated that the Japanese, so like each other but so different from the white race, were difficult to sort into loyal or disloyal groups. At another level, the phrase implied that the Japanese people's inherent loyalty made them white America's potential enemies regardless of location. For these claimants, the Japanese were America's true enemies.

The Japanese as Difficult to Sort

Chronicle letter writer Addison N. Clark's comments exemplify the notion that loyalty detection within the Japanese ranks was a difficult task: "I know that many Niseis are horror-struck at the Japanese racketeers' late acts and methods, and at heart are pro American. But how can *our* FBI sort the wheat from the rust rotted grain and the chaff, overloaded as it is today with spy detection?"[65] Clark eloquently suggested that *our* FBI could eventually decode the secrets of the Japanese heart, but he questioned whether they were fully equipped to do so when so occupied with spy detection on all fronts. As he indicated, loyal Japanese did exist, but the problem was identifying them. This task was complicated by two ostensible factors: (1) all Japanese "looked alike" and (2) Japanese were "inscrutable."

Looking Alike

Claimants often considered racial distinctions in terms of physical difference. However, within the racialized categories, claimants maintained that physical similarities outweighed difference. From this idea emerged the assertion that all Japanese individuals looked alike, which presented claimants with problem after problem. The overarching concern was that Japanese loyalty could not be discerned by "the average Caucasian."[66] For some, the problem of looking alike would cause people to confuse local Japanese from alien invaders. As California Governor Culbert Olson stated: "There is the situation where if we had parachute troops dumped on us, it would be impossible to distinguish local, and perhaps loyal, Japanese from the invaders."[67] For others, the problem was one of distinguishing the Japanese alien from the American-born Japanese citizen. Newspaper editor Manchester Boddy explained: "First, I should like to emphasize as emphatically as possible the fact that the local white men do not recognize the distinction between Japanese aliens and their sons."[68] Still others argued that looking alike prevented people from discerning loyalty—as if loyalty or disloyalty could be determined from physical features alone. California farmer H. L. Strobel stated: "The Japanese have a racial similarity so that it is very hard for the average man to note any difference between them when he sees them just occasionally."[69]

Looking alike also prevented people from positively identifying a saboteur, even if caught in the act. To illustrate, consider General DeWitt's argument against a plan to allow the Nisei to remain at large: ". . . if they are allowed to remain where *they* are, *we* are just going to have one complication after another, because you just can't tell one Jap from another. *They* all look the same. Give a sentry or an officer or troops any job like that, a Jap's a Jap, and you can't blame the man for stopping all of them."[70] Complications indeed. In DeWitt's assessment of the problem, the army would be overwhelmed with spy detection, forced to stop Jap after Jap, (maybe even the same individual over and over), unable to identify the suspicious or the friendly because they all look the same.

Although members of the same racial category were said to look alike, claimants never applied that argument to their own white grouping. Rather, they reserved this claim for non-white racial categories, for *them*. Strobel's statement, that the "average man" cannot tell individual Japanese apart, reveals an underlying common-sense presumption: the Japanese were not "average," but nonnormative, the "other." Thus, as people-categories physically indistinguishable from each other, the Japanese were objectified as a single mass—one human being of Japanese descent becoming interchangeable with another.

Inscrutability

Not only did the Japanese people look alike, but they also thought alike, so claimants maintained. Again, the similarities were presented as the province of the "other" and were popularly presented as Japanese inscrutability. The common-sense contention here was that white people were incapable of knowing any Japanese person's inner thoughts. As a *Chronicle* letter writer noted: "The Japanese more so than any other nationality, with perhaps the exception of the Chinese, who through tradition, test and trial is excepted from this issue, is a poker-faced stoic. He may be 100 percent for you or that much against you but only his inner self knows which."[71]

This inscrutability made it difficult for white people to assess Japanese loyalty. Proclaiming loyalty was not enough, claimants asserted, since the Japanese can easily dissemble their true feelings. Congressman Martin Dies gave credence to this concern when he reported of two sets of books housed in each Japanese language school. One set, the report notes, the school authorities show "occidental visitors." The other set, which is really used in the curriculum, "preaches loyalty to Japan and treason against the American Government," on "every page."[72]

As noted, most World War II-era racial claims-making was framed as common sense. However, racial discourse surrounding the inscrutability issue often slipped into a quasi-scientific mode. Frequently, people associated inscrutability with the races' propensity to "assimilate," a term with a social-scientific tinge.[73] For example, E. M. Seifert, president of the Grower-Shipper Vegetable Association, in a letter to California Congressman John Anderson referred to the Japanese people's inability to assimilate due to their inherent mental differences: "These people, you know, do not think like *we* do, nor do *we* think like *they* do. *They* cannot be assimilated. *They* will not blend with *our* peoples, and since that is true, *they* should be restricted forever from owning any land or property in *our* county." In this passage, Seifert appeals to common sense with the selection of the phrase "you know," but also employs the quasi-scientific word *assimilate* to bolster his contention that his statement "is true."[74] Using such quasi-scientific discourse in this instance discloses its appeal to the basic racial premise—that mental processes and personality traits emanate from race as a biological "fact." However, claimants imply that the Japanese mind is not just different, but primitive—hence, its impenetrable nature. Thus, members of these constructed people-categories are stripped of their humanity, descending from groups of people into groups of primitives. In fact, much World War II rhetoric depicted the Japanese as "monkey-men," with short legs, and buck teeth.[75]

The Japanese as Enemy

In the above examples, claimants implied that loyalty existed within the Japanese ranks, but it was difficult to detect. However, some claimants categorized the entire group as enemy, employing the "Jap's a Jap" phrase as a shorthand way of saying that all Japanese, regardless of location and birth, were loyal to their own race. Mississippi Congressman Rankin's remarks, quoted as part of a news article, illustrate this. After noting that the West Coast was "teeming with spies and fifth columnists," the *Chronicle* reported him as claiming: "Once a Jap always a Jap! . . You can't any more regenerate a Jap than you can reverse the laws of nature. I'm for taking every Japanese and putting him in a concentration camp."[76] As with the inscrutability argument, the phrase "A Jap's a Jap," used in this sense, was paired with appeals to quasi-scientific discourse. Here Rankin likens the "Jap's a Jap" notion with the "laws of nature," while other claimants employed the assimilation construct: "*They* do not become assimilated and *they* are Japanese to the end."[77]

Although claimants used the "Jap's a Jap" construct to demonstrate inherent racial loyalty, they also used it to racially categorized a group based upon the race-as-skin-color construct, applying the rhetoric of binary opposites. Just as the technique bolstered arguments that distanced Americas yellow friends from the Japanese race-as-nation, it also amplified positions that distinguished the yellow Japanese from white America. For example, *Bee* letter writer Ann Agard contended that it was the Japanese people's "misfortune to have been born into a race that is treacherous to the core."[78]

Developing Solutions to the Enemy Alien Problem

As white racial members, German and Italian aliens enjoyed treatment as individuals. When solutions to the white enemy alien problem were formed, claimants expressed confidence that their loyalty could be effectively assessed, as did California Governor Olson: "It is undoubtedly true that among so many of the Italian and Germans, there is also a strong loyalty to this country on their part, even though they haven't yet become citizens of the United States and hadn't heretofore declared their intention. As I say, I think espionage services and the F.B.I. can pretty much tell whether there are disloyalties among those groups."[79] One claimant argued that this sorting could be accomplished by the "rule of reason,"[80] suggesting that white loyalty assessors could apply everyday logic to determine the nature of people so like themselves.

The Japanese problem posed a more complicated loyalty assessment challenge for many claimants. To these claimants, the Japanese group contained either loyal and disloyal individuals who were difficult to properly sort, or true enemies worthy of condemnation. Adherents of both views advanced internment as the best solution to the problem, one that would effectively contain the threat. As a military report explained: "*Their* oriental habits of life, *their* and *our* inability to assimilate biologically and, what is more important, *our* inability to distinguish the subverters and saboteurs from the rest of the mass made necessary *their* class evacuation on a horizontal basis."[81]

Internment justification was a logical extension of the racial discourse surrounding the constructed Japanese problem. Positing that people looked alike and thought alike paved the way for treating them as "all alike," with one short step remaining to vilification as enemy. While one group of claimants created people-categories where individuals disappeared into one objectified mass, the other fashioned the mass into enemies, worthy of condemnation. In both cases, the actions of any member within the vilified group was irrelevant to the categorization project. Blameless individuals carried with them the stigma of enemy, and internment policy became the practical consequence of this justification process.

Discussion

This research concentrated on how common people selected from an array of racial notions to categorize the American Japanese as enemy. Focusing upon the claims-making activity of those who argued that the Japanese, as a race, should be interned, I showed how they created categories of problem people. For them, the enemy alien problem was about identifying people-categories who presented a *potential* threat to national security, not an *actual* problematic condition. Tangential to their task was direct observation of individual action. For them, containing the threat meant confining the people-category within the walls of internment camps. Although numerous people have decried the internment plan because there was no evidence of disloyal action by any American Japanese, this analysis shows that that critique would have fallen on deaf ears in 1942. Individual behavior of any Japanese was *not* the issue; the Japanese as a type of person was.

This finding extends our knowledge concerning the construction of people-categories. Loseke's formulation of the concept presents two constructed groups: victims, who incur harm, and victimizers, those deemed responsible for harm. While victims are people who are acted upon, victimizers are ostensibly *acting* in ways that earned them the label. For example, "men who batter," a condemnation-worthy people-category, are defined in terms of their behavior.[82] However, the task of constructing people as enemies is independent of action observation, due to claimants' concern with containing *potential* threats. With such a categorization project, all falling into a particular group are similarly stigmatized, regardless of their individual behavior.

Constructing people-categories is one of several steps in constructing enemies. Subsuming distinct individuals into a category allows people to react to the group, forgetting the human beings who comprise it. To devalue the category, claimants employ rhetorics of binary opposites,[83] which render it worthy of condemnation. This judgment implies a dichotomy of inferiority and superiority, where claimants see themselves as superior to those they denounce, distancing the "other" from themselves. With the category's collective denigration, claimants justify policies designed for the vilified object, regardless of the individual sentiment or action of its occupants. Moreover, once people are rhetorically placed within the category, their membership in the groups becomes a master status and any member's action can be constructed as having evil intent. As Burke states, once a category is "essentialized," all "proof" is automatic. If one points out evidence seeming to contradict the category's vilification, claimants can re-construct such action to fit within the initial classification. For example, Hitler's critics pointed out that Jewish workers were continually at odds with the "international Jew stock exchange capitalist." Hitler responded that these actions were yet more indications of the "cunning with which the 'Jewish plot' was engineered."[84]

To construct people-categories, claimants drew from an available array of rhetorics and this analysis focuses upon their employment of racial ones. Thus, constructing vilified racial categories is one way claimants "do racism," by drawing from a variety of racial constructs that shift in accordance to a particular rhetorical project. The Japanese could be members of a skin color or national category, distinct from others or part of a "racially harmonious" society. Nagel discusses how the interplay between one's self-presentation as ethnic and one's audience produces a "layering" of ethnic identities.[85] This analysis shows how a multiplicity of ascriptions existing within a political discourse can delimit people's choices of racial identification.

However, there were also limits to *claimants'* use of race. Although they lived in a world replete with racial images, they remained uncritical of them. People's debates were about properly ascribing racial traits, not the act of employing them. Recall that Mrs. Wing did not object to Asians categorization as yellow, but the *misuse* of the term.[86] Similarly, Bianchi criticized certain traits' ascription to a particular group, but not the *act of ascribing such traits*.[87] Given this racial climate, claims such as that the loyal Japanese could not be sifted from the disloyal, or that they constituted an inherently "enemy" race, were viable ones. Since people liberally ascribed qualities to other races without challenge, why would claimants suspect these racial claims to be less valid? The only way for people to effectively challenge the construction of Japanese as vilified people-categories would be to attack the credibility of racial ascriptions generally, not just in a particular case. However, such a challenge would be met with fierce resistance, as it challenged common sense. As Gusfield noted: "The most subtle forms of social control are those we least recognize as such. Precisely because the categories of understanding and meaning provide so powerful a constraint to what we experience, they prevent awareness of alternative ways of conceiving events and processes."[88]

A further limit on the ways racial constructs are used is that they were employed within a collective definition of America as a white country. Thus, being white was normative, while all other groups operated at the borders of public discourse. As Essed's comparison of U.S. with Dutch society shows, cultures that treat whites as the norm develop hidden agendas that "tolerate" racial minorities as long as they subscribe to the dominant cultural value system.[89] Any racial group's divergence from the norm would render them problematic, and as this analysis shows, dominant group members can construct racial "others" as troublesome with relative ease. Once a racial category is deemed problematic, claimants can channel their energies toward containing the threat the racialized group poses, and that group is relatively powerless to shape the tenor of public discourse due to its status as a non-white "other."

Yet, focusing upon problem people hides the group's political choice—to support the status quo rather than critique it. As Loseke points out, claimants frequently debate whether or not a category of person is victim or victimizer.[90] Often these debates involve a shifting of perspective away from the group and onto the structure in which these groups exist. To question the act of ascribing racial constructs to the American Japanese or to challenge America's collective definition of itself would mean confronting the society's underlying racist structure. Thus, blaming the Japanese merely for being members of a particular race, rather than challenging a structure which allowed racial discourse to be formulated in such a way as to justify a policy such as internment, allowed claimants to maintain social order in a world at war.

This paper expands our knowledge of Japanese internment and enemy construction generally. Operating within a historically bounded racial discourse, claimants applied appropriate racial rhetorics to construct the Japanese as problem-people who must be interned. As "social problems work,"[91] claims-making during World War II shares features with other social problems processes. Claimants must construct credible claims and connect these to their putative problem people. Framed in this way, the study of Japanese internment during World War II need not remain a singular case resulting from particular sociohistorical causes. Rather, it can provide valuable insights into racism, enemy construction, genocide and other social problems where racialized people-categories are the focus of claims-making efforts.

Notes

1. This paper in much earlier incarnations provided the basis for chapter four of my dissertation "Constructing the Enemy: Justifying Japanese Internment during World War II" (Syracuse University, 1992) and was presented at the Meetings of the American Sociological Association in Cincinnati, Ohio, August 23-27, 1991. I would like to thank Donileen Loseke, Michael Yavenditti, and all the editors of this volume for their helpful comments on the present version. Direct all correspondence to Gina Petonito, Department of Sociology and Anthropology, Western Illinois University, Macomb, IL 61455. Electronic mail may be sent via internet to <G-Petonito@wiu.edu>; Joane Nagel, "Constructing Ethnicity: Creating and Recreating Ethnic Identity and Culture," *Social Problems* 41, no. 1 (February 1994): 152-76.

2. Philomena Essed, *Understanding Everyday Racism* (Newberry Park, Calif.: Sage, 1991).

3. Malcolm Spector and John I. Kitsuse, *Constructing Social Problems* (Menlo Park, Calif.: Benjamin/Cummings, 1977); Joseph W. Schneider, "Social Problems Theory: The Constructionist View," *Annual Review of Sociology* 11 (1985): 209-29; Donileen Loseke, *Thinking about Social Problems: An Introduction to Constructionist Perspectives* (Hawthorne, N.Y.: Aldine de Gruyter, 1999).

4. Peter R. Ibarra and John Kitsuse, "Vernacular Constituents of Moral Discourse: An Interactionist Proposal for the Study of Social Problems," in *Constructionist Controversies,* ed. James Holstein and Gale Miller (Hawthorne, N.Y.: Aldine de Gruyter, 1993), 21-54.

5. Since this project draws data from a variety of sources, it is difficult to choose a term that adequately describes all claimants. In fact, some claimants were not Anglo-American, as analysis will show. However, their claims were routinely qualified as those of non-white people. Therefore, the claims given legitimacy in the public arena were those that needed no qualification, those of white Americans.

6. Donileen Loseke, "Constructing Conditions, People, Morality, and Emotion: Expanding the Agenda," in *Constructionist Controversies,* ed. James Holstein and Gale Miller (Hawthorne, N.Y.: Aldine de Gruyter, 1993), 207-16.

7. Michael Blain, "Fighting Words: What We Can Learn from Hitler's Hyperbole," *Symbolic Interaction* 11, no. 2 (Fall 1988): 257-76.

8. Ronald J. Berger, "The 'Banality of Evil' Reframed: The Social Construction of the 'Final Solution' to the Jewish Problem," *The Sociological Quarterly* 34, no. 4 (November 1993): 597-618.

9. See Emile Durkheim, *Elementary Forms of Religious Life* (New York: Free Press, 1995).

10. Howard Becker, *Outsiders: Studies in the Sociology of Deviance* (New York: Free Press, 1973).

11. Petonito, "Constructing the Enemy"; see especially chapter 5.

12. Anne Reeploeg Fisher, *Exile of a Race* (Seattle: F & T Publishers, 1965); Morton Grodzins, *Americans Betrayed: Politics and Japanese Evacuation* (Chicago: University of Chicago Press, 1949); Peter Irons, *Justice at War* (New York: Oxford University Press, 1983); Carey McWilliams, *Prejudice; Japanese Americans: Symbol of Racial Intolerance* (Boston: Little, Brown 1944); Bradford Smith, *Americans from Japan* (Westport, Conn.: Greenwood, 1948); Jacobus ten Broek, Edward N. Barnhart, and Floyd W. Matson, *Prejudice, War, and the Constitution: Causes and Consequences of the Evacuation of the Japanese Americans in World War II* (Berkeley: University of California Press, 1954); Michi Weglyn, *Years of Infamy: The Untold Story of America's Concentration Camps* (New York: William Morrow, 1976).

13. Becker, *Outsiders,* 181; Barry Glassner and Jay Corzine, "Can Labeling Theory Be Saved?" *Symbolic Interaction* 1, no. 2 (Spring 1978): 74-89.

14. Racial claims in McWilliams's *Prejudice* read similarly to those in my data, which is not surprising since he was most probably writing his book contemporaneously. For example, at one point McWilliams states that "Germans and Italians belong to the same racial stock as a majority of people" in the United States, employing the race-as-nation construct widely used in World War II-era racial discourse.

15. Irons, *Justice,* 54.

16. Michael Moerman, "Accomplishing Ethnicity," in *Ethnomethodology: Selected Readings,* ed. Roy Turner (London: Penguin, 1974), 54-68; Fredrik Barth, *Ethnic Groups and Boundaries* (Boston: Little, Brown, 1969).

17. Moerman, "Accomplishing Ethnicity," 54-68; Nagel, "Constructing Ethnicity," 152-76.

18. Michael Omi and Howard Winant, *Racial Formation in the United States* (New York: Routledge & Kegan Paul, 1986); Dana Y. Takagi, *The Retreat from Race: Asian-*

American Admissions and Racial Politics (New Brunswick, N.J.: Rutgers University Press, 1992).

19. Grodzins, *Americans Betrayed*, 10-11.

20. Barney Glaser and Anselm Strauss, *The Discovery of Grounded Theory: Strategies for Qualitative Research* (Chicago, Ill.: Aldine, 1967).

21. Edward Said, *Orientalism* (New York: Vintage, 1978).

22. Ashley Montagu, *Race, Science and Humanity* (Princeton, N.J.: Van Nostrand, 1963).

23. Miller Freeman, "Japanese Invasion," *Pacific Fisherman*, August 1908, *Papers* No. 13456-7.

24. "The Enemy," *This World, San Francisco Chronicle*, 28 December 1941, 11-12.

25. Elsie Bianchi, "Born and Raised Right Here," *San Francisco Chronicle*, 6 March 1942, 14.

26. Montagu, *Race, Science.*

27. "FBI Is Said to Be Probing Pro Japanese Drive among Negroes," *Sacramento Bee*, 5 March 1942, 10.

28. "Japanese Whispers among Negroes," *San Francisco Chronicle*, 19 March 1942, 14.

29. "Loyalty Is Asserted," *Sacramento Bee*, 17 January 1942, 8.

30. "Japanese Pilot Killed on Nihau after Taking Isle," *Honolulu Star Bulletin*, 16 December 1941, 1.

31. United States House of Representatives, *Hearings before the Select Committee Investigating National Defense Migration* (Washington, D.C.: U.S. Government Printing Office, 1942), 11354.

32. "Japanese Whispers," 14.

33. Charles E. H. Bates, "Aliens Who Did Not Become Citizens," *San Francisco Chronicle*, 4 February 1942, 14.

34. Bureau of Intelligence, Office of Facts and Figures, report to Archibald McLeish, 25 May 1942, *Papers* No. 6708-16.

35. Joseph Harech, "Loyalty of Youths Here Is Stressed by War Correspondent," *Honolulu Star Bulletin*, 20 March 1942, 4.

36. "The Chickens Will Have to Grow Up." *San Francisco Chronicle*, 19 March 1942, 14.

37. Chester Rowell, "Our Japanese Issue Is a Two Edged Sword," *San Francisco Chronicle*, 3 February 1942, 12. In this quote and hereafter, I italicize instances of similar pronouns to make their use evident to the reader.

38. *Hearings*, 11592.

39. The one exception to the lack of racial self-identification among white claimants was during the Tolan Hearings testimony of Ronald Lane Latimer a Buddhist priest. In the face of charges of Japanese Buddhist disloyalty, Latimer advocated for them, and his status as white lent credence to his claims. *Hearings*, 11807-11.

40. Elsie Jones, "Asks Democracy to Unbend a Little," *San Francisco Chronicle*, 23 March 1942, 10.

41. Lucio V. Ramos, letter to President Roosevelt, 7 March 1942, *Papers* No. 14786-89.

42. "FBI Is Said," 10.

43. *Hearings*, 11347. Many of these processes occur in similar form today. As noted in Ruth Frankenberg, *White Women, Race Matters: The Social Construction of Whiteness* (Minneapolis: University of Minnesota Press, 1993), 17, being white and Western meant being devoid of ethnicity. As such the white Western self has gone unexamined and unnamed. In many ways, being white or being American is comprehensible only with refer-

ence to the "other," peoples of color excluded from the collective definition of who "we" are as Americans.

44. *Hearings*, 11627.

45. See, for example, "German and Italian Aliens," *Sacramento Bee*, 24 February 1942, 4.

46. See, for example, "More about Aliens Giving Up Radios," *San Francisco Chronicle*, 29 December 1941, 5.

47. See, for example, Lt. Comdr. C. H. Coggins, "A War-time Problem: The Japanese in Hawaii." U.S. Navy Report, n.d., *Papers* No. 6964-84.

48. Of those positing differences between the three enemy alien groups, many argued that the Japanese presented the most danger, followed by the Germans, with the Italians the least threatening. On the distinction made between German and Italian aliens, see Bureau of Intelligence report to MacLeish, *Papers* No. 6708-16.

49. *Hearings*, 11493.

50. Note how he said "the country to which they belong," rather than the more inclusive "our" country.

51. *Hearings*, 11562.

52. T. A. Hunter, letter to Lt. Surfess, U.S. Ordnance, U.S. Army, 3 January 1942, *Papers* No. 13419.

53. Rowell, "Our Japanese Issue," 12.

54. Eve Pollard Davis, "The Way to Take No Chances," *San Francisco Chronicle*, 12 December 1942, 18.

55. D. O. Burlingame, "Japanese Not Only People of Yellow Race," *San Francisco Chronicle*, 23 January 1942, 12.

56. "Japanese Toying with Two-Edged Sword," *San Francisco Chronicle*, 14 January 1942, 14.

57. F. Wing, "Japanese Only a Bad Item in Yellow Race," *San Francisco Chronicle*, 17 January 1942, 10.

58. Robert Ivie, "Images of Savagery in American Justifications for War," *Communication Monographs* 47, no. 4 (November 1980): 284.

59. V. B. S., "Deserve No Sympathy," *Sacramento Bee*, 12 February 1942, 28.

60. Curtis B. Munson, Report on Hawaiian Islands, n.d., *Papers* No. 19500-16.

61. "Fair Treatment for Isle Japanese Asked by Hicks," *Honolulu Star Bulletin*, 11 February 1942, 4.

62. See for example, Alfred Au, "Faith in Americans of Japanese Ancestry," *Honolulu Star Bulletin*, 1 January 1942, 6.

63. Rowell, "Our Japanese Issue," 12.

64. *Hearings*, 11102.

65. Addison N. Clark, "Japanese Born and Once Removed," *San Francisco Chronicle*, 16 February 1942, 12.

66. *Hearings*, 11631.

67. *Hearings*, 11630.

68. Manchester Boddy, letter to Francis Biddle, 9 February 1942, *Papers* No. 13435.

69. *Hearings*, 11092.

70. John DeWitt, transcript of telephone conversation with Secretary McCloy, 3 February 1942, *Papers* No. 138.

71. Name obscured, "The Question of Internment," *San Francisco Chronicle*, 20 February 1942, 14.

72. "The Dies Report," *San Francisco Chronicle*, 28 February 1942, 1-3; "Dies Report Reveals Years of Japanese Espionage in State," *Sacramento Bee*, February 1942, 1, 4-5.

73. The everyday word used to describe this process was "Americanize" or "become American," as noted in Gina Petonito, "Constructing Americans: 'Becoming-American,'

Loyalty, and Japanese Internment during World War II," in *Perspectives on Social Problems*, vol. 4, ed. James Holstein and Gale Miller (Greenwich, Conn.: JAI Press, 1992), 93-108. However, when claimants discussed "inscrutability," *Americanize* was replaced with *assimilate*. An example of a conscious use of both words is presented in John DeWitt, memo to Secretary of War Henry Stimson, 13 February 1942, *Papers* No. 19424:

> The Japanese race is an enemy race and while many second and third generation Japanese born on United States soil, possessed of United States Citizenship, have become "Americanized," the racial strains are undiluted. . . . That Japan is allied with Germany and Italy in this struggle is no ground for assuming that any Japanese, barred from assimilation by convention as he is, though born and raised in the United States, will not turn against this nation when the final test of loyalty comes.

Putting quotes around the word *Americanized* suggested that it, as a vernacular construction, was deceptive. On the other hand, DeWitt employed the word *assimilate* without quotation marks, to contrast the common sense view with "scientific facts," as he saw them.

74. E. M. Seifert, letter to Congressman John Z. Anderson, 16 January 1942, *Papers* No. 13450.

75. John W. Dower, *War without Mercy: Race Power and the Pacific War* (New York: Pantheon, 1986); Sam Keen, *Faces of the Enemy* (San Francisco: Harper, 1991).

76. "Enemy Aliens: Congressmen Demand All American-Born Japs Be Moved from Coastal Areas," *San Francisco Chronicle*, 19 February 1942, 9.

77. William H. Keller, letter to Francis Biddle, 23 February 1942, *Papers* No. 10669.

78. Ann Agard, "Americans Are Naive," *Sacramento Bee*, 14 February 1942, 19.

79. *Hearings*, 11634.

80. Western Defense Command and Fourth Army, Wartime Civil Control Administration, memorandum to Col. Karl Bendetsen, 22 May 1942, *Papers* No. 858.

81. Western Defense Command, *Papers* No. 857.

82. Loseke, "Constructing Conditions."

83. Ivie, "Images of Savagery," 279-94.

84. Kenneth Burke, "Rhetorical Analysis: The Rhetoric of Hitler's Battle," in *Kenneth Burke: On Symbols and Society*, ed. Joseph Gusfield (Chicago: University of Chicago Press, 1989), 213.

85. Nagel, "Constructing Ethnicity," 154-55.

86. Wing, "Japanese Only," 10.

87. Bianchi, "Born and Raised," 14.

88. Joseph Gusfield, *The Culture of Public Problems: Drinking, Driving, and the Symbolic Order* (Chicago: University of Chicago Press, 1981), 28.

89. Essed, *Understanding Everyday*.

90. Loseke, "Constructing Conditions."

91. Gale Miller and James Holstein, "Social Constructionism and Social Problems Work," in *Constructionist Controversies,* ed. James Holstein and Gale Miller, (Hawthorne, N.Y.: Aldine de Gruyter, 1993), 131-52.

Chapter Three

Emotional Actor

Foreign Policy Decision Making in the 1982 Falklands/Malvinas War

Nora Femenia

The conflict that erupted in the spring of 1982 between Argentina and Great Britain, quickly escalating into war, stunned the world. Even today, emotions are triggered on either side when the British name, Falkland Islands, or the Argentine name, Islas Malvinas, is used to refer to the disputed islands lying 300 miles east of the Strait of Magellan at the southern end of South America and 8,000 miles away from the United Kingdom. In a surprise attempt to take possession of the Falkland Islands, Argentina humiliated a former European superpower and precipitated one of the most unpredictable wars of the century.

What drove these countries to move forcefully on their long-disputed, 150-year-old claim? What moved Argentina to recover the Malvinas and Britain to repel the invasion using force? I propose here that in the Falklands/Malvinas crisis, unacknowledged emotional factors were the central motivations behind the decisions made by both Britain and Argentina. Furthermore, I will show that such emotion-loaded factors—specifically, national self-images—are an often ignored but essential tenet of every nation's foreign policy-making.

Argentina had other opportunities to initiate forceful recovery of the islands during the 150 years of sovereignty claims against Britain, which began in 1833, such as during World War II when Britain was at its weakest. At that time, Argentina had developed concrete plans to retake the Malvinas. However, the perceived enemy against whom to secure the islands was the United States, not Britain. Maintaining the consistent image of Britain as a valued ally, Argentina waited nearly forty years to act on those plans. Strategic plans to recover the Malvinas were part and parcel of the training of military officers for a long time, though confined to the theoretical domain. Research suggests that the main impetus in 1982 to justify a change in the stalemate was partially motivated by unsatisfactory British and Argentine national self-images and their inevitable and compelling needs for international recognition.[1] The same emotion-driven self-images that had precluded a military takeover in the 1940s—because then highly satisfactory— prompted a takeover in the 1980s because of deep frustration produced by unsolved emotional needs. Shrinking British power in post-imperial times prompted a national identity crisis, directed to heal diminished national images.

When the crisis ended by Argentina's surrender on June 14, 1982, both countries were left with the symbolic treasure over which they fought; Britain was left with a renewed sense of British world greatness and Argentina appropriated the role of victimized, heroic David resisting the prepotency of the superpowers. The confrontation tragically confirmed for each national player the basic elements of their emotional scripts, reassuring them both that war is a legitimate means to get to know who they are and what they stand for.[2]

Underlying Affective Factors in Foreign Policy Decision-Making

Social groups and nations demand that their unique existence be acknowledged. They adopt varieties of symbols, which represent their uniqueness and draw attention to their existence. Denial of recognition produces a kind of narcissistic hurt that appears to stimulate wrathful reactions. Political terrorism movements have roots in this dynamic.[3] Perhaps, in a Hobbesian world, there is some gratification in gaining international recognition as a respected threat that disappears when being perceived as weak or having no recognition at all. In such a world, non-recognition really means to be perceived as powerless.

The concept of normative/affective (N/A) behavior demonstrated by actors whose choices are dominated by values and emotions is an ideal type, a baseline concept. Once it is introduced, there is room to discuss the conditions under which supposedly rational behavior shows such characteristics. In this paper, one of the main affective factors considered is the need for recognition. Burton[4] calls the need for recognition the right of any group to present a positive image in the eyes of other groups in the international arena. Non-recognition of individuals and groups is the source of their endless and relentless anger, sometimes expressed as armed aggression committed precisely against others who are valued as recognition-providers but who fail to provide it.

The need for recognition is difficult to define as an interest. However, this intangible human need of both individuals and groups is so valuable that the mere granting of acknowledgment can often bring disproportionate dividends in a negotiation process. The same dynamic response is elicited whether at the individual or social level. Recognition at the nation-state level is much more difficult to achieve, insofar as sovereignty problems are experienced by the national citizenry as factors threatening the integrity of the group self. This explains one of the newly emerged states' needs to obtain immediate recognition from peer states so as to be internationally accepted as its equal member.

In this field, N/A factors are often associated with or conditioned by symbols and self-images.[5] Perceptions of symbols and self-images are constructed within a national group at the same time as outside perceptions develop. National elites as international actors are often preoccupied with constructing their own actions in the most positive light in the eyes of the whole world. Self-images constructed by elites in each country through the support of national myths are promoted among its own citizens and other nations.[6] Those that are chosen and enforced are final products of an active process of reality construction that addresses both the elite's and public's needs to maintain self-esteem. Through this process, nations develop myths and dramatic scripts selected precisely for their ability to enhance and promote the valued national image.[7]

In this essay, I suggest that *national self-images and underlying national self-esteem needs are important elements that determine and influence foreign policy decision-making considerations.* In some cases, a perceived threat to a national self-image can be as serious as a territorial threat, if not more so. I would also argue that self-esteem needs at a nation's highest level are unacknowledged because of self-presentation needs to appear rational in the decision-making process. To save face, leaders repress awareness of these needs, while simultaneously promoting aggressive behavior to repair a weak image or to replace it with a more assertive or powerful one. The flip side of rational foreign policy decision-making consists of a level of semi-conscious anxiety which strives to maintain and restore a positive self-image vis-à-vis domestic public opinion, along with the need to force recognition by other international actors through whatever means possible.

The main focus of this paper is to show how N/A factors—embodied in national self-images—shaped the Argentine decision to invade and recover the Falkland/Malvinas and the British response. In this armed confrontation, elite decision-making and group-think on both sides were shaped and motivated not by alleged rational calculations, but by hidden affective factors. I will follow a general proposition that "the majority of choices people make, including economic ones, are entirely or largely based on normative-affective considerations not merely with regard to selection of goals but also of means. The limited zones in which logical/empirical (L/E) considerations are paramount are themselves defined by N/A factors that legitimate and otherwise motivate such decision-making."[8]

In this way, I hope to highlight the importance of N/A factors in foreign policy decision-making. Each issue will be addressed from opposing perspectives—both the British and the Argentine processes of self-image construction, along the seventy-four days of the Falklands/Malvinas war. Each country had a set of self-images assembled in a script that had developed over time in a patterned sequence of events, each in timely response to the other's propositions in the hostile interaction process. By exploring the respective self-images of Britain and Argentina and demonstrating how the perceived images affected the decisions of the elites, I will make a clear linkage between emotional motivations and foreign policy decision-making.

The Inadequacy of Realism

While the realist model of foreign policy decision-making is the most widely accepted and applied of the existing foreign policy paradigms, it is an incomplete model for understanding and predicting national decisions in the international arena. By assuming that nations make their foreign policy decisions in a logical, unemotional process guided solely by national interest considerations, the realist

Table 3.1. The Falklands/Malvinas War: A Short Chronology

December 20, 1981 With British authorization to exploit his two-year contract, aboard the naval ice-breaker *Almirante Irizar* Argentine scrap dealer C. S. Davidoff visits South Georgia to inspect some purchases and plan the dismantling of the equipment of a former whaling station.

February 27, 1982 In New York, Argentina and Britain reach an agreement to establish a permanent negotiation commission.

March 18, 1982 Argentine workers contracted by Davidoff, sailing in the *Bahia Buen Suceso* land at the Leith station in South Georgia without British authorization. Official confirmation of departure is given on March 22, but some men and equipment and a flag are left behind.

March 22, 1982 Britain protests against what is regarded as a violation of "British sovereignty," warning that if any further attempt is made to land in South Georgia without proper authorization, the British government reserved the right to take whatever action might be necessary.

March 23, 1982 The Thatcher government sends the ship *Endurance* to expel the Argentines from the islands.

March 24, 1982 The Argentine navy, reluctant to comply with the removal of the party left under the threat of force, orders the *Bahia Buen Suceso* to South Georgia.

April 2, 1982 Argentine troops land on the Falkland/Malvinas Islands. Royal marines surrender.

April 3, 1982 Argentina takes South Georgia Island. First House of Commons is seated since Suez. United Nations Security Council passes Resolution 502 calling for the withdrawal of Argentine troops from the islands and the immediate cessation of hostilities. First RAF transport aircraft deploy to Ascension Island.

April 5, 1982 Lord Carrington resigns as foreign secretary. British-owned *Task Force* sails.

April 7, 1982 Britain declares a 200-mile military exclusion zone around the Falkland/Malvinas (effective April 12).

April 8, 1982 The U.S. secretary of state, Alexander Haig, arrives in London to begin shuttle mediation.

April 10, 1982 The EEC approves trade sanctions against Argentina. Haig arrives in Buenos Aires for talks with the military *junta* in power.

April 17, 1982 Haig meets again with Argentine *junta*. After breakdown in mediation talks, he returns to Washington April 19.

April 23, 1982 British Foreign Office advises British nationals in Argentina to leave.

April 25, 1982 Royal marines recapture South Georgia, with the surrender of Cap. Astiz. Submarine *Santa Fe* is attacked and disabled.

April 30, 1982 Haig's mission is officially terminated. President Ronald Reagan declares U.S. support for Britain and economic sanctions against Argentina. Total exclusion zone comes into effect.

Table 3.1 (Continued)

May 1, 1982 British Harriers and a Vulcan attack Port Stanley (renamed Puerto Argentino) airfield. Three Argentine are aircraft shot down.

May 2, 1982 Belaunde Terry, president of Peru, presents a peace proposal to Argentine President Leopoldo Galtieri, who gives a preliminary acceptance with some proposed modifications. Before the Argentine junta ratifies the acceptance, the British submarine HMS *Conqueror* sinks the cruiser *General Belgrano*. The *junta* rejects the proposal.

May 4, 1982 Argentina sinks the HMS *Sheffield*, hit by an Exocet missile. A British Harrier plane is shot down.

May 5, 1982 Peru drafts a peace plan.

May 7, 1982 The UN enters peace negotiations.

May 9, 1982 Islands are bombarded from sea and air. Two Sea Harriers sink the Argentine trawler *Narwal*.

May 11, 1982 The Argentine supply ship *Cabo de los Estados* is sunk by HMS *Alacrity*.

May 14, 1982 Three Argentine Skyhawks are shot down. Prime Minister Margaret Thatcher warns that peaceful settlement may not be possible. Special forces conduct a night raid on Pebble Island; 11 Argentine aircraft are destroyed on the ground.

May 18, 1982 A peace proposal presented by the United Nations secretary-general, Javier Perez de Cuellar, is rejected by Britain.

May 20, 1982 Thatcher accuses Argentina of obduracy, delay, and bad faith.

May 21, 1982 British forces land on San Carlos, at East Falkland. HMS *Ardent* is sunk by air attack. Nine Argentine aircraft are shot down.

May 22, 1982 Consolidation day at bridgehead.

May 23, 1982 HMS *Antelope* is attacked and sinks after an unexploded bomb detonates. Ten Argentine aircraft are destroyed.

May 24, 1982 Seven Argentine aircraft are destroyed.

May 25, 1982 HMS *Coventry* is lost and *Atlantic Conveyor* hit by an Exocet (sinks May 28).

May 28, 1982 Second Battalion, Parachute Regiment, takes Darwin and Goose Green. More air raids on Port Stanley.

May 29, 1982 Warships and Harriers bombard Argentine positions: 250 Argentines are killed, 1,400 captured and 17 British are killed.

May 30, 1982 Shelling continues as British troops advance. Forty-five Commando units of the Royal Marines secure Douglas settlement, 3rd Battalion of The Parachute Regiment. recaptures Teal Inlet.

June 1, 1982 Britain repeats cease-fire terms.

June 2, 1982 British troops take Mount Kent.

June 4, 1982 Britain vetoes a Panamanian-Spanish cease-fire resolution in the UN Security Council.

June 6, 1982 The Versailles summit supports the British position on the Falklands.

June 8, 1982 Argentine aircraft attack landing craft *Sir Galahad* and *Sir Tristam* at Bluff Cove, with the loss of 50 British.

June 12, 1982 British forces seize Mount Tumbledon.

June 14, 1982 Argentine forces, led by Gral. Menendez, surrender in Port Stanley.

July 20, 1982 Britain formally declares an end to hostilities, and the two-mile exclusion zone established around the islands during the war is replaced by a Falklands Protection Zone (FIPZ) of 150 miles.

Sources: D. Morrison and H. Tumbler, *Journalists at War* (London: Sage, 1988) and N. Femenia, *National Identity in Times of Crises: The Scripts of the Falklands War* (New York: Nova Science, 1996).

model fails to take into account a number of other important factors affecting such decisions. Some of the most significant factors which realist paradigm fails to account for are normative/affective or emotional factors.

The failure of social theory, and specifically rational choice theory, to explain the constitution of identity is increasingly accepted among scholars. In the realist tradition, either states share the logic of self-help or they are at the mercy of others, but the complex aspects of redefining national identity and its affective components are not included. When the state is the central focus as the sole rational agent capable of action, defining security in self-interested terms, other considerations are necessarily left out. Thus realism undervalues sociological and psychological understandings of international interaction as they relate to security considerations. It is no surprise that the collapse of the Cold War as a theoretical milieu now allows different perspectives as changing conceptions of "self and interest" come to the fore.[9] For example, Kleiboer[10] is opening the field of international relations by including theories describing relational and socio-psychological behavior as factors determining outcomes. Considering identity and interest formation allows students of international relations to address the problem of how historical group-subjects' motives are generated. These considerations point to a basic question of my research: if viewed from the N/A framework, how was the motivation for the military invasion of the Falkland/Malvinas islands produced in Argentina in 1982? A reciprocal search is important in a study of the forceful British recovery.

The Falklands/Malvinas war makes a good case study because rarely are conflicts as remotely situated, as limited in time frame, and as easily isolated from the media as this war was. The unique, "research-friendly" characteristics of the Falkland/Malvinas war make it appealing in many ways for different research communities, as is apparent in the wealth of research done not only by both sides of the conflict but also by the international community.

Argentina's Growing Isolation on the International Scene

Argentina's military and economic superiority in South America was established at the beginning of the twentieth century, because of a prosperous relationship with the powerful British Empire begun in the previous century. But Argentina's fortune rose and fell with Britain's, and by 1939, the world was on the verge of dramatic change. Despite these evident impending changes, Argentina's ruling elites maintained the same relationship they had for over a century through World War II. Di Tella and Watt[11] argue that from 1920 on, Argentina's allegiance to Britain was counterproductive.

World War II thrust Argentina and the entire world into a sea of change. Argentina was forced to confront the existing socioeconomic conditions of 1945: national depression and humiliation due to misguided decision-making during World War II; working-class alienation due to changes from agrarian to industrial modes of production; and the growing lack of prestige and influence of traditional elites.

Figure 3.1 Map of Argentina

With the passing of British imperial might, the fundamental problem for Argentine elites was that the power of their long-standing "protector" country appeared to be fading away. But having modeled their identities upon those of their British counterparts, national elites could not bring themselves to relinquish such a cherished identification with their former allies in due time. Failure to do so would leave domestic leadership in dire need of new models on which to build self-images vis-à-vis domestic and international publics. By failure to resolve the impossible choice, a long period of frustration and isolation ensued.

Internal upheaval generated by conflicts between the old, landed oligarchy and the rising masses of immigrants' children, combined with the national ideology championed by the Peronist movement, produced a cycle of military coups d'état. Beginning in September 1930, these military takeovers led to alternating civilian and military governments until 1983, when the military junta that planned and executed the military recovery/invasion of the Falklands/Malvinas fell. Three top-level military officers from the Army (General Galtieri, designated president), the Navy (Admiral Anaya) and the Air Force (Brigadier Lami Dozo) composed the third Argentine junta, which continued to rule until elections were called in 1983. Reversal of development[12] and endless political crises were followed by growing international concern and helped shape a conflictive international image. In the recent history of Argentina's international relations, a permanent tension between acceptance and rejection by the Western world shaped a national role that would alternate between the image of the traditional continental leader and an "international pariah" status.[13]

Between the 1950s and 1970s, Argentina—like most other Latin American countries—was subjected to a U.S. policy of benign neglect. But this "benign neglect" was transformed into widespread, unanimous international criticism during the Carter years, when the first news about the junta's policy of "domestic control by means of state terror" became public. As more and more reports of atrocities against unarmed, defenseless civilians were made public, instituting the new figure of the "*desaparecidos*," the international community began reacting against the policy of domestic repression (denominated the "dirty war") and pressing the military regime for reforms. The Carter administration, beginning in 1977, instituted a new approach towards human rights violations, primarily motivated by Argentina's domestic terror. Maintained through the last part of the 1970s and the beginning of the 1980s, this policy provoked a rancorous response from the Argentine military then in power. The Argentine military perceived this policy to be an unjust attack upon behavior previously approved of and even taught by the U.S. military. The following statement reflects a deep reaction towards a policy of rejection and isolation: "We are left alone, we that are the Western defense reserves are attacked by people who should be defending our cause; we are the combat front against communism that is left alone."[14]

Even after the Malvinas fiasco, the experience of being Britain's enemy compounded the military junta's sense of "*being excluded from the family of Western countries, whose interests we were defending, where we feel that we belong.*"[15] The elites' need for international recognition was evident; how those needs impinged upon foreign policy decision-making will be shown. However, first it is necessary to look at how both international and domestic recognition needs intertwine.

> In recovering the islands, Argentina has carried out an action endorsed not only by the totality of its people, but also by the mandate of each succeeding generation ever since the day in which that part of its territory was snatched away from it. . . .
>
> Therefore, at the same time that the immutable Argentine disposition to negotiate honorable formulae for resolving the conflict has been made clear, it is necessary to state with the same firmness, the will of its authorities and its people to defend its sovereign rights and have them recognized.[16]

Domestic recognition needs are a strong motivating factor. Immediately after mobilizing national identity by recovering/invading the islands, it was impossible for the junta to withdraw the troops from the islands without jeopardizing the bases of their support. On the one hand, the junta was under intense domestic pressure, and on the other hand, it was cornered by British intransigence. Public support was so overwhelming for the members of the same junta, previously rejected by a massive hate demonstration two days before, that it blocked the initial design to remove the troops in the two-day period after the landing and take them back home, leaving only a symbolic presence. Having Argentine soldiers there, in the sacred Malvinas soil, became the essence of being Argentine; the *"ser nacional"*—that elusive national essence—was there alive and glowing. Common citizens could recognize themselves as being actors in the historic recovery of the long-lost islands, and so recover an identity also long lost in the era of military dictatorship.

How could the military junta possibly retreat without committing treason against this emotional, warming wave of public support that they had inadvertently unleashed? Admiral Anaya warned his colleagues of this situation and urged them to come to a decision, which was, not surprisingly, to stay and wage an impossible war. Thus, the emotional domestic situation, coupled with other pressures, locked Argentina into an armed conflict with Britain from which there was no possibility for withdrawing without losing national and international face.

Emotional Underpinnings

Argentina, throughout the nineteenth and much of the twentieth centuries, based its self-image on its profitable relationship with Britain, which was the most important commercial ally in the region. It drew strength from its assets in the fertile, extended pampas, natural resources and selective immigration that had also inspired faith in the concept of "Argentina Potencia"—Argentina's destiny to be the preponderant Latin American regional power.[17] When, after World War II, this relationship began to change because Britain's decline affected both Argentina's own self-image and its international trade, it brought internal strife and growing international isolation throughout the 1950s, 1960s, and 1970s. This isolation—coupled with the desperate need of Argentina's military junta for relief from domestic rejection—bred the rage, defensiveness, and emotional desire for an improved national self-image, which ultimately led to its decision to invade the Malvinas in 1982. An early self-affirming posture can be seen in Argentina's response to the British threat to send the *Endurance* to evict workers landed in the Georgias: "If we give way, in this case to a kind of British sudden impulse to eject our people by force, and in a British ship, then this is an affront to national honor."[18]

The Falkland/Malvinas Islands themselves were a long-standing source of tension between Britain and Argentina. First colonized by Argentina, and then taken by England in 1833, they would either be relegated to the background of the relationship or put to the fore, as by the communications agreements of 1971. But international negotiations were protracted and leading nowhere in 1982, as described by Foreign Relations Minister Costa Mendez: "The invasion of the Malvinas, or the occupation of the Malvinas, was caused by a long-time British attitude and, in my judgment, prompted by mismanagement of the Georgias crisis by the British government. Really, it is a gross exaggeration of the Georgias crisis."[19]

Given this history, it is no surprise that the Argentines, frustrated as they were with their relationship with Britain, chose the Falkland/Malvinas Islands as a

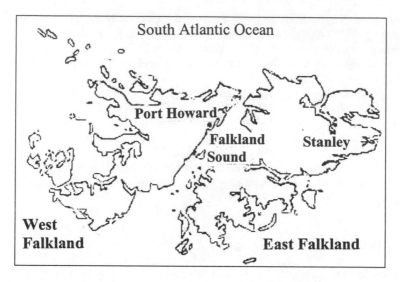

Figure 3.2 Map of the Falklands/Malvinas Islands

symbol of their fight for international recognition and legitimacy. The Malvinas, held in the public consciousness by almost a century of indoctrination through the school system,[20] meant more than merely a piece of territory. Argentines were seeking not only to right more than a century of perceived wrongs, but also to resolve now the deeper dispute of where Argentina stood vis-à-vis Britain and its position in the world system. The invasion of the Falklands/Malvinas, it was hoped, would spur a consideration of more substantive issues and, as a result, boost Argentina's international image to a more adequate level of importance. As Costa Mendez would say, "This occupation would make it possible for us to negotiate once and for all the underlying dispute. It would also *induce the international community, the interested parties and even the U. S. to pay more attention to the reasons for the dispute, its character and the need for a rapid solution.* The United Nations would not be able to procrastinate if faced with military action and would have to discuss it at the highest possible levels."[21]

But the emotional appeal of the Malvinas recovery had the unintended consequence of deeply mobilizing and inspiring the entire nation. As *La Nación*,[22] a popular newspaper, put it: "*An emotional wave washed the streets on April 2, with so much impetus, the same rolling over that of the forces on the beaches of Malvinas.*" At the same time, the elites' strategy in Argentina demanded that, in order to rally domestic support and engage the citizens on an emotional level, the invasion should be repeatedly portrayed as mandated by an anthropomorphic, mythological entity—the *entire Argentine public as an unitary actor: "A profound sentiment of all sectors of society. . . . This step has been thought of in the name of all and every one of the Argentines.*" This strategy was successful.

Argentine national elites appealed again and again to this mythological supraentity's pride and honor. They were followed enthusiastically by the public, which grasped the opportunity to see itself in a more positive way—no more the beaten, terrorized subjects of state terror, but a proud people, deserving a better future, as shown in these examples:

> As the Governor of the Southern Argentine territories, I am sure to reflect the deep faith that Argentines have, with a heart full of joy and love for the Fatherland, at this time when it begins to heal the *bleeding wound that during a century and half injured national dignity.*[23]

> *British pride needs respect as much as Argentine pride,* and if it has been hurt by Argentine military occupation of the Islands on April 2nd, *the Argentine pride was hurt by not only a century and half of occupation,* but also by the British *disdainful attitude* concerning the [unattended] need to continue examining the political aspects of the dispute.[24]

An essential element of the emotional appeal of leaders to their citizens is the ability to draw a clear line between right and wrong, good and evil. Specifically, the leaders must convince the people that theirs is a right and just cause. Argentina's leaders repeatedly reminded their citizens of the "justness" of their cause. Both Argentine elites and the media produced emotional appeals that portrayed the Falklands/Malvinas recovery as producing the healing of Argentina's identity and self-image as a whole nation, severely diminished by so many years of state terror under military juntas from 1976 on. They did so by comparing the recovered Islas Malvinas with lost family members who were finally found.[25] It is inevitable to find in these powerful emotional undertones an allusion to the fruitless search for so many disappeared children that were never found by their relatives:

> The day has arrived in which we can embrace that unknown missing Argentine, called Malvinas. We are very conscious about recovering these pieces of our motherland. We are very proud to be in the age of the rescue of our pieces, our islands that we feel as family and rejoice in the reunion of missing parts of our identity.[26]

> A son previously taken away from us has been reintegrated into the maternal fold; an act of justice has been accomplished.[27]

These metaphors demonstrate how the affective dynamics of "things lost and never to be recovered" impregnated the imaginary contents of public discourse. Contrary to researchers' theoretical assumptions, most of the psychological content of public Argentine discourse was not dedicated to building up enmity against the enemy, Britain, but to the process of working through and healing national emotional wounds. This furthers the hypothesis of such constructions as being more revealing of the internal processes' needs of the constructing entity than providing information about the described target enemy.

The "Touch and Go" Plan to Recover the Malvinas

From the beginning, according to Gamba-Stonehouse,[28] Argentina's military elites had foreseen the following course of events: military action would capture the attention of both the United Kingdom and the United States and would lead to resumption of negotiations under the terms of the 1966 United Nations accords. If necessary, the United States would be brought in as a mediator; and if that failed, the United Nations would be on Argentina's side, assuming that the Security Council would only take action after a breach of peace.

A short operation, that is, a show of military teeth followed by a turn to the negotiation table, was the plan. Busser[29] confirms that the operation—short, bloodless, and a surprise, so as to minimize casualties—seemed within Argentina's capabilities. The "touch and go" plan was driven by rational calculations that also involved the psycho-political need to seek due recognition of the seriousness of Argentina's intentions from the United Kingdom, the United States and the United Nations. In addition, the urgent Argentine need to negotiate the islands' sovereignty projected an image of equal importance to both contending nations.

Actions and not words would convince the international community of the importance of the Malvinas problem for the Argentine public; force was the only road open to achieve this objective. For Argentine elites, within the frame of their imagined "national parity" with Britain, a "touch and go" operation would succeed in moving the British stance to mandatory negotiation. This meant, in the military junta's calculations, an implicit assumption about Argentina's great importance in world rankings.

According to the perceptions of the British elites, the impudent demands of the imagined "lesser party" were perceived as an affront. The invasion of United Kingdom territory fueled an international perception both of British deterrence failure and its overall military weakness, compounding an unmistakable affront. The intended Argentine message—*We are equals; let's take each other seriously and acknowledge our needs for honorable negotiations*—had to be utterly ignored.

The British response was also conditioned by the strategic fact that recognition of Argentina's needs would do nothing to provide a badly needed boost in British self-image. Moreover, it was almost impossible—after the Suez 1956 crisis—to tolerate another "touch and go" humiliation from a Third World nation without answering it with a show of resolve.

Miscalculation by the junta included support for national self-images that disproportionately enlarged Argentina's strategic importance in world affairs. A vital part of Argentina's risk analysis, such as a more realistic self-appraisal, was missing in the decision to intervene in 1982. This delusion of self-importance, which compensated for so many years of international isolation and pariah status, permeated almost all the elites' decision-making after April 2, and this delusion injured Argentina's chances of accomplishing even the most modest goals of its invasion/recovery.

A Feeling of Rage, a Failure of Deterrence

Underneath the motivation of Argentina's military elites in 1982 was rage at their humiliating treatment by the United Kingdom and wholesale rejection by the international community because of persistent human rights violations. Domestically, the junta never accepted foreign perceptions, always considering itself a victim of an alleged "systematic international campaign against Argentina's prestige." Wedge[30] asserts that the phenomenon of narcissistic rage is precipitated by various forms of humiliation based on a sense of unfairness or injustice. While defeat in a fair competition is accepted by the prideful self (for example, the Argentine Air Force's behavior in the combat fields of the Malvinas), it is only when one is forced to accept unequal rules and finds oneself helpless or unable to gain acceptance that narcissistic rage ensues.

In the Falklands/Malvinas dispute, these unequal rules would be evidenced by Britain's past tendency to make strategic decisions about using military deterrence instead of meaningful negotiations. In the long history of the dispute between the two countries over the islands, this treatment had happened before. When Britain responded aggressively with threats and military actions to Argentina's invasion of the Falklands/Malvinas, it dealt a blow to Argentina. Argentina was doubly humiliated because it considered itself an equal partner to Britain, with a long partnership that merited a more egalitarian treatment than the subordinate position implied by threats of force. Admiral Busser[31] viewed the British decision to send military reinforcements—instead of pursuing negotiations—as a signal of British low interest and disdain for Argentina's rightful claims.

Due to this set of circumstances, Britain was naturally singled out to be the enemy at this time. In the recent past, Chile could have been Argentina's enemy because it also confronted Argentina with territorial disputes. Confrontations like these were taken as challenges to a glorious and important national image as continental leader. As described in a military speech pronounced to justify the first military junta's takeover in 1976, the promised Argentina of the immediate future was one of unmitigated splendor. Those images were overwhelmingly consistent with issues concerning Argentina's due status in the Western world, always focusing on a national drive to recover a proper place in the world order in accordance with its historical and strategic importance, and the consequent recovery of greatness, honor, and prestige. Argentina's relentless search for international recognition and status involved correcting disastrous image problems, by means such as coups d'etat or international confrontations. These image problems are described as fueling a "crisis waiting to happen."

> The progressive disintegration of Argentine optimism caused a real national neurosis, observable in certain social phenomena, such as compulsive attention to the 1978 World Soccer championship. There, the triumph against the best teams of other countries gave back the public the lost certitude that they could be the best of the world. Such glory . . . gave an ersatz consolation for national soul wounds, lacking other significant triumphs in areas of international competition.[32]

It is clear in the Falklands/Malvinas case that traditional deterrence can produce contradictory results. Lebow[33] clearly points out *"the apparent failure of states practicing deterrence to identify and address, at the same time, what may be the most important causes of foreign policy aggression."* One of these causes is the degree to which would-be challengers are inner-directed and inwardly focused on their own political interests. Lebow suggests that "their own political interests" are often grounded in self-image preservation and enhancement. Using defensive avoidance, elites try to reconcile incompatible domestic imperatives (the redefinition of the military junta from a perceived genocidal machine into a valued national leadership) and geopolitical-foreign relations objectives. The faltering legitimacy of the junta in Argentina increased its desperate need to do something to shore up its public support. The threat of domestic rejection overrode all deterrence considerations, precisely because at the same time there was an urgent need to redress the perceived lack of British recognition of Argentina as its worthy, equal partner. Fear of Britain's military might was not enough to deter brinkmanship decision-making when considerations about lack of international prestige, loss of face and narcissist hurt provoked the rage of the military junta members.

This rage originated with the frustration of the junta's need to be internationally acknowledged in their dual self-representation as valid and respected Western leaders, aptly exterminating the communist menace, and with the need to be accepted domestically as legitimate warriors in the fight against leftist guerrillas. Lebow, and also Levy,[34] observe that the principal incentive for aggressive foreign policy appears to be a state's own perceived domestic vulnerabilities. Perceived vulnerabilities lead state policy-makers to challenge an adversary, even when the external opportunity to act, in the form of an opponent's vulnerable commitment, is absent. Lebow and Stein, as well as Burton,[35] are proposing new research directions for a "human needs" theory that would explain and predict cases when strategic vulnerabilities and domestic political needs can create compelling incentives to use force.

By initiating military operations in order to avoid more humiliation, the line between mere "saber-rattling" and concrete military actions was crossed. Referring to the decision to retake the Malvinas, and the preliminary events that led to that decision, Busser maintains:

> It was not possible to accept taking back Davidoff's team of workers from Georgias without suffering a national humiliation. Whether using a British ship or an Argentine one would do it, it would be always under duress, by using force or the threat thereof. *By sending war ships to the area on March 25, and with all certainty on March 29, the United Kingdom had already begun its aggression.* When the ships arrived, workers would be evacuated from the place and *our humiliation would be unavoidable.*[36]

Busser's argument here confirms that the self-system of individuals provides a powerful linkage with the behavior of groups in social conflict. Non-rational human needs, in particular the need for recognition and "justice," provide a driving force in conflict behavior and need to be taken into account more than is commonly the case. Busser's claim to success illustrates how aggressive measures applied in order to recover a respected place within a valued relationship become validated: "We can see now that the British approach to the problem has changed, from utter disdain of Argentina's capacity of action or reaction, to the adoption of serious preventative measures. To the contrary, disdain and conceit were shown in the March 23rd ultimatum."[37]

Confirming pieces of evidence are the self-enhancing results of an image obtained by a courageous challenge—even if a nation fails, then it fails gloriously. Later, Busser when describing his perception of a new place for Argentina in the world's appreciation, supports the contention that crisis generation was an appropriate strategy for Argentina to regain national pride:

> Today, nobody can ignore that due to the British usurpation, a less powerful country confronted one of the most powerful military, economic and social superpowers. . . . *Nobody can deny that today Argentina has another place in these countries' consideration.* Admiration so gained would endure and have transcendence impossible to suspect today. *Prestige and an image of moral courage during the conflict gave to Argentina moral leadership;* because of the Malvinas we now are regarded with admiration and respect, because we showed ourselves as a country committed to defend what is its own.[38]

The generic psychological result of internal and external mobilizations, stemming from a pride-enhancing script, is a renewal of the sense of identity and dignity among human populations that feel (and often are) excluded not only from the centers of power but from a legitimate "home" and recognized "roots" in the order of societies: "As we are in the southern part of the continent, we looked like a terminal country; we are not being that anymore but a nation included, by necessity, in the Western world. . . . Malvinas is an episode of something much more important. *It is Argentina's place in the world.*"[39]

In challenging Britain, Argentines assumed that the United Kingdom could assure the defense of the Falkland Islanders through the negotiation of a number of guarantees for their lifestyle preservation, but that in the long run, Argentina's claim for sovereignty on the islands would be internationally accepted. The illusion that Argentina and Britain were on the same footing and that Argentina's forceful attempts to be heard would be successful was a natural conclusion for a people seeking affirmation of its self-image. Given that national identity mobilization is such a powerful force,[40] it is not surprising that the pressure from below (Argentine and other South American countries' public expectations) influenced the decision-makers in Buenos Aires by frustrating the "touch and go" operation and restricting their ability to seek creative and flexible solutions with Britain. Even though they lost the challenge, the symbolic rewards of forcing Britain to recognize Argentina as a suitable military enemy were more satisfactory for humiliation and rage compensation than any formal agreement.

The management of narcissistic rage requires that offended groups be given every opportunity to assert in public their identity and to explain their complaint.

They must not be yielded to, but they must be heard and acknowledged. This prescription runs flatly counter to the normal rational decision to restore international order by isolating and silencing such unrestrained actors. Thus, the realist politics that advocate ignoring, controlling and/or destroying dictators is in this aspect counterproductive and futile. Such was clearly the case in the Falklands/Malvinas crisis, as the British, motivated by their own emotional needs, were unwilling and unable to acknowledge Argentina's emotional desires and thus responded aggressively to Argentina's perceived affront to British sovereignty and pride. If emotional needs were included in the threat evaluation, perhaps other conflict resolution methods would have been attempted, without the need for a military confrontation. Conflict resolution succeeds only when war is regarded more as a waste of much-needed resources instead of a necessary compensation for hurt pride at any price.

The United Kingdom: In Need of a Good War

Britain's long history of success in battle, its long reign as the world's foremost empire, and its decline following World War II are well known and need not be chronicled here. Britain always had a glorious vision of itself as a world leader, a conqueror, and an imperial power, but following World War II, domestic and international reality began to challenge that self-image. Even in the early 1980s, Britain was still coming to grips with the reality of its decline in prestige and influence in the world. In 1982, overstretched in military capabilities, foreign policy elites feared a replay of the Suez crisis of 1956 during which Britain was forced to abandon its military response to Egypt's attack because it lacked U.S. military support. Thereby Britain had to accept humiliation at the hands of a Third World nation. During the Falklands episode, seen as a replay of the Suez crisis, that fear was compounded by the rage and shame of having been surprised in their defense planning vis-à-vis their NATO partners. These feelings cast a long shadow, as Canetti[41] explains: "No one ever forgets a sudden depreciation of himself, for it is too painful. Unless he can thrust it on to someone else, he carries it with him for the rest of his life. And the crowd as such never forget its depreciation."

The political and psychological consequences of the Suez crisis of 1956 changed, once and for all, the world's perceptions of Britain and demonstrated its declining world role and influence with the United States. It also demonstrated the frightening proposition that poor countries sometimes do not even need to be nuclear powers to reveal a superpower's military weakness. To heal that historic wound, some definite kind of U.S. support was needed that would provide explicit recognition, as Christie[42] says: "After the terrible psychological shock of our defeat at Suez, *the Falkland Islands recovery was an element of redemption.* The Americans let us down; they betrayed us, at Suez. This time, they stood by us. This time, they did the right thing."

During the Falklands/Malvinas crisis, Britain and Argentina engaged in an "event definition process" that is an integral part of reality construction. According to Edelman,[43] reality is best understood as a phenomenon that is inter-subjective but certainly not verifiable in the positivist sense. Whatever seems real to a group of people is real in its political consequences regardless of how absurd, hallucinatory, or shocking it may look to others in different situations or at other times. Any definition of the situation by elites has this impact. Multiple realities are inherent in politics and they are built upon policy rationalizations that justify choosing particular interpretations of the political scene and ignoring others. Argentine takeover of the Falkland Islands prompted Prime Minister Thatcher's early characterization:

> The House meets this Saturday to respond to a situation of great gravity. We are here because, for the first time for many years, British sovereign territory has been invaded by a foreign power. . . . The Falkland Islands and dependencies remain British territory. No aggression and no invasion can alter that simple fact. It is the Government's objective to see that the Islands are freed from occupation and are returned to British administration at the earliest possible moment.[44]

Dillon explains the reality construction process that took place in Britain in the following manner:

> The task confronting British decision-makers at the beginning of the invasion crisis was the construction—under great pressure and changing circumstances—of a new and sustainable interpretation of the whole Falklands affair: an interpretation that would express the War Cabinet's appreciation of what was now at issue in the Falklands, *mobilize the maximum amount of national and international support* for the ultimatum it had issued, seek a diplomatic way out of the ultimatum if possible and govern its progressive implementation if Argentina refused to withdraw. [45]

> As in all policy-making, the interpretation was created and edited as it was enacted. In the process, the language and thus the character of the Falklands issue was transformed into a great symbolic drama composed of a wide variety of *interweaving national themes,* all of which focused on the future of the Islands and the outcome of the conflict. *The Government's political will thus became closely identified with the validation of the country's values and symbol system.*[46]

A perceived disparity between a glorious and stable past and a tarnished and unstable present leads to the selection and characterization of certain events as a focus for a process of purposeful self-esteem recovery. Selection criteria for those events consist of their ability to provide emotional compensation for the deficits of the present situation to domestic publics in dire need of self-esteem reinforcement. That this was long overdue was Mrs. Thatcher's opinion: *"Too long submerged, too often denigrated, too easily forgotten, the springs of pride in Britain flow again."*[47]

British Emotions: Humiliation and Shame

Members of the British Parliament, known worldwide for their theatrics and impassioned delivery of remarks, made quite explicit to the world that the British emotional answer to the Falklands crisis humiliation meant an aggressive response:

> Last Saturday's debate was *a very sad occasion for all of us*. It has not been made any the less sad since then by the departure of Lord Carrington from the Foreign Office. I am sure that today we are all bound together, as we were on Saturday, by feelings of *sorrow, shame and anger*. [48]

> Last Friday, *as the House knows to its pain*, Argentine military aggression took place on British sovereign territory in the Falkland Islands. This was, as we all feel, a *humiliating experience, and a grave affront* to the people of the Falkland Islands above all, and to the people of the United Kingdom. That action was totally and utterly unacceptable to all of us. [49]

> Of course we have suffered *indignity and humiliation*. Of course we are *angry and shocked* that the country should have been taken completely by surprise when we might have been warned and prepared. [50]

If one accepts as valid the hypothesis that Britain's self-image necessarily includes world leadership, the "recovery" of the islands by Argentina was necessarily a challenge to that belief. By exposing a self-designated world power and the third naval power of the world as unable to deter a surprise attack by a neglected former "almost colony," Argentina's recovery/invasion of the islands struck at the core of Britain's self-image. [51] It was an emotionally shocking situation to be globally perceived as unable to control an actor so insignificant that it never made Britain's "adequate contenders" list.

In this way, Argentina's sheer ignorance of the British public's tolerance limits for Third World aggression provided enough justification for the military response. [52] Britain's past experiences and its fears of future humiliations constitute important, if largely repressed, explanatory determinants of its international behavior. As Dillon explains:

> British sovereign territory invaded by a Third World nation is an international humiliation impossible to deny, because it is perceived under the memory of another international humiliation: the Suez crisis and the Egyptian challenge of 1956. The meaning was clear: When the British Empire breathed its last at Suez in 1956, it was confirmed to world opinion that Britain had lost the imperial will. [53]

Whatever the Argentines thought the impact of their "non-aggressive recovery" would be on the British mindset, they never suspected the depth of the humiliation, shame and outrage experienced by the British public towards its own historical background: "The third naval power in the world and the second in

NATO have suffered a *humiliating defeat.* . . . We should recognize that we have suffered the inevitable consequences of the combination of *unpreparedness and feeble counsels.*"[54]

Steinberg[55] defines shame as an unpleasant emotional experience implying an acute lowering of self-esteem. Furthermore, it is a specific form of anxiety evoked by the imminent danger of unexpected exposure, humiliation and rejection. Shame involves feelings ranging in intensity from bashfulness to embarrassment, as well as the experience of being slighted, put down, dishonored, disgraced, humiliated or mortified.

The experience of shame and unacknowledged alienation has been described as the emotional trigger for vengeful thinking.[56] What is called "war fever" is no more than the aggressive reaction that attempts to redress what is perceived as a public embarrassment with unforeseen harmful consequences:

> We feel *sorrow* for the people of the Falkland Islands, the framework of whose lives has been smashed; *shame for ourselves* that undertakings of assurances given, perhaps unwisely, by successive Governments to defend the Islands to the best of our abilities, in the event have meant so little; and *anger at a piece of gross international misconduct. Sorrow, shame and anger* may not be good counselors now.[57]

As shame is the public signal of a threatened social bond, reaction by members of Parliament concerned with their constituencies' support had to be immediate and swift:

> *My gut reaction is to use force.* Our country has been *humiliated.* Every Honorable Member *must have a gut reaction to use force,* but we must also be sure that we shall not kill thousands of people in the use of that force. I am in favor of the firmest possible diplomatic action and sanctions against the Argentines. I am in favor of asking the United States and all our allies to unite against the Argentine.[58]

Could Britain have been spared this international humiliation? If humiliation could not be avoided, then Britain was a lesser power than Argentina. Those that believed that the invasion could have been prevented by Britain's intelligence and defense services simultaneously asserted that humiliation ought to have been prevented. The failure of British deterrence, despite their intelligence capabilities, was exposed by the surprise invasion:

> The real question is this. *Was the available evidence of such a character that she should prudently have taken precautions at an earlier date?* My answer to that question must be "Yes." . . . That is my first charge against the Government today. . . . Today our Fleet is sailing towards *hostilities that could have been prevented.* . . . We are sending an aircraft carrier that has already been sold to meet cash limits from a port that is to be closed and with 500 sailors holding redundancy notices in their pockets. I find that *humiliating,* too.[59]

Not only the House but also the domestic press widely confirmed humiliation and shame perceptions and also harshly criticized the Thatcher government's deterrence failure:

> *The Government last night rounded off a day of spectacular military and diplomatic humiliation* with the public admission by the Foreign Secretary, Lord Carrington, and the Defense Secretary, Mr. John Nott, that Argentina had indeed captured Port Stanley, while the British Navy lay too far away to prevent it. . . . The irony of a government elected to strengthen Britain's defense posture of finding itself in this position, will not be lost on MPs and some were saying that the debacle in the Falkland Islands was the *Government's most dramatic single humiliation. The British Lion is caught with his trousers down.*[60]

Shame is derived from helplessness and loss of self-control together with foreign over-control. British lack of interest in the previous negotiations with Argentina—which occupied the forty-seventh place in a ranking of its strategic interests—was reflected in nonchalant attitudes. Postures like "talking with Argentina only for the sake of talking" or "buying time, having nothing to offer" were balanced only by ineffectual good intentions, as stated in the Franks Report[61] as well as other sources, including Charlton,[62] Dillon,[63] and Freedman and Gamba-Stonehouse.[64] Dooming to failure the British strategy of "substituting procedure for substance," Lebow [65] predicted that, sooner or later, Britain would run out of new negotiation proposals and Argentina would tire of the waiting game. By invading the Falkland/Malvinas Islands, Argentina denounced this weak strategy in the most dramatic way.

The emotional motivations underlying the British response to the Falklands crisis are clearly stated by British elites throughout the crisis.[66] Humiliation stemming from a declining international image and an uncertain self-image were turned to rage by the Argentine invasion of the Falkland Islands. The resort to aggression appeared to be a needed means to redress the pain that humiliation had brought upon Britain.[67] The Argentine elites failed to perceive the depth of British emotional reaction, assuming, according to the rational actor model, that the British would reciprocate in a logical and diplomatic manner by negotiating a solution. By acting out its own emotional needs, Argentina's leadership failed to realize that British elites had emotional needs of their own.

A Compensatory Response: Shame Becomes Pride

The compensatory response to the pervasive sense of shame and humiliation among both the British elites and the British public was swift aggression. Argentina had "touched a nerve" with the British, and in elite discourses, revenge appeared instead of atonement, and shame was turned into pride. Lord Shackleton[68] at the House of Lords declared, *"The war showed us to be prepared to stand up for what we believe to be right, this is our pride."* Traditionally, lost pride was recovered by enforcing British imperialism through the deployment of the Royal Navy. Professing to see *"this ancient country rising as one nation,"* Thatcher stated, *"The Navy sets out to win back Britain's pride."*[69]

By invading the Falkland Islands, Argentina had given to British elites a perfect opportunity to restore some of its lost pride and honor using the famed British Navy against a British territorial invader, and so to reaffirm an imperiled role. In the Falklands crisis, *"both national honor and the traditional Royal Navy,"* were at stake. The future of the Royal Navy and how it would share military burdens with the Americans "east of Suez" was in question. To save one was to save both.[70]

Pride and shame are opposite emotions that describe polar situations in self-esteem. They serve as intense and automatic signs of the state of a system that is otherwise difficult to observe. While pride is the sign of an intact social bond, shame is the sign of a threatened one, and domestic unrest is its corollary. Britain seized the opportunity to transform the shame of the Falkland Islands invasion by the Argentines into a glorious naval victory, which restored the pride of Britain's past. In addition, the conflict offered the perfect rationale for restoring naval capabilities, which were more threatened by British budget cuts than by Argentine Exocet missiles.

The power of Britain's elites' emotional construction of events and the effects of the episode on the British psyche are summed up by a media report on the event. It is quite clear how the emotional overtones play a role as building blocks in the construction of national identity:

> After victory, certain things will follow. *The British have become a nation again, on the back of the Falklands war.* Several ministers have said so. *The whole thing has been a kind of therapy.* As a result, from victory in the South Atlantic, Mrs. Thatcher will stride to triumphs on a wider plane. Supporting this optimism are the opinion polls. The latest poll, showing 89% of the British in favor of the invasion, is surely unanswerable. The war cabinet can scarcely believe its luck.[71]

Conclusion

This research supports the claim that normative/affective motivations underlie all foreign policy decision-making. Domestic concerns for positive national-image recognition are a permanent powerful force still unaccounted for by most foreign policy decision-making paradigms. Superpowers attempt to project images of global superiority, but these images must be maintained continually as constructs recognized by other countries. Image-maintenance efforts can generate circumstances that make international violence possible and may even produce it, as this research has proven, to stage a confrontation that would confirm resolve and military might.

A vital lesson of the Falklands/Malvinas conflict is the acknowledgment of the importance of emotions connected with national self-images in foreign policy decision-making. This is a hidden element that indeed shapes presupposed rational decision-making, from a balanced self-assertion to the extremes of mythological self-righteous crusades. Conversely, public needs for self-appreciation can be manipulated and used to provide symbolic, emotional substitutions for more concrete subsistence needs, which national leadership somehow perceives itself unable to deliver. This is an impossible trade-off, as symbolic goods are easily spent, and more misery waits in the future if no concrete development plans are made. This research has described how those emotional, symbolic constructs were created, developed and provided to the public in the case studied, but more information about the emotional aspects of foreign policy decision-making is needed if we are to better understand and perhaps prevent armed conflict between nations.

It has been proposed that a comprehensive approach to understanding foreign policy decisions must combine deterrence and assurance.[72] I argue that we must move beyond a merely enhanced version of power politics, to build a new paradigm of conflict resolution based on human needs approach. It has also to acknowledge such unexpressed national drives for recognition and consequent needs for self-esteem maintenance that a contending nation is trying simultaneously to express and resolve through deterrence challenges.

If it is true that war begins in the minds of men, a thorough review is needed of the social psychological components of the decision-making process of elites who decide that war has an acceptable cost and wage it with constructed domestic support. Given social structures as they are now, we have just begun to search beneath theoretical rationales for aggressive decision-making (the "rational man" hypothetical construct) by looking at more subconscious motivations (the "emotional man").

From the point of view of the peace researcher, it is regrettable that intersubjective international understandings, friend-images and communities of recognition have no similar dramatic impact and are not able to gather the same world attention and interest in motivations and needs as armed (televised) confrontation. The positive outcome of Argentina's defeat was in providing it with a needed contrast to the mythical self-image, allowing the internalizing of painful new understandings of self and other, and in beginning the process of acquiring new and more accurate national role identities. Along this path, self-presentation and stage management in a different, non-conflictive setting would provide the opportunity to frame alternative definitions of social situations in ways that create more positive international roles. To teach the rest of the world that Argentina could be trusted, it had to design unilateral initiatives showing strong positive intentions, such as the return to democratic rule in 1983. To reassert moral leadership, Britain had to review the much-neglected relationship with the Falkland Islanders and grant them benefits previously denied, such as the right to British citizenship, so as to assure the lessening of their colonial dependency from London.

Perhaps Kriesberg[73] points in this direction when he calls for an international relations paradigm that encompasses not only the security of individual countries but also a commonality of interests defending world peace. In a new multipolar world, more voices may be integrated into a shared standing, in different capacities, so as to give some symbolic assurances of the proper place in the international order to all nations, great and small. Failure to do so forces nations to accept being mobilized to wage wars they cannot afford and which basically only seek to redress symbolic wounds.

Notes

Except where noted emphasis in quoted material throughout this chapter is my own.

1. Nora Femenia, *National Identity in Times of Crises: The Scripts of the Falklands-Malvinas War* (New York: Nova Science Publishers,1996).

2. M. Cottam and Shih Chih-yo, eds., *Contending Dramas: A Cognitive Approach to International Organizations* (New York: Praeger, 1992).

3. Theodor Scheff and S. Reztinger, *Emotions and Violence: Shame and Rage in Destructive Conflicts* (Lexington, Kans.: Lexington Books, 1992).

4. John Burton, ed., *Conflict: Human Needs Theory.* (New York: St. Martins, 1990).

5. Amitai Etzioni, "Normative-Affective Factors: Towards New Decision-Making Models," in *Decision Making: Alternatives to Rational Choice Models,* ed. Mary Zei (New York: Sage, 1992), 91.

6. Noel Kaplowitz, "National Self-Images, Perception of Enemies, and Conflict Strategies: Psychopolitical Dimensions of International Relations," in *Political Psychology* 11, no. 1 (March 1990).

7. Femenia, *National Identity.*

8. Helena Flam, "Emotional Man: Corporate Actors as Emotion-Motivated Managers," in *Decision Making: Alternatives to Rational Choice Models,* ed. Mary Zei (New York: Sage, 1992), 90.

9. Alexander Wendt, "Anarchy Is What States Make of It: The Social Construction of Power Politics," in *International Organization* 46 (1992), 301-425.

10. Marieke Kleiboer, "Understanding Success and Failure of International Mediation," in *Journal of Conflict Resolution* 40, no. 2 (1996), 60-389.

11. Guido Di Tella and D. Cameron Watt, *Argentina between the Great Powers, 1939-1946* (Pittsburgh, Pa.: University of Pittsburgh Press, 1990), 195.

12. Carlos Waissman, *Reversal of Development in Argentina: Postwar Counterrevolutionary Policies and Their Structural Consequences* (Princeton, N.J.: Princeton University Press, 1987).

13. Carlos Escude, *La Argentina, Paria Internacional?* (Buenos Aires: Editorial de Belgrano, 1984).

14. Horacio Verbitsky, *La Ultima Batalla de la Tercera Guerra Mundial* (Buenos Aires: Legasa, 1986), 30.

15. President Galtieri, National Address, *La Nación,* 2 May 1982.

16. Argentina Military Junta Communiqué, no. 25, 15 April 1982.

17. Mario Rapoport, *Aliados o Neutrales? La Argentina frente a la Segunda Guerra Mundial* (Buenos Aires: Eudeba, 1980), 76-79.

18. Admiral Fraga, *La Nación,* 28 March 1982.

19. Nicanor Costa Mendez, quoted in Michael Charlton, *The Little Platoon: Diplomacy and the Falklands Dispute* (London: Blackwell, 1989), 122-24.

20. Carlos Escude, *Patología del Nacionalismo* (Buenos Aires: Editorial de Belgrano 1987).

21. Nicanor Costa Mendez, "El Papel de los EE.UU. en el Conflicto del Atlantico Sur," part 2, *Revista Argentina de Estudios Estratégicos* (Buenos Aires: Ejército Argentino, 1983):15; Where it is useful to highlight the aspects of propositions that support this chapter's contention regarding the role of emotions, I add emphasis (italics) to paragraphs which include emotionally based content.

22. Editorial comment, *La Nación,* 20 April 1982, 6.

23. Gral. Mario Menendez, governor of Malvinas, *La Nación,* 3 April 1982, 13.

24. Editorial comment, *La Nación,* 21 April 1982, 6.

25. Femenia, *National Identity.*

26. Amelia Borthagaray, letters to the editor, *La Nación,* 3 April 1982, 10.

27. Colonel Callioni, *La Nación,* 3 April 1982, 12.

28. Virginia Gamba-Stonehouse, "International and Inter-Agency Communication Failures in the Period Previous to and during the Falkland/Malvinas War of 1982 between the United Kingdom and Argentina," (Washington, D.C.: United States Institute of Peace, 1991), 400-408.

29. Carlos Busser, *Operación Rosario* (Buenos Aires: Atlántida, 1985), 16.

30. Bryan Wedge, "Psychology of the Self in Social Conflict," in *International Conflict Resolution,* ed. Azar and Burton (Sussex: WheatSheaf, 1986), 61.

31. Busser, *Operación Rosario,* 92.

32. Norberto Ras, "Saber Perder," *La Nación,* 3 June 1982, 6.

33. Richard Ned Lebow, "Miscalculation in the South Atlantic: The Origins of the Falklands War," in *Psychology and Deterrence,* ed. Jervis, Lebow and Stein. (Baltimore: Johns Hopkins University Press, 1985), 340.

34. Lebow, "Miscalculation," 340; Jack Levy, "External Scapegoating by Authoritarian Regimes: Argentina in the Falklands/Malvinas Case," (Rutgers University, 1990).

35. Richard Ned Lebow and Janice Gross Stein, "When Does Deterrence Succeed and How Do We Know?" (Ottawa Canadian Institute for International Peace and Security, Occasional Paper, 1990); John Burton, *Conflict, Resolution and Provention* (New York: St. Martins, 1990).

36. Carlos Busser, *Malvinas, la Guerra Inconclusa* (Buenos Aires: Francisco Reguera Editor, 1987), 97.

37. Busser, *Malvinas, la Guerra,* 12.

38. Busser, *Malvinas, la Guerra,* 62.

39. Brigadier Ricardo Lami Dozo, Air Force Commander, *La Nación,* 15 June 1982, 10.

40. William Bloom, *Personal Identity, National Identity and International Relations* (Cambridge: Cambridge University Press, 1990).

41. Elias Canetti, *Crowds and Power* (New York: Continuum, 1976), 187.

42. W. Hunter Christie, in Michael Charlton, *The Little Platoon: Diplomacy and the Falklands Dispute* (London: Blackwell, 1989), 91.

43. Murray Edelman, *Constructing the Political Spectacle* (Chicago: University of Chicago Press, 1988), 66.

44. Margaret Thatcher, 3 April 1982, in *The Falklands Campaign* (Official Record of Members of Parliament's debates) (London: HMSO, 1982).

45. M. Dillon, "Thatcher and the Falklands," in *Belief Systems and International Relations,* ed. R. Little and S. Smith. (London: Blackwell. 1988), 112.

46. Dillon, "Thatcher and the Falklands," 112.

47. Thatcher, 29 April 1982, in *The Falklands Campaign.*

48. MP John Peyton, 7 April 1982, in *The Falklands Campaign.*

49. MP Richard Luce, 7 April 1982, *The Falklands Campaign.*

50. MP Michael Mates, 7 April 1982, in *The Falklands Campaign.*

51. Andrew Thompson, "Informal Empire? An Exploration in the History of Anglo-Argentine Relations, 1810-1914," in *Journal of Latin American Studies* 24 (1991): 419-36.

52. Christoph Bluth, "The British Resort to Force in the Falklands/Malvinas Conflict, 1982: International Law and Just War Theory," in *Journal of Peace Research* 23, no. 1 (1987): 5-20.

53. Dillon, "Thatcher and the Falklands," 99.

54. MP Julian Amery, 3 April 1982, in *The Falklands Campaign.*

55. Blema Steinberg, "Shame and Humiliation in the Cuban Missile Crisis: A Psychoanalytic Perspective," in *Political Psychology* 12, no. 4 (1991): 655.

56. Scheff and Reztinger, *Emotions and Violence,* 137.

57. Peyton, *The Falklands Campaign.*

58. MP George Foulkes, 3 April 1982, in *The Falklands Campaign.*

59. MP Leonard Callaghan, 7 April 1982, in *The Falklands Campaign.*

60. M. White, 3 April 1982, in *The Falklands Campaign.*

61. Lord Franks, "Falkland Islands Review, Report of a Committee of Privy Counsellors" (London: HMSO, 1982): 61, 63, 71, 75.

62. Michael Charlton, *The Little Platoon: Diplomacy and the Falklands Dispute* (London: Blackwell, 1989), 71-75.

63. Dillon, "Thatcher and the Falklands," 117.

64. Lawrence Freedman and Virginia Gamba-Stonehouse, *Signals of War: The Falklands Conflict of 1982* (London: Faber and Faber, 1990), 9.

65. Lebow, "Miscalculation in the South Atlantic," 105.

66. Ygael Vertzberger, *The World in their Minds: Information Processing, Cognition and Perception in Foreign Policy Decision-Making* (Stanford, Calif.: Stanford University Press, 1990).

67. Vamik Volkan, *The Need to Have Enemies and Allies* (New York: Jason Aronson, 1988).

68. Lord Shackleton, 14 June 1982, in *The Falklands Campaign.*

69. Margaret Thatcher, 14 June 1982, in *The Falklands Campaign.*

70. Charlton, *The Little Platoon,* 188.

71. Hugo Young, "Can This Really Be a Triumph?" *London Times,* 30 May 1982, 17.

72. Lebow, "Miscalculation in the South Atlantic.

73. Louis Kriesberg, "Explaining the End of the Cold War," in *New Views of International Security* Occasional Paper Series (Syracuse, N.Y.: Syracuse University, 1990).

Chapter Four

David versus Goliath

The Big Power of Small States

Ross A. Klein

A cursory review of the literature on inter-nation conflict suggests that little attention has been given to conflicts in which the government of a relatively weaker state has successfully confronted and won in a dispute with a state that is militarily and economically more powerful. One possible reason that these types of conflicts have not been studied is that conventional wisdom would indicate that the outcome of such disputes is obvious—the state that is relatively stronger militarily and economically will ultimately prevail. However, there are instances in which states that are militarily weaker have confronted and won in disputes with stronger adversaries.

Conflicts in which a relatively weaker party is able to prevail in a dispute with a stronger adversary provide a unique opportunity to study the dynamic of a dispute in which military and economic strength are not the sole factors determining the outcome of a conflict. Study of these conflicts focuses attention on tactics and strategies that are nonmilitary in nature and which would appear to be effective in neutralizing or minimizing the role of the military of the government of a stronger state. Success in these conflicts is likely to depend on the use of nonviolent (i.e., negative sanctions that fall short of military force) or noncoercive (i.e., positive inducements and persuasion) actions.

The purpose of this chapter is to explore several conflicts in which the government of a militarily weaker state has been successful in challenging a state that is militarily and economically stronger. Of interest in this study are two issues: (1) what strategies or factors make it possible for the government of a militarily weaker state to successfully challenge a state that is militarily stronger? and (2) what strategies or factors appear to neutralize the government of a militarily stronger state from using the full force of its military? These questions will be answered through case studies of three sets of protracted disputes over claims of coastal fishery limits in which a militarily weaker state has successfully challenged a stronger adversary.

The Cases

The three sets of disputes over international fishing rights chosen for this study have several characteristics in common: (1) each involves a militarily weaker state extending the coastal area over which it claims exclusive jurisdiction; (2) each involves a direct challenge to a stronger state by the government of a militarily weak state; (3) in the case of each, the government of the militarily stronger state resisted the claims of the weaker state; and (4) each conflict was resolved with the government of the militarily weaker state being able to claim, at least in part, success.[1] These commonalities allow for a comparative analysis and for tentative conclusions about how it is possible for the government of a militarily weaker state to win in a conflict with a militarily stronger adversary. The cases include a series of four disputes between the United Kingdom and Iceland (a country about the size of Kentucky), popularly known as the Cod Wars; and both concurrent and separate disputes involving the United States and Ecuador (a country about the size of Colorado) and the United States and Peru (a country roughly twice the size of Texas), which have commonly been referred to as the Tuna Wars.

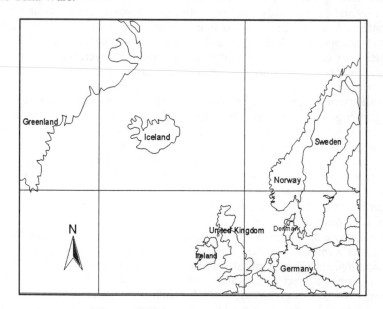

Figure 4.1 Geographic Location of Iceland

The Cod Wars

In October 1949, in accordance with a 1901 treaty between Great Britain and Denmark which established three-mile fishery limits around Iceland, the Icelandic Government notified the British Government that it was giving the required two years notice that the agreement would be terminated in October 1951. On 22 April 1950, the Icelandic Ministry of Fisheries issued regulations providing for a four-mile conservation zone off the north coast of Iceland wherein all fishing by foreign countries would be prohibited as of 1 June 1950, with the exception of British fishing vessels which would be allowed to continue fishing in these areas until 3 October 1951. This extension was followed on 19 March 1952 with regulations extending the four-mile limit to all Icelandic coasts and providing for a new system of drawing baselines from which the four-mile limit would be calculated. British Government and industry protests of this four-mile limit led to the first Cod War, which was resolved four years later after a two-year mediation effort by the Organization for European Economic Cooperation (OEEC).

The Icelandic Government again extended its fishery limit in 1958—this time to twelve miles—which led to a renewed dispute between the United Kingdom and Iceland and which lasted until 1961, when the two governments were able to settle their differences. Settlement came only after the second United Nations Law of the Sea Conference failed to reach agreement on an internationally acceptable law relating to the breadth of fishery jurisdictions and contiguous zones. Iceland's Government extended the fishery limits around the island again in 1972 to fifty miles and in 1975 to two hundred miles.

Each of these extensions led to renewed conflicts; the first being resolved in 1973 after mediation by NATO and the second in 1976 following direct intervention by the Governments of Norway and the United States, and NATO. In each of the latter three disputes, the British Government resisted the Icelandic challenge with the use of its navy, and in two of them the British fishing industry countered with a ban on the landing of Icelandic products in the United Kingdom.

Table 4.1. The Cod Wars: A Short Chronology

October 1949 Iceland declares its intent to extend limits to 4 miles.

May 1952 Limit extended to 4 miles. British Government protests extension; landing ban imposed on Icelandic products at British ports. Iceland shifts exports to Soviet Union.

February 1953 British Government offers to lift ban in return for referring dispute to International Court of Justice; blocked by the British fishing industry.

November 1954 Organization for European Economic Cooperation (OEEC) appoints special committee to resolve the dispute.

March 1956 Icelandic Government requests closure of NATO base at Keflavik.

November 1956 Agreement reached: British government accepts fishing limit; landing ban lifted; Iceland agrees not to extend further while Law of the Sea under consideration by United Nations (i.e., the next six months).

April 1958 Law of Sea Conference concluded with no agreement.

Table 4.1 (Continued)

May 1958 Iceland announces extension of fishery limits to twelve miles, effective September, 1958.

July 1958 British Government announces it will provide armed escorts for British trawlers to fish within the 12-mile limit.

September 1958 Limits extended; Royal Navy deployed. Several confrontations occur wherein Icelandic Coast Guard boards and tries to arrest British trawlers and trawl wires are cut; 70 incidents in first 18 months. Iceland appeals to international organizations to stop British gunboat diplomacy.

March 1960 Second Law of the Sea Conference convened; British trawlers agree to pull out of Iceland's 12-mile limit.*)*

April 1960 Law of the Sea Conference ends with no agreement. British Government refuses to protect trawlers with Royal Navy; trawlers remain outside 12-mile limit.

October 1960 Negotiations between Iceland and the U.K. begin, following trawlers' threat to re-enter 12-mile limit.

February 1961 Agreement reached: 6-mile limit now; 12-mile limit to be phased in over three years. British trawlers go on strike to protest.

July 1971 Iceland announces intent to extend limits to 50 miles September 1, 1972.

April 1972 British Government applies to International Court of Justice; Icelandic Government rejects the Court's authority.

August 1972 International Court of Justice renders decision against Iceland.

September 1972 Iceland extends fishery limits to 50 miles, begins cutting trawl wires.

January 1973 British trawlers demand protection by Royal Navy; rejected by British Government but Government sends tug to interpose between Coast Guard and trawlers. Harassment stops because Coast Guard is needed for cleanup from volcanic eruption on Iceland.

March 1973 Harassment resumes—17 trawl wires cut in nine days; Coast Guard uses warning shots across bows of trawlers; Icelandic Government begins public relations campaign in Britain.

May 1973 Third tug sent to protect trawlers. Negotiations break down; British Government sends Royal Navy to protect trawlers. Iceland appeals to NATO to arrange withdrawal of the Royal Navy.

June 1973 Iceland serves notice to NATO to renegotiate treaty for NATO base.

September 1973 Iceland announces intent to break diplomatic relations with U.K. if Royal Navy continues to ram its Coast Guard vessels.

October 1973 Royal Navy withdrawn; negotiations resume and agreement is reached.

July 1975 Iceland announces extension to 200 miles, effective October 15.

November 1975 Iceland begins to defend 200 miles; negotiations break off. Six trawl wires cut in first week; Royal Navy sent for protection.

December 1975 Iceland appeals to UN Security Council and NATO.

January 1976 Mediation efforts by secretary general of NATO lead to withdrawal of Royal Navy and bilateral talks; talks fail.

February 1976 Royal Navy returns to Icelandic waters; Icelandic Government breaks diplomatic relations with U.K. Collisions, ramming, and trawl wire cutting intensifies.

May 1976 At meeting of NATO foreign ministers, Iceland threatens to leave NATO unless conflict settled in six months; Norway's foreign minister (with U.S. pressure on the U.K.) mediates an immediate resolution of conflict in Iceland's favor.

The Tuna Wars

The disputes between the United States and Peru and between the United States and Ecuador have as their basis both individual claims by the Peruvian and Ecuadoran Governments of jurisdiction over waters adjacent to their coasts to a distance of two hundred miles and twelve miles respectively—the Peruvian claim being promulgated in 1947, the Ecuadoran claim issued in 1951—and a joint proclamation in 1952 by the Governments of Ecuador, Peru, and Chile (the Santiago Pact) of jurisdiction over a two-hundred-mile maritime zone adjacent to their coastlines. The Government of the United States protested each of these proclamations, even though it was earlier claims by the United States that served as a basis and precedent for the extensions.

The Peruvian decree claiming a two-hundred-mile fishery zone was issued in accordance with the Truman Proclamation—which conceded the right of any state to establish conservation zones off its shores as long as recognition is given to any U.S. fishing vessels already fishing in the area—since U.S. fishing interests did not yet exist in the area. By 1951, however, when the Ecuadoran claim of a twelve-mile territorial sea was issued, U.S. fishing vessels had begun operating off the South American coast; the United States protested the Ecuadoran extension in the same way it protested the earlier claim by Peru. The Ecuadoran Government responded to the U.S. protests and its continued fishing within its twelve-mile limit by seizing and fining U.S. fishing boats found within twelve miles of its coast. At the same time, Peru's tuna industry, which had been built during the Second World War at the request of the United States Government for export to the U.S. market, was being threatened by the U.S. tuna industry's

Figure 4.2 Geographic Location of Ecuador and Peru (South America)

Table 4.2. The Tuna Wars: A Short Chronology

1947 Peru extends fisheries jurisdiction to 200 miles.

March 1951 Ecuador extends territorial sea to 12 miles, arrests U.S. tuna boats and levies fines equal to license fees.

August 1952 Ecuador and Peru join Chile in forming Santiago Pact; arrest of U.S. boats continues.

March 1954 Five U.S. boats arrested and fined $10,000 each. U.S. Congress passes Fisherman's Protection Act of 1954.

November 1954 Onassis challenges Peru's limits; Peru begins arresting U.S. tuna boats.

October 1955 Negotiations between U.S. and Chile, Ecuador, and Peru fail; U.S. tuna boats voluntarily agree to buy licenses to avoid arrest.

Fall 1962 U.S. tuna boats stop buying licenses; arrests resume and continue.

July 1963 Military junta takes control in Ecuador.

September 1963 Ecuador stops arrests in return for foreign aid (contained in secret agreement).

March 1966 Agreement made public; military government overthrown. Ecuador claims 200-mile territorial sea. Nineteen tuna boats arrested by Ecuador and Peru in next year.

1967 U.S. proposes referral to International Court of Justice (rejected) and multilateral conference (rejected). Preliminary talks about conservation begun, but are strained by U.S. threats to suspend loans and economic aid.

April 1968 Informal talks between U.S., Ecuador, Peru, and Chile. Ecuador and Peru want to discuss conservation; U.S. wants rescinding of 200-mile limit. No agreement.

May 1968 U.S. Congress suspends $57,500,000 in loans to Peru. Peru expropriates the U.S.-held International Petroleum Corporation.

August 1968 Amendment to Fisherman's Protection Act requires secretary of state to withhold foreign aid in amount of fines levied. In October, U.S. Congress sanctions governments that seize or fine U.S. fishing vessels.

December 1968 U.S. Government cancels delivery of military equipment to Ecuador; Ecuador orders U.S. military mission off its territory.

June 1969 U.S. agrees to lift sanctions; Ecuador and Peru agree to formal conference on the dispute. Talks limited to conservation issues; reconvened in September 1970.

Spring 1970 Arrest of fourteen vessels in 1969 and five more in early 1970. American Tunaboat Association calls for military escorts are rejected by Congress and the State Department. U.S. and Soviet Union attempt to have Ecuador and Peru agree to a 12-mile territorial sea; proposal is rejected and efforts are made to strengthen claim to 200-mile limit.

May 1970 Ecuador and Peru convene nine-nation Latin American Territorial Limits Conference; outcome supports Ecuador's/Peru's position.

September 1970 Quadpartite talks among U.S., Ecuador, Peru, and Chile. No progress.

Spring 1971 After nine arrests in one week (and 51 in the year), American Tunaboat Association renews its call for armed escorts (rejected); U.S. Congress imposes economic sanctions. Ecuador calls emergency meeting of the foreign ministers of the OAS, which leads to resumption of talks between U.S., Ecuador, and Peru.

December 1971 U.S. Congress imposes additional economic sanctions; Ecuador continues to arrest and fine U.S. vessels.

February 1972 U.S. tuna boats begin to voluntarily purchase licenses

1975 U.S. claims its own 200-mile fishery zone, though conflict continues at low level because U.S. refuses to accept a 200-mile limit when it involves migratory species of fish. The deadlock continued until final resolution of the Law of the Sea by the United Nations.

campaign to increase tariffs on imported tuna. These two factors—increased tariffs and U.S. defiance of Ecuadoran claims—in combination with a draft resolution before the Organization of American States (OAS) sanctioning a two-hundred-mile fishery limit, led to agreement by the Governments of Ecuador and Peru to join Chile in coordinating their policies with regard to fisheries as embodied by their joint proclamation in 1952, and establishment of a tripartite Commission of the South Pacific to coordinate exploitation and conservation of fisheries off the South American coast.

The resulting dispute between the United States and South American governments regarding the breadth of jurisdiction over coastal waters persisted until 1956, when agreement was reached between the American Tunaboat Association, which represented the U.S. tuna industry, and the Governments of Ecuador and Peru, assuring that the U.S. tuna boats would purchase licenses to fish within the disputed areas. The dispute periodically re-emerged during the 1960s and 1970s (sometimes involving both Ecuador and Peru, other times involving only one or the other) when U.S. fishing vessels stopped purchasing licenses and fished illegally in South American waters. The conflicts became especially heated when there was heavy migration of tuna into Peruvian and/or Ecuadoran waters and after Ecuador (in 1966) and Peru (in 1968) became relatively independent of possible U.S. political and economic sanctions.

The Big Power of Small States

A number of different reasons have been suggested by social scientists to account for the ability of the government of a militarily weaker state to successfully challenge a militarily stronger adversary. It has been suggested that the government of a militarily weaker state may be successful in its challenge of a stronger adversary: (1) when there is an asymmetry in the importance or vitality of the issue(s) at the center of the dispute; (2) when there is an asymmetric dependence of the militarily stronger state on the weaker state; (3) because of the greater diversity of constituents and interests within the stronger state than its weaker adversary, which provides the opportunity for the militarily weaker state to play its adversary against itself; (4) because of the interdependent nature of the world system, which may mediate the intensity of the actions taken by one or both parties; and (5) through its involvement in and use of international organizations and alliances. Each of these will be considered, in relation to the cases studied, in order to gain insight into the degree to which they account for the success of the government of the militarily weaker state. In addition, other possible explanations for the success of the weaker state will be considered.

The Importance/Vitality of the Issue

It would be expected that in any conflict there is a difference in the importance to each party of the issue at the center of the dispute and that there is greater likelihood that an issue will be of national importance for a smaller state than a larger state. Because the government of a militarily weaker state is generally concerned with a relatively narrow range of issues, it is able to concentrate on a small number of vital interests. In contrast, a greater power is faced with a broader range of problems and concerns, which forces it to carefully choose the issues on which it will use strong political, economic, or military force,[2] generally reserving the use of force for issues of broad and common concern.

This asymmetry in the importance of the issue in dispute is reflected in both the Cod Wars and the Tuna Wars. For the Icelandic people, the fishery limits issue was of practically universal interest and of prime importance. If not affected directly by their employment in the fish industry or a fish-related industry, most Icelanders were affected indirectly by the Icelandic economy's near-total dependence (as high as 95 percent in the 1950s; as high as 70 percent in the 1970s) on the country's ability to catch and market its fish on the international marketplace.

With the protection of the fishery at the core of the collective identity of Icelanders, each decision by the Icelandic Government to extend its exclusive control over coastal fisheries was met with almost total public support. Where there was dissent, it was generally over the degree to which the government could make concessions, generally involving criticism of the government for being too generous in its dealing with the United Kingdom. These criticisms were used to advance the agenda of internal political parties, but did not undermine the actions or the resolve of the Government.

Iceland's collective identity around the fishery was further reinforced by a view that the disputes arising from its extension of fishery limits was a direct challenge to the nation's sovereignty. This served as a catalyst sparking Icelandic nationalism, which allowed the dispute to become linked to another nationalist cause—expulsion of the U.S.-leased NATO base at Keflavik and, for a small minority of Icelanders, withdrawing from the North Atlantic Alliance. The arousal of Icelandic nationalism by the dispute, and overwhelming public support for the fishery limit extensions, gave the Government a relatively free hand to be as harsh as it saw fit in dealing with the British, but it also prevented the Government from retreating from positions once they were publicly stated.

Defense of national sovereignty was also a key element in Peru's and Ecuador's dispute with the United States. By linking the dispute to issues of national sovereignty, the Governments were able to foster a collective identity which provided a sense of pride in confronting the dominant country in the hemisphere. As Loring points out with regard to Peru (though the same would be true of Ecuador):

> The two-hundred mile question is probably one of the most effective political issues in Peruvian politics. Defense of national sovereignty has emotional appeal. In a country where bravery and courage are more important than friendship with the United States . . . the picture of tiny Peru standing up against the "great economic colossus of the north" wins votes. The fact that no Peruvian interest group is greatly harmed by the claim could allow politicians to take extreme positions in its defense . . . [and] no political figure, including members of a

military government, could advocate a change in Peru's position without risking political suicide.[3]

There were two interests served by Peru's and Ecuador's extension of their fishery limits. First, like Iceland, they had an interest in conservation and controlled exploitation of fishery resources. Even though they were not yet fully exploiting their fishery resources, they wanted to assert their inherent right to regulate and control, through a requirement to purchase licenses, fishing by foreign (as well as domestic) vessels. Their secondary interest in requiring the purchase of licenses to fish within their coastal waters was to replace the revenues lost by U.S. fishing vessels landing their catch in the United States in order to avoid landing taxes in Ecuador and Peru, and by lowered tuna exports to the United States because of increases in U.S. tariffs on imported tuna. The tactics used by Ecuador and Peru in enforcement of their claims were designed to forcibly collect license fees from those fishing boats that refused to do so voluntarily.

In contrast to Ecuador, Peru, and Iceland, the issue in dispute varied with different actors in the United States and United Kingdom. In both countries, a variety of actors had diverse interests in the fishery limits issue and dispute, their perceptions of the dispute and issue being colored by these interests. As such, different actors in and outside the Governments of the United States and United Kingdom were protagonists for contrasting, and sometimes conflicting, courses of action. In stark contrast to the unified collective identity in the smaller states, the Governments of the United States and United Kingdom were faced with competing national interests that undermined their ability to foster a collective identity around the issues in conflict.

In each of the disputes, there was agreement with the Governments that the primary issue to be decided was the legality of any extension of fishery limits beyond those claimed and traditionally recognized by the United States and United Kingdom. While the Government of the United States and United Kingdom did not disagree with their weaker adversaries on the issue of conservation, they did view the issues differently. They insisted that conservation measures could only be decided by and through multilateral discussions and not by unilateral decisions. But this is where agreement between the United States and United Kingdom ended.

Probably the largest factor working against the ability of the U. S. or British Government to reach amicable settlements with their weaker adversaries was the complex structure and interaction of domestic politics. In the United Kingdom, the distant-water fishing industry, represented by the British Trawler Federation, played a key role in the determination of Government policies and strategies through its ability to maintain a relatively strong hold over the leadership and civil servants in the Ministry of Agriculture, Fisheries and Food. This influence was maintained through active public relations campaigns directed at the British public and politicians, through direct lobbying of Government ministers and bureaucrats, and by adding to its political clout, when necessary, by joining forces with the Transport and General Workers' Union, which represented the fish handlers in power and the trawlerpersons.

There was opposition to the positions advocated by the British Trawler Federation both within and outside the fishing industry. Within the industry, the near-water fisherpersons (predominately from Scotland), who were increasingly in competition with fishing vessels from other parts of Europe that fished off the British coast, favored extensions of British fishing limits similar to those claimed by Iceland. Outside the fish industry, the disputes were viewed either indifferently or with distaste by the British public—a view that was exploited by Icelandic public relations campaigns in the United Kingdom. To the British public, the disputes were generally seen as a nuisance and embarrassment that should be terminated as early as possible.[4]

There were also divisions about the disputes within the British Government. Most notable was the division within the Foreign and Commonwealth Office. The legal advisers within the Foreign Office took a firm stand against recognition of any and all extensions of fishery limits, while the foreign service officers provided suggestions, from inside Iceland, how to best negotiate and solve the conflict. As a rule, the legal advisers exerted greater control over the Foreign Office than the foreign service officers whose suggestions for solutions were generally set aside. The position taken by the legal advisers was supported by the British defense department in the second Cod War. The Ministry of Defence viewed Iceland's extension to twelve miles as a threat to British naval authority and superiority and felt that a quick show of force would put Iceland in its place. Instead, naval presence made the conflict much more intense and added to the British objectives: how to get the Navy out of Icelandic waters without losing face. This experience caused the Ministry of Defence to be more reserved in its support for the use of the Navy in subsequent disputes.

Like the United Kingdom, there was not a singular and collective view within the United States with regard to the fisheries issue and dispute. On the one hand, there was the American Tunaboat Association, which had considerable influence over legislators in the State of California and other western states. As a result of its political clout in the West, the American Tunaboat Association was able to secure legislation in the U.S. Congress that imposed sanctions against countries that seize U.S. fishing vessels (almost exclusively tuna boats) for operating outside U.S.-recognized limits. But the American Tunaboat Association also had to deal with East Coast fishing interests, which, like the near-shore fishing interests in the United Kingdom, favored extensions of U.S. fishery limits in order to limit competition with European distant-water fleets operating off the New England coast. Even though the American Tunaboat Association was able to secure passage of the Fisherman's Protection Acts (which reimbursed U.S. vessels for fines and losses caused by arrest and/or seizure) and amendments to foreign aid and naval loan extension legislation that specified retaliatory action for seizure of their boats, the issue of fishery limits was one on which it could not consistently influence Government policy in its favor.

Within the executive branch of the Government, the American Tunaboat Association had an ally in the Department of Defense, which also favored, for purposes of national security and freedom of navigation, narrow fishery and territorial limits. While the other arms of the executive branch—the Department of

State and White House—supported the Defense Department's desire for narrow limits, they opposed the coercive sanctions specified in legislation and avoided imposing these sanctions whenever they had the option. By not imposing sanctions legislated by Congress, the State Department encouraged Congress to pass new legislation that eliminated any discretion the executive branch may have had.

The extent to which other interests affected U.S. Government actions is not entirely clear. But it needs to be noted that U.S. companies had extensive investments in Ecuador and Peru. U.S. tuna canners had majority interest in three of Ecuador's five largest tuna processors, U.S. oil companies had holdings in both Ecuador and Peru, and Grace and Company operated sugar refineries in Peru. There is no reason to believe that these various interests did not do as the oil companies had and "lobbied vigorously for Washington to reduce tensions over the fishing dispute for the companies' sake."[5]

From the foregoing discussion, it is apparent that there is an asymmetry in the importance of the fishery limits issue to the militarily stronger and militarily weaker states and consequently a clear difference in the ability of the governments to foster a collective identity about the conflict among their constituents. In the militarily weaker states, there is an almost unitary view of the issue of fishery limits, both within the Government and among its constituents. In contrast, the issue of fisheries and fishery limits solicits the interest of many diverse groups within the militarily stronger state. Contrary views are taken within the government and within the fishing industry. As such, it is more difficult for the government of the militarily stronger state to develop a clear and consistent policy with regard to the dispute.

In both the Tuna Wars and the Cod Wars, special interests prevented the stronger state's government from compromising its fundamental position. In the Tuna Wars, the political clout of the U.S. tuna industry—unionized by the International Longshoreman's and Warehouse-man's Union, financed by the Bank of America, and owned by companies such Van Camp and Ralston Purina—has helped in preventing the U. S. Government from recognizing the South American claims to two-hundred-mile conservation zones. The ability of the British Government to negotiate mutually agreeable terms with the Icelandic Government in ending the last three Cod Wars rests not in a retreat by the British fishing industry but rather in a decision by the British prime minister and foreign minister to take charge of negotiations and to act in a way that was free from the direct influence of special interest groups over certain government ministers/ministries. Within that framework, the foreign minister or prime minister extracted all that he believed he could from the Icelandic Government and then settled the dispute.

Dependence

A second reason that may account for the government of a militarily weaker state succeeding in its challenge of a stronger adversary is asymmetric dependence. A review of the Cod Wars and Tuna Wars indicates different types of relationships with regard to dependence: the relationship between the United Kingdom and Iceland can be characterized as asymmetric dependence; the relationship between the United States and Ecuador and the United States and Peru can be characterized as interdependence. In this section, the nature of the relationships will be discussed, and the impact of asymmetric dependence versus interdependence on the outcome of the dispute will be considered.

The relationship between Iceland and the United Kingdom is perhaps unusual in the modern world system given the asymmetry in dependence of the United Kingdom on Iceland. While the United Kingdom depended on Iceland for both its fish products exported to British markets and its coastal fishing grounds, Iceland had little if any dependence on the United Kingdom. Everything for which Iceland traded with the United Kingdom was easily available from other sources. This is illustrated by Iceland's ease in finding new trading partners each time British trawlerpersons and unions imposed boycotts on Icelandic fish products. Since the Icelandic Government allowed no foreign investment in the country, it was also free from any obligations to other governments.

As a consequence of this asymmetric dependence, there was very little that the British could offer Iceland in the Cod Wars. Consistent with power-dependence theories, which suggest that in situations of asymmetric dependence, coercive force will be necessary if the dependent party wishes to overcome its adversary,[6] the British Government had two choices: it could accede to Iceland's claimed extensions or it could attempt to coerce the Icelandic Government into retreating from its proposed fishery limit extension. After all, its use of persuasive arguments that the extensions had no basis in international law had had no impact on the Icelandic Government, and its use of positive inducements in the form of trade concessions offered in 1972 by the European Economic Union provided no real incentive, so also had no real effect.

Rather than give in to Icelandic demands, the Government of the United Kingdom attempted to coerce the Icelandic Government into retreating from its extended fishery limits in the latter three Cod Wars by using the Royal Navy to protect its fishing vessels from harassment by the Icelandic Coast Guard, thereby defending its claim to the right to fish within the disputed areas. The use of the Royal Navy was generally counter productive. It further solidified the collective identity within Iceland, caused the Icelandic Government to become more resolved in its claims, and escalated the hostility of the conflict by encouraging the Icelandic Government to link settlement of the fishery dispute to its continued participation in NATO and its willingness to allow the NATO base at Keflavik to continue to operate.

For its part, the Icelandic Government had a full range of strategies available for pursuing the conflicts. It used persuasion within and outside international forums; used coercive tactics directly through its harassment of British fishing vessels and direct confrontation of the Royal Navy, and indirectly through linkage strategies which coerced third parties to put pressure on the British Government; and used positive inducements in the form of concessions that would allow some fishing in areas that it had proclaimed no fishing would be allowed, or higher levels of catches in existing areas. In 1961, these concessions amounted to a phased-in extension, which was accepted by the British Government; in 1973, they consisted of acceptance of a larger catch limit than was first proposed as acceptable, but still less than would have been given in a negotiated settlement prior to hostilities escalating.[7] No conciliatory inducements were offered in the first (1952-1956) and last disputes: in the first Cod War the British acquiesced; in the last Cod War Iceland was successful with its use of coercion.

As already indicated, the relationship between the United States and Ecuador and the United States and Peru is best characterized as interdependent insofar as each is dependent on the other for trade and they are involved in cooperation within a number of international and hemispheric organizations. Beside U.S. imports of bananas (from Ecuador only), sugar, and fish products from Ecuador and Peru, U.S.-based companies are also heavily invested in these industries and have sizable interests in the exploration for and refining of oil in both countries. With Peruvian and Ecuadoran import of industrial products, trade is skewed to a very small extent toward the United States. But with the continuation of U.S. resistance to Ecuadoran and Peruvian two-hundred-mile claims and escalation of the dispute, the balance of trade and trading partners began to change. While the balance of trade remained somewhat constant, the value of that trade steadily decreased during the late 1960s and early 1970s.

In addition to its expropriation of the U.S. company-owned International Petroleum Corporation in 1968, Peru in the late 1960s and early 1970s began to diversify its trade to include Eastern Bloc countries from which industrial products traditionally supplied from the United States were sought in trade for its fish products. This search for new trading partners was spurred largely by U.S. threats and sanctions imposed on Peru, first for the seizure of U.S. fishing vessels and later for the expropriation of U.S.-owned property.

Ecuador also diversified its trade by opening channels of economic relations with both Western and Eastern European markets. Rather than doing as Peru had done and expropriating Texaco and Mobil holdings in the country, the Ecuadoran Government sought advance royalties from the companies to make up for U.S. economic sanctions. While the United States' choices were limited to directing its fishing vessels to abandon fishing for tuna once the fish migrated into the South Pacific, to purchase licenses required by Ecuadoran and Peruvian law, or to allow them to continue fishing and tolerate seizures and fine, the Governments of Ecuador and Peru had the freedom to seek from others that for which they had come to depend on the United States.

Given its dependence on the South Pacific for tuna fisheries and knowledge that retribution against U.S. holdings in Peru and Ecuador could be linked to the fisheries dispute, the U.S. Government was prevented from using its full military and/or economic force to coerce the South Americans into submission. The Governments of Ecuador and Peru, on the other hand, given their ability to find alternative trading partners and thereby lessen their dependence on the United States, removed a wedge that could be used to splinter the collective identity within the country, and also freed themselves from most sanctions the United States could impose. This allowed them to continue their defiance of U.S.

threats and requests that they abandon the two-hundred mile concept. They regularly seized and fined U.S. tuna boats found violating their fishery limits (see table 4.3).

Playing One's Adversary against Itself

In discussing differences in the importance to each state of the issue in dispute, the range of diverse interests within the militarily stronger states were contrasted with the unitary view of the dispute found in the militarily weaker state. As illustrated, the range of interests within the United States and United Kingdom meant that there was an absence of a collective identity. This was exploited by the militarily weaker states and, in turn, affected the actions available to and taken by the Government.

Table 4.3. Seizures of U.S. Tunaboats by Ecuador and Peru

	ECUADOR		PERU	
Year	Seizures	Fines($)	Seizures	Fines($)
1951	2	13,500		
1952	1	12,600		
1954	7	50,000		
1955	2	49,362	6	12,000
1962	1	150	3	19,000
1963	3	28,720		
1965	1	13,950	7	34,000
1966	2	*	7	59,000
1967	9	130,410	2	22,000
1968	6	211,664	3	*
1969	2	122,575	4	55,692
1970	2	133,700	1	20,552
1971	51	2,640,000	1	18,154
1972	30	1,538,920	1	19,450
1973	23	1,616,136	23	703,080
1974	2	82,450		
1975	7	1,9222,641		
1977			2	59,040
1979			6	420,723
1980			3	146,631
Totals	**151**	**8,566,778**	**69**	**1,589,322**

*Data are not available

Sources: "Seizures, Detentions, and other Harassments of Tuna Vessels," *Congressional Record-Senate*, March 28, 1968, 8093-8094; *Fishing Rights and United States-Latin American Relations* (Washington, DC: GPO, 1972), 7-11. Figures provided by the U.S. Department of State and by the Commission for the South Pacific.

These diverse interests prevent a single coherent view of the conflict from emerging and provide fertile ground for persuasive, coercive, and noncoercive efforts that exploit potential or existing splits within the state. There are three levels on which efforts that play an adversary against itself can be directed: (1) government officials or offices can be pitted against one another; (2) public opinion can be targeted in order to erode the support for a government; (3) special interest groups can be played off one another or against the government.[8]

Analysis of the Tuna Wars indicates that none of the parties appeared to actively attempt to create or exploit divisions within its adversary. In contrast, an important part of the way in which the Icelandic Government pursued its dispute with the United Kingdom was to create and/or exploit splits among the various constituent groups within the country. In the two most recent Cod Wars, the Icelandic Government employed a British public relations firm to coordinate a campaign directed toward persuading the British public that the dispute was senseless and truly not in the best interest of the British consumer/public. The three most effective tactics involved: (1) community meetings in which Icelanders were brought into British fishing communities from which distant-water and near-water fleets operated and in which they presented the Icelandic case for the extension of limits and the effect that opposition to these claims were having on Icelanders; (2) use of newspaper advertisements presenting the Icelandic position and challenging the British Trawler Federation and British Government to respond to its assertions; and (3) providing tours of fishing villages around Iceland and regular flights over disputed areas—particularly when there were active confrontations between Royal Navy frigates and unarmed Icelandic Coast Guard vessels which were harassing British trawlers—to British and other foreign news reporters in order to solicit sympathy for its extension from the British and world press. Perhaps most effective in eroding British public support for its Government's continued opposition to the Icelandic extensions were the images on the evening news in Britain of the Royal Navy chasing or being rammed by the much smaller vessels of the Icelandic Coast Guard (see table 4.4).

The Icelandic Government also made a concerted effort to exploit divisions within the British Government. Regular weekly briefings were held with members of Parliament in order to present the Icelandic view. As well, frequent efforts were made to lobby ministers in the Government. Overall, these efforts, combined with those directed at the British public, proved quite productive. Similar attempts by a British public relations firm acting on behalf of the British Trawler Federation to run a campaign in Iceland proved to be counterproductive.[9] While Iceland was able to construct an image of the United Kingdom which made it appear as a bully, attempts by the United Kingdom to drive a wedge in the collective identity of Icelanders only solidified and strengthened that identity and increased the Icelandic resolve in its conflict with the British.

Table 4.4. Trawl Cutting and Ramming in Third and Fourth Cod Wars

Cod War #3 1972-1973			Cod War #4 1975-1976		
Month	Trawl Cutting	Collisions	Month	Trawl Cutting	Collisions
Sept	5	0	Nov	0	7
Oct	2	0	Dec	5	6
Nov	1	0	Jan	3	3
Dec	1	0	Feb	9	16
Jan	7	0	Mar	13	1
Feb	0	0	Apr	12	12
Mar	20	0	May	12	4
Apr	13	1			
May	1	1			
June	0	4			
July	0	2			
Aug	18	4			
Sept	0	3			
Totals	**68**	**14**		**49**	**54**

Sources: "Fisheries Disputes between the United Kingdom and Iceland" (London: HMSO: Cmd. 5341, 1973); Bjorn Thorsteinsson, *Tiu Thorskastrid, 1415-1976* (Reykjavik: Sogufelagid, 1976).

The Interdependent World System

It has been suggested that military force is unlikely to be used and will play a minor role in disputes between governments in an interdependent world system.[10] This hypothesis is predicated on the assumptions that social norms and collective values will oppose and sanction the use of military force by a government and that similar negative reaction may be forthcoming from internal factions. It appears that, in both sets of disputes studied, the stronger state's government was constrained in its use of military force. The British Government only reluctantly decided to use its military force in each of the Cod Wars, and then only because of direct pressure from domestic interest groups. Consequently, British use of the Navy was limited; its objective was to prevent Icelandic harassment of British fishing vessels by interposing its ships between the Icelandic Coast Guard vessels and British trawlers. There was very little else the British Government could do to prevent Icelandic enforcement of its limits without arousing negative reactions from the international community. In the third and fourth Cod Wars, hoping to avoid use of its Navy, the British Government deployed oceangoing tugs to protect its fishing vessels. Initially, the tugs did not solicit as negative a response as the Royal Navy, but they tended to be more aggressive and their presence precipitated a rash of collisions and rammings which in turn led to negative reactions to the dispute,[11] and which led in the end to deployment of the Royal Navy.

The Government of the United States, on the other hand, recognized the futility, in view of the British experience (and French experience in a fishery dispute with Brazil), of using its navy to defend its fishing boats from a friendly neighbor. The Government was aware that world public opinion would be opposed to U.S. gunboat diplomacy, as would many interest groups within the country. The Government considered it to be in its long-term interest to allow Ecuador and Peru to seize U.S. fishing boats and to reimburse the U.S. fishing vessels for fines and lost income.[12]

The Governments of Ecuador, Peru, and Iceland did not appear to be similarly constrained from using their navies or coast guards for offensive actions in the defense of a wider coastal authority. There was obviously a negative reaction from distant-water fishing interests in the United States and United Kingdom to the use of force, even though it was generally nonviolent. But there was virtually no domestic response, and little if any public reaction, against the use of force. Most of the public (world community) opposition toward Iceland, Ecuador, and Peru was directed toward the controversial claims and not the use of force to defend those claims.

A second feature of an interdependent system is the availability of linkage strategies. It is suggested that strategies of linking unrelated issues is more accessible to weak states than strong states and that strong states are likely to resort to linkage of economic issues to issues in dispute since their military force has likely been rendered useless. Governments of militarily weaker states, in contrast, are likely to link the issue at the center of a dispute to issues of concern to international organizations.[13]

This hypothesis is reflected in the Cod Wars and Tuna Wars. The United States and United Kingdom relied heavily on economic sanctions. The United States commonly offered help to Ecuador and Peru in securing necessary loans from the Inter-American Development Bank and World Bank in return for rescinding their two-hundred-mile claims; in 1963 Ecuador actually rescinded its two-hundred-mile claim in negotiating a secret agreement with the United States, but when the agreement was made public in 1966 the Government was replaced with one that was more strongly anti-U.S. than any of its predecessors.[14] When offers of rewards failed, the Government of the United States would generally impose economic sanctions in the form of cut-offs of foreign and military aid and would block those same loans for which help was promised. With the exception of the secret agreement with Ecuador, U.S. promises of reward were unsuccessful and generally had the effect of aggravating South American perceptions of the United States. The United Kingdom similarly tied the fisheries dispute to economic considerations. In three of the four Cod Wars (the second dispute excepted), British industry immediately imposed landing bans on all Icelandic products, and in 1972, the Government offered inducements through the European Economic Community that would have provided Iceland with immediate tariff reductions if it agreed to abandon its fifty-mile claim. These efforts had no apparent effect on the Icelandic Government. Sanctions did however constitute an external threat to the constituents of the government of the militarily weaker states and only strengthened the collective identity in the country.

International Organizations and Alliances

The Governments of Ecuador, Peru, and Iceland linked (or allowed to be linked in the adversary's perceptions) their participation in certain international organizations or summits to the fisheries disputes. Iceland, being in the position of having the North Atlantic defense system dependent on the country for the stationing of surveillance equipment to monitor the movement of Soviet and Eastern Bloc military aircraft and naval vessels, quite skillfully took advantage of its unique position in relation to NATO to influence British perceptions and behavior. By threatening the collective identity of a multinational body such as NATO, Iceland was able to isolate the United Kingdom. In the three latter Cod Wars, the Icelandic Government threatened withdrawal from NATO; in the third Cod War it actually gave notice of its intent to renegotiate the treaty that provided for the NATO base at Keflavik. The fourth Cod War was resolved after the Icelandic Government made a similar threat of withdrawal, which led to direct pressure on the British Government by its European allies and the United States to quickly resolve the conflict. The conflict ended one day after the Icelandic Government's final ultimatum to NATO.[15]

The Governments of Ecuador and Peru linked their disputes with the United States to international organizations in a somewhat different way, but their actions also threatened to cause internal conflict that would isolate the United States within these organizations. Both Governments, individually and at different times, linked their participation in hemispheric meetings to withdrawal of U.S. sanctions or to U.S. agreement to enter discussions. The Government of Ecuador also used the threat of censure by the Organization of American States as a means to influence U.S. behavior toward it in 1971. Involvement of the OAS likely prevented further escalation of the dispute, but did not lead to resolution.

There are a number of other ways in which international organizations became involved in the disputes under study. In all the disputes, international organizations were used as forums for each adversary to present the merits of its respective case. These presentations, made in organizations in which one or both of the partisans were members, were directed as much at persuading others that one was correct in its stance as at a domestic audience in order to maintain support for the Government's representation of collective national interests.

The Governments of Ecuador and Peru also formed new organizations in an effort to further their cause. By joining with others with similar interests, they were able to more clearly define a "we" and "they." In 1952, Ecuador and Peru joined Chile in forming the Commission of the South Pacific, which was charged with overseeing the conservation and exploitation of resources off the South American coast. In 1970, in reaction to U.S./Soviet efforts to win support for a twelve-mile fishery limit, they convened Latin American states which together issued the Montevideo Declaration and a couple of months later the Lima Declaration on the Law of the Sea. Both declarations asserted the coastal state's right to jurisdiction over the fisheries off its coast. Iceland, in contrast, didn't form coalitions as much as it lobbied other groups of states (e.g., Organization for African Unity, nonaligned third world governments) to take similar positions in relation to their fisheries. It also drew on the collective identity of Nordic states (i.e., Denmark, Sweden, Finland, and Norway) through its membership in the Nordic Council. However, the use of international organizations appeared to have little real effect, other than providing a basis for both adversaries to claim that public opinion was on their side.

As expected, international organizations also became involved in the disputes as intermediaries,[16] but their role as mediators or intermediaries differed when invited by the militarily weaker state or by the stronger state. The United States and United Kingdom both repeatedly suggested appealing their respective disputes to the International Court of Justice, but this was never an acceptable channel for the Governments of Ecuador, Peru, or Iceland. The Government of each claimed that there was not sufficient international law on which the Court could base a decision. When prospects for adjudication disappeared, and when coercive sanctions, positive inducements, and persuasion proved unsuccessful, the stronger state tried referring the dispute to a third party in which the militarily weaker state was a minority member—in Britain's case, to the North Atlantic Fisheries Commission; in the case of the U.S., to a yet-to-be-formed commission in which Ecuador and Peru would share membership with the U.S., Canada, and Japan. These efforts proved unproductive.

In contrast, the Governments of the militarily weaker states tended to refer their disputes to a third party only after the conflict had escalated beyond tolerable limits. In referring the dispute to a third party, these governments did not request mediation. They simply asked the third party (e.g., OAS, NATO) to secure retraction of a coercive act by its stronger adversary. These third parties often became involved in the conflicts, particularly the Cod Wars, at their own initiative. In these cases, the third party had a direct interest in the outcome of the dispute. This is certainly true of NATO, which became involved in each of the Cod Wars through its own concern for the military installations in Iceland, and of Norway, which faced with the prospects of closure of the base at Keflavik the need to increase the size of its military force and to allow a similar base to be built on its territory. At the very least, international organizations were able to cause the dispute to de-escalate; in the case of NATO, the organization was able to coerce the stronger state to resolve the conflict.

Other Factors

There are two other factors that appear to be important to understanding the Tuna Wars and the Cod Wars and their outcomes. First, a large part of the militarily weaker state's success is attributable to its ability to find a means of coercion that is relatively inexpensive and easy to use, but to one's adversary costly to sustain and difficult to escape. Iceland's, Ecuador's, and Peru's tactics of harassment and seizure of foreign fishing vessels added very little, if any, cost to the overall operating expenses of the Icelandic Coast Guard or Ecuadoran or Peruvian Navy since, if not involved in the enforcement of fishery limits, the same vessel would be used in other ways. But coast guard/navy action was quite costly to the Governments of the United States and United Kingdom and to the American and British fishing industries. In the Tuna Wars the United States Government absorbed the cost of excessive fines and the U.S. tuna boats tolerated losses in fishing time. In the Cod Wars, trawlers absorbed the costs of lost fishing time and diminished catches, while the British Government bore the expense of leasing the tugboats, of reimbursing trawlers for lost gear, and of repairing extensive damage done to Royal Navy frigates by rammings by Iceland Coast Guard.[17]

A second factor that influenced the pattern of escalation and de-escalation and outcome of the Tuna Wars was seasonal migration patterns of tuna and variations in these patterns from year to year. Unlike the Cod Wars, in which the fishery is exploited year-round, tuna rarely migrate to the South Pacific for more than six months each year, normally entering Ecuadoran waters between November and January and migrating north again between March and April. Seizure of U.S. vessels followed this pattern, beginning in November or December, peaking in January and February, and ending in March or April. Peaks in the use of coercive measures similarly coincided with this pattern. This built-in pattern seemed to provide a regular time in which the dispute could de-escalate and hostile feelings could dissipate. But it also made it difficult for coercive action by the Government of Ecuador and Peru to be effective since seizures were, at best, sporadic.

Conclusion

At the beginning of this chapter, two issues were raised as of interest: (1) the strategies or factors that make it possible for the government of a militarily weaker state to successfully challenge a state that is militarily stronger; and (2) the strategies or factors that neutralize the government of a militarily stronger state from using the full force of its military. The disputes discussed provide insight into each of these issues.

The success of the militarily weak states, even when only partial, depends on a number of factors. None of the reasons suggested above for the possible success of a weaker state is individually sufficient to guarantee that a challenge to a stronger adversary will have the desired results. However, the fact that a smaller state has fewer competing interests appears to be a major factor in its Government's ability to pursue the conflict as it sees fit, in part because of a unified constituency and in part because of the difficulty that an adversary would have in creating and/or exploiting divisions within the state. Quite simply, the smaller states were able to take advantage of (and further foster) a collective identity that saw the larger state as a threat. This gave the Governments of Iceland, Peru, and Ecuador a relatively free hand in dealing with the conflict. In contrast, the United States and United Kingdom were comprised of competing collective interests which prevented a coherent national interest from developing. The Governments' actions were constrained by the need to balance competing interests in an attempt to restrain emergence of internal conflict.

Of similar importance to the ability of the government of a militarily weaker state to challenge a stronger adversary is its independence from possible economic and political sanctions that the stronger adversary has available. Independence allows the militarily weaker state to withstand sanctions that are applied. Where there is asymmetric dependence of the stronger state on its militarily weaker adversary, the weaker state has good prospects to be able to prevail in the dispute. These factors combined produce a situation where a militarily weaker state may be able to absorb any sanctions used against it, and where it is able to develop sanctions (including the use of linkage strategies and strategies that exploit competing domestic interests) that have little if any cost to use but which are very costly for its adversary to absorb.

Another crucial factor in the ability of a militarily weaker state to succeed in challenging a stronger adversary is its ability to neutralize the adversary's options around the deployment of its military force. The world system generally mediates the stronger nation's ability to use its military, but perhaps a larger factor is the image created by a militarily stronger state "bullying" a state that has a small military, or in the case of Iceland no military at all. Even if a militarily strong state can justify the use of its military to others in the world system, it is still left with convincing its constituents that its use of military force is justified against an unarmed or poorly armed adversary. As shown above, Iceland was able to project a negative image of the United Kingdom to both the international community and the constituents of the British Government.

While the world system may mediate against a militarily strong state using its military, it may tolerate the limited use of force by a militarily weaker state. Had the Icelandic Government had a military, and had it used its military in more belligerent ways than it had used its coast guard, it is possible that the United Kingdom would have had greater freedom to use the Royal Navy and to use it with greater force. Similarly, the fact that Ecuador and Peru refrained from a violent use of their navies likely contributed to the U.S. Government's decision to avoid gunboat diplomacy.

In sum, the success of militarily weaker states in their conflicts with militarily stronger states appears to rest on three crucial factors: (1) fostering a collective national identity among their constituencies while creating and exploiting intergroup conflict within their adversaries; (2) the use of international organizations to present a negative image of the militarily stronger state and to thereby threaten the collective identity on which these organizations depend; and (3) the use of strategies and tactics that make resolution of the conflict much more attractive and less costly to the militarily stronger state than continuing the conflict.

Notes

1. The case studies are based on four different types of information: (1) newspaper accounts and news summaries (e.g., *New York Times, London Times, Kee-sings Contemporary Archives: A Weekly Diary of Important World Events, Survey of Current Affairs,
Latin America*); (2) academic and nonacademic articles and books, including memoirs;
(3) documents produced by parties to the conflict (i.e., trade journals and press releases of
concerned special interest groups; official records of congressional hearings and parliamentary debate; official records and publications of international organizations; government position papers, reports, press releases and public speeches, and white papers);
(4) interviews with people who were involved with the dispute (e.g., diplomats, civil
servants, government ministers, news reporters and social scientists, leaders of special
interest groups).

2. Robert O. Keohane, "The Big Influence of Small Allies," in *Foreign Policy* 2 (April
1971): 161-182.

3. David C. Loring, "The Fisheries Dispute," in *U.S. Foreign Policy and Peru*, ed.
Daniel Sharp (Austin: University of Texas Press, 1972), 106.

4. This was the way in which the British ambassadors to Iceland during the third and
fourth Cod Wars characterized the British public; it was a perception that appeared to
pervade the British Foreign Office. Statements reflecting the public's impatience with the
disputes were also common in parliamentary discussions of the dispute.

5. Bobbie Smetherman and Robert Smetherman, *Territorial Seas and Inter-American
Relations* (New York: Praeger, 1974), 49.

6. See Richard M. Emerson, "Power Dependence Relations," *American Sociological
Review* 27, no. 1 (January 1962): 31-41. See also Roderick Martin, *The Sociology of
Power* (Boston: Little, Brown, 1977).

7. The agreement ending the third Cod War allowed the British a catch limit of
130,000 tons per year for each of the next two years. It was indicated in interviews with
two Icelandic officials that Iceland would have accepted a ten-year agreement with a
catch limit of 139,000 tons up until September 1972.

8. Keohane, "The Big Influence of Small Allies."

9. This was disclosed in an interview with the director general of the British Trawler
Federation.

10. Robert O. Keohane and Joseph S. Nye, *Power and Interdependence* (Boston: Little, Brown, 1977).

11. The Icelandic Coast Guard took advantage of the fact that its vessels were built
with thick hulls for the strength necessary to cut through ice and manage through Icelandic winters. In contrast, the Royal Navy's frigates were built with a thin aluminum
shell since they were designed for speed and needed to be lightweight. In a collision between the two, the coast guard vessel would obviously sustain less damage than the frigate—and any damage that was sustained by the coast guard vessels was insured against
by Lloyd's of London. So long as it had the right of way, the Icelandic Coast Guard vessels would take no action to avoid a collision with a British vessel. Coast guard vessels
would also commonly come alongside a frigate and turn suddenly away so as to cause its
rear-end to "bump" against the side of the frigate. Aggressive tactics were also adopted
by the British tugs, which would ram Icelandic Coast Guard vessels (N.B. These accounts
were disclosed in confidential interviews with British and Icelandic officials).

12. Keohane and Nye, *Power and Interdependence*, 134.

13. Keohane and Nye, *Power and Interdependence*, 30-31.

14. Following a coup in 1963, the military junta that took control of the Ecuadoran
Government made a secret agreement with the United States which provided that the U.S.

would secure loans needed by Ecuador in return for Ecuador enforcing only a twelve-mile fishery limit. On March 29, 1966, the Ecuadoran foreign minister disclosed the existence of the agreement and denounced it as not being in the interest of the Ecuadoran state. Denouncement of the agreement led to renewed arrests of U.S. tuna boats and to the ouster of the military junta that had made the agreement. The new Ecuadoran Government claimed an unequivocal two-hundred-mile territorial sea and the new constituent assembly honored the foreign minister for his exceptional service to the Fatherland (N.B. This account is based on unclassified State Department documents).

15. At the opening session of the Spring meeting of the NATO foreign ministers, the Icelandic foreign minister, Einar Agustsson, indicated Iceland's intention to give formal notice that it would leave NATO unless there was a settlement of the Cod War within six months. He warned NATO that it would have to decide which is more important: the NATO base at Keflavik or British fishing off Iceland. The next day, the Norwegian foreign minister held a number of meetings to work toward resolving the dispute. As well, there was meetings between Iceland's and West Germany's foreign ministers, after Mr. Agustsson said he would not be surprised if the German foreign minister would meet with the British foreign secretary, Anthony Crosland, to discuss lifting EEC sanctions against Iceland. Agustsson also met with Henry Kissinger, the U.S. secretary of state, who indicated to Agustsson that he had already emphasized to the British Government that the Government of the United States was interested in seeing that the fisheries dispute was solved in such a way that the Icelanders would be pleased with it (Jonsson, 1978). Later that day, in a meeting convened by Norway's foreign minister and the secretary general of NATO with the foreign ministers of Iceland and the United Kingdom, an agreement was reached which ended the dispute (N.B. These meetings were disclosed by their participants in confidential interviews).

16. See Peter Wolf, "International Social Structure and the Resolution of International Conflicts, 1920-1965," in *Research in Social Movements, Conflicts and Change*, vol. 1, ed. Louis Kriesberg (Greenwich, Conn.: JAI Press, 1978), 35-59.

17. While exact figures are not readily available, it was disclosed that the cost to the Royal Navy for its involvement in the Second Cod War was £670,000, and the cost for repair of damage caused in each of the last two Cod Wars was in excess of £3,000,000. The cost of leasing each of the three tugs used in the last two Cod Wars was £1,500 a day.

Chapter Five

Conflict and Children

Integrated Education in the Segregated Society of Northern Ireland

Sean Byrne

Developmental psychologists have formulated important theories about the process through which children develop workable constructs of their external environment.[1] Individuals organize information about their political world from direct experience or information conveyed by agents of political socialization into ideological schemata or information storage menus.[2] Schemata allow children to make sense of and construct meaning from their political milieu and to organize knowledge about politics, society, and conflict.[3] Different socioeconomic backgrounds and educational experiences ensure that individuals have particular schemata to organize and store political information.[4] Political socialization, as well as interpersonal and intergroup socialization, plays an important role in the development of political understandings.[5] We need to examine the cognitive and evaluative components of children's political images if we are to better understand their political world view and help to build democratic values among children residing within intercommunal conflict regions.

Northern Irish children are socialized into accepting the ethnoreligious and national identity of the in-group as it distinguishes itself from the out-group along the religious-nationality cleavage.[6] Lack of physical contact between the Protestant and Catholic communities fosters and preserves extraordinary stereotypes that shape the schemata and political cognitions of these children.[7] A widespread sense of social futility permeates their schemata as they develop their political world views. They come to believe that the Northern Ireland conflict is intractable and to accept violence as a way of life. It is important to recognize the children's political imagery as it relates to conflict, identity, and stereotyping. Hence, two significant social and institutional factors need to be explored to understand the specific nature of the Northern Ireland conflict—the history of the development of a Protestant Unionist national identity and the role of segregated education in supporting that process.

This chapter demonstrates the possible effects of the historical basis of identity and integrated and nonintegrated education on the socialization and political cognitions of two groups of Protestant schoolchildren. Schools are important agents of political socialization, especially regarding civic education.[8] Education influences the way children perceive the reality of everyday life, and in turn affects their understanding and development of sensitivities toward their political milieu. For children, these understandings underlie their sociopolitical behavior and their approach to conflict and identity at interpersonal, intergroup, and structural levels.

Protestant Alienation and Identification with the Monarchy: The Role of Education

Although confusion and uncertainty about national identity lead to fear, anxiety, and insecurity among the Protestant population, the symbolism of the monarch remains very important to their ethnoreligious identity.[9] The queen is a "mother figure" who provides the same stability a child may find at home.[10] In a study of the sociopolitical identities of 475 sixth-year pupils, whose mean age was 17.3 years, it was found that Protestant children regarded themselves as British, while Catholics chose an Irish identity.[11] Other surveys have demonstrated that even though Protestants are not as homogeneous in their national identity preferences as Catholics, Protestants are more likely than Catholics to think of themselves as British.[12] To understand the Protestant ideological position in Northern Ireland, therefore, one has to explore the central role the queen plays in Northern Irish politics.[13] Protestants of Northern Ireland are psychologically bound to the queen "with bonds of blood, history and common adversity which cannot be bartered away in some logical package no matter how attractive that might seem."[14] The queen, as head of state and head of the Reformed Church, symbolizes the allegiance of the Protestant population of Northern Ireland.[15] The queen becomes an important political and religious symbol for Protestants, especially during political crises.[16] Protestants are ultimately loyal to the symbols of their religion because it is the only secure identity for them.

Loyalty to the queen is, however, dependent on the queen's obligations and commitment to keep Northern Ireland British. Protestants believe that they entered into a political contract and a religious covenant with the monarch when Ulster was being colonized during the seventeenth century.[17] The concept of the contract or the covenant becomes politically significant when Protestants perceive the British government as not fulfilling its side of the bargain.[18] Loyalists or extremist Protestants believe that it is not disloyalty to the queen to refuse to obey the laws of "ministers or governments that fail in their duty to give loyal subjects the blessing of the queen's peace."[19] They believe that Protestants have to behave in a disloyal manner to the British government to demonstrate their constitutional and religious attachment or loyalty to the crown.

Miller argues that if the British government negates its political covenant with Northern Irish Protestants, they should not discard the contract—rather they

Figure 5.1 Map of Ireland

should break the law and force the government into maintaining the political bargain. Consequently, national and religious attachment to the monarch enhances the ethnoreligious identity of the Protestant community while excluding the Catholic community that is not perceived to be loyal to the monarch. National identity and religious allegiance are directly correlated in Northern Ireland because the religious label assists in categorizing the national identities of Protestants and Catholics.[20] However, Protestants are divided into moderates and extremists and do not constitute a monolithic and cohesive ideological bloc.[21] Members of the extremist group work to prevent the Catholic Nationalist community from gaining political power because they believe "the maintenance of Ulster depends upon the political unity of Protestants."[22]

Some of the major historical and political causes of the Protestant community's fear and suspicions underlie that community's mistrust toward the British government's political actions toward Northern Ireland.[23] The Protestant community believes that the British government does not wish to honor its promise to keep Northern Ireland British. A couple of applications of Protestant intransigence clearly outlines this psychological mechanism.

First, the Home Rule political crisis of the late nineteenth and early twentieth centuries, for example, clearly illustrates how the Protestant community adopted the language, symbols, and images of conditional loyalty to thwart the political challenge of Charles Stuart Parnell's Irish Parliamentary Party to usher in a new political era in Ireland.[24] During the 1880s, Ireland remained a predominantly agricultural country, with few concentrations of industrial population.[25] The landlord class in Ireland was replaced by conservative, Catholic peasant proprietors living in a rural Ireland alienated from the Protestant industrial basin of northeast Ulster. The Home Rule controversy of the 1880s effectively established a militant Catholic nationalist ideological movement in the early 1900s that sought political autonomy.[26]

The political mobilization of a pan-Nationalist Catholic front drove an ideological wedge between an agrarian South of Ireland and an industrial Protestant Unionist Ulster.[27] The Protestant community sought the protection of the union with Britain to secure its endangered ethnoreligious identity, liberal value system, and British strategic economic markets.[28] Home Rule for Ireland promoted the division of the island and the predominance of the ethnoreligious cleavage and the national identity question that shape the politics of a divided Northern Ireland today.[29]

Second, the next major political crises the Protestant community faced came in 1972 when the Northern Ireland parliament was abolished by the British government. Since the implementation of Direct Rule from London, Northern Irish Protestants have become increasingly alienated or estranged from the British government.[30] A number of political issues have combined to create uncertainty and fear among the majority community of Northern Ireland.[31] Loyalists banded together in 1972 to resist any attempt by the British government to reform the political system in Northern Ireland. Direct Rule was perceived as a political threat to the religious identity and liberty of the Protestant community.

Similarly, opposition to the 1985 Anglo-Irish Agreement (AIA), an international treaty signed by both the British and Irish governments, illustrates the depth of Protestant alienation.[32] Protestants were not consulted in the formulation of the AIA and felt betrayed by the British government, which gave the Irish government a consultative status in the government of Northern Ireland.[33] Many Protestants believed that it was an attempt to drive them out of the union and into a Catholic-dominated united Ireland.[34] However, Protestant protests against the 1985 AIA revealed the limitations of the politics of conditional loyalty. Because of the violent reaction of the Loyalists, British public opinion became less interested in maintaining a political attachment to Northern Ireland. The British public appeared unsympathetic to Protestant attempts to preserve

Figure 5.2 Inset of Northern Ireland

their culture and history.[35]

Finally, the latest political crises to affront Northern Irish Protestants has intensified feelings of betrayal, frustration, fear, and isolation. Some believe the April 1998 Good Friday Agreement unveiled by British Prime Minister Tony Blair and his Irish counterpart, Bertie Ahearne, promises to usher in a new era of peace, prosperity, and political stability in a region that has been plagued by political violence over the last 27 years.[36] Less optimistic savants, however, believe that the British and Irish governments have made a huge blunder by expecting Protestants to consent to what they perceive as a paved road to a united Ireland.[37]

In fact, the outraged reaction of the Protestant community against the 1995 Framework Document for Peace indicated its opposition to what it saw as a pathway to a united Ireland and civil war.[38] Protestants fear that the document's provisions for an all-island or cross-border institution with executive powers was tantamount to threatening Northern Ireland's sovereignty within Britain. They insisted that Paragraph 47 promoted the substance of Joint Authority by the British and Irish governments and eventual Irish unification.[39] The Rev. Dr. Ian Paisley even went as far as to claim that the document was the result of a pan-Nationalist front established to dragoon Protestants into a united Ireland against their will.[40] Protestants rejected the process as undemocratic and against their political interests.[41] Hence, perceived Protestant alienation has important implications for their political relationship with the British government and the Catholic community in Northern Ireland.

Northern Ireland's ambiguous constitutional position within the United Kingdom leads to political polarization along national identity lines.[42] People are not willing to compromise because the most important need is to combat perceived or imaginary threats emanating from the other side.[43] The February 9 1996 breakdown in the PIRA cease-fire intensified fear and polarization and heightened segregation between both communities. Both ethnoreligious groups seek to maintain their separate and distinct identities.[44] This leads to segregation in sports, the work force, the neighborhoods, and the education system because children develop their national attachments through the structures by which they are educated.[45]

Segregated education preserves a Protestant and Catholic "way of life" and minimizes contact between children.[46] Studies of children who have been exposed to violent political environments have been conducted with children from South Africa,[47] Israel,[48] and Northern Ireland.[49] These studies indicate that children's attitudes mirror those of society because they are molded by its particular culture, values, and norms. Before reaching adolescence, a child begins to be able to identify members of the out group.[50] For children, these understandings will underlie their social and political behavior and their approach toward identity issues.

One of the earliest and most consistent arguments in the scholarly literature was the association of segregated education with the segregation of the Protestant and Catholic communities coexisting in Northern Ireland.[51] The school systems in Northern Ireland mirror the larger segregated societal forces that drive both communities apart. Children receive their political learning from the static historical nature of Northern Ireland's sociopolitical world.[52] Significant historical and cultural events impact on their political development. However, different histories and religions are taught in the segregated schools, shaping the ethno religious identities of Protestant and Catholic children.[53] Further dividing the communities is the fact that cricket and rugby are played at Protestant state schools while Gaelic football and hurling are played at Catholic schools.[54]

Today, integrated schools comprise only 3 percent of the education structure throughout Northern Ireland.[55] The steadily growing sector of integrated schools in urban and rural areas is populated by young people from a variety of religious and class backgrounds who are working together to create long-term social change in Northern Ireland.[56] An increase in demand for integrated schools from the grassroots level indicates that integrated schooling is providing important opportunities for more understanding and positive communication to develop between Protestant and Catholic children.[57] In response to a demand for more integration in the society, the Northern Ireland Department of Education enacted legislation in 1988 to allow for the right of parents to choose to send their children to integrated schools.[58]

More recent scholarly evidence suggests, however, that the influence of integrated schooling may not be as important as previously thought in promoting intercommunal relations.[59] Children in a mixed school environment may be aware of the out-group and avoid controversial political and religious issues to preserve harmony and avoid intercommunal conflict.[60] Sensitive and taboo issues may be avoided by Protestant and Catholic children to preserve peace and tranquility within the integrated school context.[61]

Methodology

This analysis is part of a larger research study of interviews with 24 Protestant and 11 Catholic children in two schools in Belfast in the fall of 1991.[62] I am only using a portion of the data for the purposes of this chapter, which focuses on Protestant rather than Catholic schoolchildren. In order to address the continued debate over children, education, and identity, this sub-study examines the political development of 15 Protestant children in a nonintegrated grammar school and nine Protestant children in an all-ability integrated school in the southeast side of Belfast—13 first-year (11-12 years old) and 11 fifth-year (15-16 years old) students. The children from the nonintegrated school live predominantly in upper-middle-class neighborhoods in suburban Belfast. However, five of the nine Protestant children from the integrated school live in polarized working-class areas, and the remaining four schoolchildren come from either fairly well-to-do middle-class Protestant or mixed religious neighborhoods. All respondents are referred to by pseudonyms to protect anonymity.

The 35 children who were interviewed for the overall research study (including the 24 Protestant children in this sub-study) were selected to be representative of the gender and age spread within each school.[63] Children were asked, in sessions lasting approximately 80 minutes, to respond creatively to five stories set in their immediate sociopolitical world. Each session was tape recorded in a classroom in the integrated school and the ladies staff room in the nonintegrated school. After the field research was completed, I transcribed the stories. I then drew up an applicable coding instrument after intensive examination of the open-ended data. This chapter focuses specifically on the qualitative rather than the quantitative data. The qualitative data are striking because of the richness of the children's stories.

I spent approximately eight weeks collecting the data using the semi-projective incomplete storytelling method at both schools, which was used to allow each child to report on his or her personal experiences and the interpretations of these experiences.[64] This technique gave the children the beginning of a story and asked them to finish it. The process allowed for creativity in design and enabled children to elaborate on what they perceived to be the most salient criteria to be included within the story structure. This research method is not unlike the life-history and storytelling method that connects the individual with collective group histories and memories.[65] Empirical findings are organized around Protestant schoolchildren's schemata, including age and school differences. Patterns are identified and supported by evidence provided by the children's stories.

Three of the five stories in the interviewing schedule invited the participants to discuss how the queen should have acted or responded to the dilemma posed in each story. The stories were then analyzed to elicit patterns or themes to discover similarities and/or dissimilarities in the children's interpretation of the monarch. These children's images of the queen illustrate the richness of detail and nuance depicted in their stories. For analysis purposes, the children were classified into two separate categories of school type and age.

Consequently, the overall research study design was set up to determine the extent of political and religious identification with the British queen, looking at the internal processes of a group of 24 Protestant schoolchildren. This sub-study maps their political images of the queen and prime minister and how these images relate to national identity. It describes the sociocultural dynamics of these schoolchildren but does not generalize to the whole society.

Results

These children's perceptions of the political and religious role of the queen in the government and politics of Northern Ireland are reflected in the following quotations from their stories. The children were asked to explain the role of the queen and the prime minister to a foreign child. The quotations are presented to illustrate the points that these children found to be important about both political authority figures. The following discussion is interwoven with selected excerpts from their stories that clearly illuminate the significance of the queen for these young schoolchildren.

Images of the Queen: Children at the Nonintegrated School

Younger Children

The majority of younger children at the nonintegrated school extol the virtues of the monarch as benevolent leader and absolute ruler of Britain. Those that recognize the prime minister's role as head of government also believe that the queen will protect the Protestant community against legislative and administrative practices of the government to detach Northern Ireland from the union.

Jacycln is from a predominantly middle-class neighborhood in Ballymena. She describes the historical symbols of the monarchy with great clarity, highlighting the benevolent behavior of the queen and the Royal Family toward Northern Ireland Protestants.

> Interviewer: For example, suppose he says, "Tell me what the queen is." What would you say?
>
> Jacycln: If he was ever in England he should go to Buckingham Palace and then he would know. But if he ever goes to an important castle, like Windsor, and if he sees a flag flying outside, he knows she's in there. All the people here are expected to respect her as their queen. With their family and all the grandchildren, I think the Royal Family is growing, and that's good. Because then, if something happens you always have something to fall back on. I think the queen's a nicer person to have, rather than the prime minister, because the prime minister does ignore you sometimes. He doesn't know our country. [12-year-old]

While Jacycln describes the prime minister as an uncaring person, another child, Cynthia, relates the head of government's behavior to that of a dictator operating in an undemocratic political system. She is from a middle-class district in Newcastle, County Down. Here is how she describes the role of the monarch:

> Interviewer: For example, suppose he says, "Tell me what the queen is." What would you say?
>
> Cynthia: She's good and she can stop the government from doing anything she doesn't like. I think that the queen has a lot of power, that she can really do what she likes. She's a nice person and understands democracy. Then she can stop the government from doing anything that would hurt people. She can stop them being dictators and just going around bullying everybody like Sadaam Hussein. She can stop them from just doing anything they want. She has the most power in the country. [12-year-old]

George is from a fairly well-to-do neighborhood in Holywood, a suburb in the northern sector of the city. He emphasizes the importance of the queen in protecting the people of Northern Ireland.

Interviewer: For example, suppose he says, "Tell me what the queen is." What would you say?

George: She has to speak out on wars and stuff just to make sure that everybody knows that she knows what's happening and she's not just standing by and letting it happen. She knows what's happening and what to do about it. And if there is anything she can do to help us like take part in some campaign. [12-year-old]

In his story George expresses a clear understanding of the role of the queen in keeping Northern Ireland British:

Interviewer: Who is more important for Northern Ireland, the queen or the prime minister?

George: The prime minister knows how to deal with the country, while the queen just recognizes it as part of Britain. She just looks after it as well.

Dale is from a middle-class district near the coastal town of Larne. Implicit in his story is the belief that the monarch is in charge of government actions and policies in Northern Ireland:

Interviewer: For example, suppose he says, "Tell me what the queen is." What would you say?

Dale: She goes away to places to other countries to talk to other presidents, queens and kings, princes. She goes to all sorts of social events like Veteran's Day. Because she really rules Northern Ireland, it's her country. [11-year-old]

Dale seems to feel that the prime minister rules while the queen reigns but the monarch has the final decision on possible political action and policy development toward Northern Ireland:

Interviewer: How do the queen's powers differ from the prime minister's?

Dale: He's the one that makes all the big decisions 'cause if there is something really important, the queen would be consulted. He makes the normal decisions. But if it's something very important, she'd be consulted about it before it was announced.

The fact that these children identify with and believe that the queen is the effective political leader of politics in Britain illustrates the salience of the monarch as an intricate part of their identity. National identity is at the very heart of the intercommunal conflict in Northern Ireland.[66]

Older Children

Relatively few of the older children use the governance theme in describing the queen, but many do in connection with the prime minister. However, while recognizing the ceremonial activities of the queen as symbolically representative of the nation, these children believe that the queen is considerably more than a figurehead. They believe that the monarch rules and governs Northern Ireland, persuading the prime minister to represent the political interests of the Protestant community.

Heather lives with her parents, three brothers and two sisters in a middle-class neighborhood in Newtownards, a suburb of Belfast. She describes the queen in a benevolent and positive light:

> Interviewer: For example, suppose he says. "Tell me what the queen is." What would you say?
>
> Heather: It's just great to have somebody there to feel that you're safe under someone. She's very much in the public eye and she does lots of charity work. I like the queen and the people here love her 'cause she's nice and gentle. [15-year-old]

Kristi is from a well-to-do neighborhood in Newcastle. She was very positive in her spontaneous and lively description of the monarch.

> Interviewer: For example, suppose he says, "Tell me what the queen is." What would you say?
>
> Kristi: The queen is, well, Northern Ireland is, part of the United Kingdom, which is a monarchy. So the queen is effectively ruling over Northern Ireland as it is part of the United Kingdom. But she doesn't have any political power because everything is decided by the government. Although she is the head of the country, she doesn't actually make decisions. But everything she has decided she must sign. Acts that were passed in Parliament must be signed by the queen. The prime minister can put forward party suggestions like how to govern Northern Ireland, or if Northern Ireland should become part of the South. [15-year-old]

Russell lives in Newtownards. He feels that the queen is more important for the people of Northern Ireland:

> Interviewer: So is the queen the one you like best?
>
> Russell: I like the queen best, because the prime minister can change, but the queen sort of keeps the myth about our country, and England has been run on that framework for thousands of years. The queen is important to Loyalists here, 'cause she rules them. John Major is loyal to England but not to Northern Ireland. He wants to sell Northern Ireland to the South. [15-year-old]

Colin lacks a clear understanding of the effective power of the prime minister with regard to the government and politics of Northern Ireland. Colin is from a mixed religious middle-class neighborhood off the Malone Road. He portrays the queen in a benign and positive way in his story:

> Interviewer: So is it the prime minister that you like the best?
>
> Colin: I would like to see the queen doing something because everybody looks up to her as being the ruler of England and here. And the prime minister is just a man that debates and stuff. He doesn't actually rule the country, the queen has a higher authority and doesn't do much, just appoints him. The prime minister thinks about what he thinks would be good for the country. Because in 1917 Northern Ireland was separated from Ireland, because England, Scotland and Wales wanted to rule part of it and many of the Irish people didn't want that. So soldiers were sent in and they separated it, and there's always been fighting since. So the prime minister is pretty important and he has a lot to do with the rule of law in Northern Ireland. [15-year-old]

In general these children hold more benign views of the queen, whom they regard as their nation's effective ruler, than do the younger children and are distrustful of the prime minister's political behavior toward Northern Ireland. They make strongly positive references to the benevolence of the head of state. As these stories indicate, Protestants are suspicious of the political actions of the prime minister and feel that the monarch is sensitive to their needs, fears, and security.

Images of the Queen: Children at the Integrated School

Younger Children

These young schoolchildren portrayed the queen in a benign and friendly manner. They believed that the monarch is the effective head of government, the most powerful political figure in Northern Ireland. Their political images demonstrate that they have not fully grasped the intricate behavior of modern and democratic political actors.

In the following case Tamara, who is from a working-class housing estate in Glengormley in the southside of the city, articulates the political influence of the monarch in making laws in Parliament. She believes that the queen looks after Northern Ireland like a caretaker, and she depicts the queen as a motherly figure:

> Interviewer: For example, suppose he says, "Tell me what the queen is." What would you say?
>
> Tamara: She's part of the Royal Family. She lives in Buckingham Palace in London, and she rules Parliament, and makes the laws of the country. And she's in charge of the country and all that. Every year she goes to Parliament to open the Parliament, or something like that there. She makes the laws there. Her name is Elizabeth II. When

she dies or leaves the throne, Prince Charles will be on the throne. He
will be king. [11-year-old]

Tamara continues to explain the effective powers of the monarch vis-à-vis the
former Tory prime minister, John Major:

Interviewer: Who is more important for Northern Ireland, the queen
or the prime minister?

Tamara: The queen, because the queen rules Parliament and John
Major, the prime minister, just goes to Parliament alone. And the
queen makes the laws of our country, and rules the country. He goes
to Parliament, and he is not as famous as the queen. Some people
were against John Major when he was being picked for the prime
minister, but nobody is really against the queen.

While Tamara displayed limited knowledge about the actual political role of
the head of government, Diana was explicit in relegating the prime minister to a
second-rate political status. Diana is from an upper-middle-class neighborhood
in the suburb of Newtownabbey. This is what she had to say about the queen:

Interviewer: For example, suppose he says, "Tell me what the queen
is." What would you say?

Diana: She meets other kings of other countries and goes to other
people's houses and dines. She goes to Parliament sometimes and she
rules over the prime minister. She looks after us here in Northern
Ireland. [11-year-old]

Richard is from the Loyalist working-class enclave of the Village near the
Queen's University. In his story Richard views the Royal Family in terms of the
political attachment of Protestants to the monarch:

Interviewer: For example, suppose he says, "Tell me what the queen
is." What would you say?

Richard: The queen is a person that rules the land and if she says
jump, you jump. She's a member of the Royal Family and is very
important for the people in this country. She's a nice lady and she's
very friendly. [12-year-old]

Robert is from a mixed religious working-class housing estate in Legoniel. In
describing the queen to a foreign child, Robert focuses on the Royal Family. He
has not fully absorbed the limitations of the queen's actual political power.

Interviewer: For example, suppose he says, "Tell me what the queen
is." What would you say?

> Robert: She is part of the Royal Family. She is the head of the Royal
> Family. I like the queen because she is famous. She is very famous,
> like. [12-year-old]

In general these young Protestant children's stories portray benevolent images
of the queen which are associated with positive affect. They perceive the queen
as the dominant political figure at the apex of a political structure in which the
political role of the prime minister pales into insignificance.

Older Children

The older children at the integrated school have a more realistic knowledge
about the actual limitations to the queen's power compared to the effective political role of the prime minister. Their level of political information is certainly
more developed and sophisticated than that of the younger children in this sample.

Lora, who is from a Protestant working-class neighborhood in Dundonald,
illustrates the benevolence of the monarch in protecting the Protestant community against the encroachment of central government:

> Interviewer: Who is more important for Northern Ireland, the queen
> or the prime minister?
>
> Lora: I think if you were to ask me that question politically, then the
> prime minister's more important because he's the person who can
> get laws changed, whereas the queen is a sort of an ornament. She
> doesn't have that kind of power. But the queen cares for the people
> in Northern Ireland and they see her as their protector, or like a
> mother. The parties are not really worried about us because we don't
> have as much voting power as the people on the mainland so they're
> not that concerned we can't put them out of power. [16-year-old]

Donna, on the other hand, is from the Loyalist working-class enclave of Ti-
gers Bay in the city of Belfast. She displays an emotional attachment to the
queen rather than the prime minister:

> Interviewer: So is the prime minister the one you like the best?
>
> Donna: I would think the queen would be more interesting. The
> prime minister is okay but he would bore you. The queen would be
> better to get on with because all the prime ministers would be talking
> about would be politics. She hasn't really bothered for Northern Ire-
> land because I've never really seen the queen over in Northern Ire-
> land. You never really see them over here. All you really see them is
> over in England and they're always taking trips abroad. But they
> must be interesting though. But if I had to sit and talk speeches and
> politics all day that would kill me. [15-year-old]

While Donna's story portrays the former prime minister as a boring person,
Rodger is explicit in depicting the former prime minister as an untrustworthy

character, ready to abandon Northern Ireland's Protestants into a united Ireland. Rodger is from a mixed religious middle-class neighborhood in the town of Lisburn, outside Belfast. This is what he had to say about John Major:

> Interviewer: Who is more important for Northern Ireland, the queen or the prime minister?
>
> Rodger: The prime minister works out the laws and tells us how to live our life so I suppose we would really be more worried about him than the queen. If he took away the Anglo-Irish Agreement, some people would be annoyed that there isn't a united Ireland and other people would be annoyed that there is an Irish government input. So he's not liked by everybody. I don't love him, it's more of a personal kind of view. Whereas the queen is a nice lady. [15-year-old]

Ronnie is from a working-class family of five in the staunchly Loyalist neighborhood of the Shankill Road. He believes that the intercommunal conflict perpetuates itself because of terrorism, stereotyping, and ignorance. He does not have a good impression of either the queen or the prime minister. However, his story implies that British politicians and the monarch are not the cause of the conflict:

> Interviewer: How important is the integrated education in changing the people and the society?
>
> Ronnie: The queen or the politicians have nothing to do with the troubles here; it's all based on ignorance. It's definitely necessary for change because if people keep going on being ignorant, they'll just keep going around in circles. The paramilitaries don't have as much support as it would seem. There are people that are ignorant, but they're not violent. The general people wouldn't want someone going out and killing people just because they're a stereotype. [16-year-old]

Here is one of Ronnie's ideas to help resolve the Northern Ireland conflict:

> Interviewer: Why don't the 90 percent that don't support terrorists get together about changing the situation?
>
> Ronnie: It's just the ignorant people don't realize that the Catholics aren't like Catholics, they're individuals and the Protestants the other way round. It has to be put down, a lot of it, to these paramilitaries, they're the main problem. They should do something about them, like internment. Internment is quite unjust, but it does solve the problem if you do it properly. It's not a bad idea but it would have to be very strictly governed.

Similarly, Maude depicts levels of political cynicism in her story about the head of state. Here is how Maude, a Protestant girl from a fairly well-to-do Protestant neighborhood in Ballymena, describes the queen in a sarcastic tone and content to a young child from another country:

Interviewer: What does the queen do?

Maude: She queens, basically, I don't know. I don't actually think she does very much because she spends a lot of her time doing, like, opening places and talking to the public and basically being queen. She goes out and about and just shakes people's hands and talks to people and sits on her backside and does nothing. She sends letters to people who are 100, that's about it, really. [16-year-old]

While some of these older schoolchildren identify with the queen rather than the prime minister, others highlight the roles of ignorance and terrorism in exacerbating intercommunal divisions rather than the symbolic roles or political actions of either the queen or the prime minister.

Discussion

This study examined the images of integrated and nonintegrated Protestant schoolchildren in Belfast, Northern Ireland, regarding the significance of the British queen for ethnoreligious identity. Focusing on evaluations of the queen and the prime minister, we see that the majority of children in both schools are more likely to describe the monarch in a positive light than the head of government. However, in the integrated school, there is variation among some of the older children's references to the queen. Maude and Ronnie were extraordinarily negative in their descriptions of the head of state reflecting, perhaps, the complexity of the Northern Ireland conflict.

Apart from the overwhelming number of references to the theme of "symbolic representative of the nation," the queen is perceived by the younger children from both schools as the effective leader of the nation. Yet, in comparison to these more simplistic images of the monarch, older children from both schools indicate a sophisticated cognitive development in their depiction of the queen's ceremonial and symbolic characteristics. Their stories typically indicate that the head of state reigns while the prime minister rules.

Younger Children

The results indicate that the evaluations of both political incumbents were very similar for the younger children from both schools. The younger children are still in a concrete stage of cognitive development. The imagery used by these children suggests a queen who is a very important person with a high level of political control over the British system of government. In all of the responses the monarch appears as the sole decision-maker in the political system. The younger children at the integrated school say, for example, that the queen is "friendly," "motherly," "a caretaker," "a very powerful ruler," and, in three instances, is a "member of the Royal Family."

Turning to the nonintegrated school, we find a similar quality in the linguistic usages of the younger children who made very positive statements describing the queen in their stories. The monarch is portrayed as "benevolent leader," "absolute leader," "protector," "symbol of the nation," and "historical figure." Also, this group of children describe the prime minister as "uncaring" and "dictatorial."

Thus, the majority of these young children in both schools think of their queen as more than a political figurehead. Their responses reflect considerable affective content in their description of the monarch and, to a lesser extent, that of the prime minister. The queen is portrayed in a positive light compared to the prime minister.

Older Children

Regarding the cognitive content of political imagery, we note that older children at both schools display more accurate knowledge about the roles of both political incumbents than do the younger schoolchildren. They are aware that the prime minister, not the queen, is the effective leader of the nation. However, virtually all of these children indicate that the role of the head of government is important politically but the individual holding it cannot be trusted. Hence, the prime minister is described as "powerful," yet "untrustworthy." This evidence suggests, perhaps, the levels of anxiety and uncertainty these children feel over the national question. They seem to realize that the prime minister has the political power to detach Northern Ireland from the union. Opinion polls in Northern Ireland since 1972 make it clear that Protestants fear that the British government will betray them into a united Ireland.[67]

In sharp contrast to the mixed evaluation of the head of government by most of this sample, some of the older schoolchildren in the integrated school are drastically less positive in their general descriptions of the queen than are their nonintegrated counterparts. Ronnie and Maude, for example, exhibit political negativism, distrust, and cynicism in the tone and content of their stories. In contrast, the other older children display a deferential attitude and emotional attachment to the monarch. Their positive use of verbs and nouns are associated with their emotional portrayal of the queen. Again the head of state is "motherly," "benevolent leader," "symbol of the nation," "a protector," and "representative of Protestants." Yet this group of children also has a comprehensive knowledge of the queen's limitation of power. Thus, the queen is portrayed as "a figurehead," "not powerful," and useful for "ceremonial functions."

The contrast between the mixed findings of political perceptions of the monarch by older children in both schools is of special interest, given our concern with the possible effects of integrated education on Protestant children's national identity and political world views. The open environment of the integrated school and close friendship ties across the religious divide may be influencing how Ronnie and Maude, for example, look at politics, conflict, and identity. However, the findings from this qualitative study are suggestive and should not be generalized to the Northern Ireland population as a whole. More extensive research, with a larger sample population of integrated and nonintegrated schools, is needed to test the research findings from this exploratory study.[68]

Conclusion

The deeply held fears, traditions, and aspirations of the Protestant community must be accounted for if we are ever to reach a stage for future reconciliation and peacebuilding in Northern Ireland.[69] Protestants believe that they owe their allegiance to the queen subject only to the monarch's providing protection for the community under the umbrella of the British nation. Their loyalty is conditional on the queen's fulfilling her sacred duty to protect and nourish the loyal Protestants of Ulster against the threat, perceived or otherwise, of Catholic domination, IRA violence, and possible betrayals by the British government.[70]

Many Protestants consider the Catholic ethos in the Republic of Ireland to be undemocratic, authoritarian, and insensitive to their religious and political needs. Protestants feel vulnerable and threatened by the very fact that they constitute a minority community on the island of Ireland.[71] Protestants fear that in a united Ireland they would be treated as second-class citizens.[72] In fact, Provisional IRA violence has reinforced Protestant allegiance to a British identity.[73]

By focusing on the political images of these children during their formative stages, we can assess how they are likely to behave as adults. Among this sample of Protestant schoolchildren, we notice a deep and emotional attachment to the queen as a symbol of the nation. Given John Major's distinctive leadership style, it is remarkable that very few of the children refer to the former prime minister in a positive light. Could it be that in a period of uncertainty over Northern Ireland's political future within the United Kingdom, this sample of children would rather embrace the symbolism of the monarch as an expression of their national and ethnoreligious identity than identify with the head of government? Russell, a 15 year-old, for example, believes that the island of Ireland will unite eventually because "we cannot really stop the prime minister letting it [Northern Ireland] go back to the South." Since the 1985 Anglo-Irish Agreement, Protestant adults in Northern Ireland are uniform in their negative attitudes toward the prime minister and the British government.[74] Protestants fear the intentions of the British government to create a united Ireland where they would be a minority community.[75]

While on the basis of these preliminary research findings one cannot extrapolate to the larger societal context, this exploratory study is useful for assessing whether integrated schooling in Northern Ireland may be making a difference in the political attitudes of these schoolchildren. The safety and openness of the integrated environment allows the children, at the same time, to explore political and religious differences in an objective manner while retaining their ethnoreligious identities and political attachments, yet creating a "shared identity."[76] A school population mixed by religion, gender, and class allied to a wholistic yet integrative curriculum context may have impacted the political attitudes of these Protestant children by expanding the identity pie or cultural tent.[77]These children come to the integrated school from different socioeconomic and religious backgrounds with life experiences that allow for different responses and interpretations of their political environment when compared to the political images of the nonintegrated schoolchildren. However, a study with a larger sampling frame is necessary to build on this work and test the hypotheses suggested by the findings.

Notes

1. R. W. Connell, *The Child's Construction of Politics* (Melbourne University Press, 1971); Fred I. Greenstein, *Children and Politics* (New Haven, Conn.: Yale University Press, 1965); Fred I. Greenstein, "The Benevolent Leader Revisited: Children's Images in Three Democracies," *American Political Science Review* 69, no. 1 (1975): 1371-98; Lawrence Kohlberg, *The Philosophy of Moral Development: Essays on Moral Development* (New York: Harper and Row, 1981).

2. R. C. Shank and R. P. Abelson, *Scripts, Plans, Goals and Understanding* (Hillsdale, N.J.: Erlbaum, 1977); Deborah Welch-Larson, "The Role of Belief Systems and Schemas in Foreign Policy Decision-Making," *Journal of Political Psychology* 15, no. 1 (1994): 17-35.

3. Ed Cairns, *Children and Political Violence* (Cambridge, Mass.: Blackstaff, 1996).

4. Welch-Larson, "The Role of Belief Systems," 17-35.

5. Sean Byrne and Aimee Delman, "Group Identity Formation and Intra-Group Conflict," *The Journal of Intergroup Relations* 25, no. 4 (1999): 35-57.

6. Sean Byrne, *Growing Up in a Divided Society: The Influence of Conflict on Belfast Schoolchildren* (Cranbury, N.J.: Associated University Presses, 1997); Sean Byrne, "Belfast Schoolchildrens' Images of Conflict and Social Change: Signs of Hope in Integrated Education," *Mind and Human Interaction* 8, no. 3 (1997): 172-85; Ed Cairns, "Impact of Television News Exposure on Children's Perceptions of Violence in Northern Ireland," *Journal of Social Psychology* 130, no. 4 (1990): 447-52; Robert Coles, *The Political Life of Children* (Boston: Houghton Mifflin Co., 1986); J. E. Greer, "The Persistence of Religion: A Study of Sixth-form Pupils in Northern Ireland, 1968-1988," *Journal of Social Psychology* 130, no. 5 (1990): 573-81.

7. Coles, *The Political Life*; Neil Waddell and Ed Cairns, "Identity Preference in Northern Ireland," *Journal of Political Psychology* 12, no. 2 (1991): 205-13; John Whyte, *Interpreting Northern Ireland* (Oxford: Carendon Press, 1990).

8. Coles, *The Political Life*; Rona Fields, *Society under Siege: A Psychology of Northern Ireland* (Philadelphia: Temple University Press, 1976); Morris Fraser, *Children in Conflict* (London: Secker and Walton, 1973); Ken Heskin, *Northern Ireland: A Psychological Analysis* (Dublin: Gill and Macmillan, 1980).

9. Byrne, *Growing Up*; Byrne, "Belfast Schoolchildrens' Images."

10. John Whyte, "How Is the Boundary Maintained between the Two Communities in Northern Ireland?" *Ethnic and Racial Studies* 9, no. 2 (1986): 219-34; Whyte, *Interpreting Northern Ireland*.

11. Greenstein, *Children and Politics*.

12. Waddell and Cairns, "Identity Preference."

13. Edward Moxon-Browne, *Nation, Class, and Creed in Northern Ireland* (Aldershot: Gower, 1983); Richard Rose, *Governing without Consensus: An Irish Perspective* (London: Faber and Faber, 1971).

14. Steve Bruce, *God Save Ulster! The Religion and Politics of Paisleyism* (Oxford: Clarendon Press, 1986); Steve Bruce, *The Red Hand: Protestant Paramilitaries in Northern Ireland* (New York: Oxford University Press, 1992).

15. Robert L. McCartney, Sean Hall, Bryan Somers, Gordon Smyth, H. L. McCracken and Peter Smith, "The Unionist Case" (Belfast: Typescript, 1981), 5.

16. Sarah Nelson, *Ulster's Uncertain Defenders: Protestant Political, Paramilitary and Community Groups and the Northern Ireland Conflict* (Belfast: Appletree Press, 1984).

17. Whyte, *Interpreting Northern Ireland.*

18. Bruce, *God Save Ulster*; Nelson, *Ulster's Uncertain Defenders*; Roy Wallis, Steve Bruce, and David Taylor, "No Surrender! Paisleyism and the Politics of Ethnic Identity in Northern Ireland" (Belfast: Department of Social Studies, Queen's University, 1986), 1-34.

19. A. T. Q. Stewart, *The Narrow Ground: Aspects of Ulster, 1609-1969* (London: Faber and Faber, 1977).

20. David Miller, *Queen's Rebels: Ulster Loyalism in Historical Perspective* (Dublin: Gill and Macmillan, 1978).

21. Miller, *Queen's Rebels*, 155.

22. John Agnew, "Beyond Reason: Spatial and Temporal Sources of Ethnic Conflict," and Terrell Northrup, "Dynamics of Identity in Personal and Social Conflict," in *Intractable Conflicts and Their Transformation*, ed. Louis Kriesberg, Terrell Northrup, and Stuart Thorson (Syracuse, N.Y.: Syracuse University Press, 1989), 41-83; Whyte, *Interpreting Northern Ireland.*

23. Paul Bew, Peter Gibbon, and Henry Patterson, *The State in Northern Ireland, 1921-1972: Political Forces and Social Classes* (Manchester: Manchester University Press, 1979); Paul Bew, Peter Gibbon, and Henry Patterson, *Northern Ireland, 1921-1994: Political Forces and Social Classes* (London: Serif, 1995); Rosemary Harris, *Prejudice and Tolerance in Ulster: A Study of Neighbors and "Strangers" in a Border Community* (Manchester: Manchester University Press, 1972); Jennifer Todd, "Two Traditions in Unionist Political Culture," *Irish Political Studies* 2, no. 1 (1987): 1-26; Frank Wright, *Northern Ireland: A Comparative Perspective* (Dublin: Gill and Macmillan, 1987).

24. Frank Wright, "Protestant Ideology and Politics in Ulster," *European Journal of Sociology* 14, no. 1 (1973): 221.

25. Sean Byrne and Neal Carter, "Social Cubism: Six Social Forces of Ethnoterritorial Politics in Northern Ireland and Quebec," *Peace and Conflict Studies* 3, no. 2 (1996): 52-72; Harold Jackson and Ann McHardy, "'The Two Irelands': The Problem of the Double Minority," vol. 2 (London: The Minority's Rights Group, 1984), 1-38.

26. A. Jackson, *The Ulster Party: Irish Unionists in the House of Commons, 1884-1911* (Oxford: Clarendon Press, 1989); James Loughlin, *Gladstone, Home Rule and the Ulster Question, 1882-1893* (Cranbury, N.J.: Humanities Press, 1987); Stewart, *The Narrow Ground.*

27. Paul Bew, *Land and the National Question in Ireland, 1858-1882* (Cranbury, N.J.: Humanities Press, 1979).

28. Byrne, *Growing Up*; Byrne, "Belfast Schoolchildrens' Images."

29. Peter Gibbon, *The Origins of Ulster Unionism: The Formation of Popular Protestant Politics and Ideology in Nineteenth-Century Ireland* (Manchester: Manchester University Press, 1975); Loughlin, *Gladstone*; Stewart, *The Narrow Ground.*

30. Jackson, *The Ulster Party*; Jackson, *The Narrow Ground.*

31. John McGarry and Brendan O'Leary, *Explaining Northern Ireland: Broken Images* (Cambridge, Mass.: Blackwell, 1995).

32. Sean Byrne, "Power Politics As Usual: Divided Islands and the Roles of External Ethno-Guarantors," *Nationalism and Ethnic Politics* 6, no. 1 (2000).

33. Seamus Dunn and Valerie Morgan, "Protestant Alienation in Northern Ireland: A Preliminary Survey" (Coleraine: Centre for the Study of Conflict, University of Ulster, 1994), 1-68.

34. Byrne, "Power Politics as Usual."

35. Brendan O'Leary and John McGarry, *The Politics of Antagonism: Understanding Northern Ireland* (Atlantic Highlands, N.J.: Athlone Press, 1993).

36. Paul Bew and Henry Patterson, eds., *Scenarios for Progress in Northern Ireland* (London: Clarendon Press, 1990).

37. Bruce, *God Save Ulster*; Steve Bruce, *The Red Hand*.

38. Sean Byrne and Michael Ayulo, "External Economic Aid in Ethnopolitical Conflict: A View from Northern Ireland," *Security Dialogue* 29, no. 4 (1998): 219-33.

39. Paul Dixon, *Northern Ireland: Power, Ideology and Reality* (London: Macmillan, 2000).

40. Cynthia Irvin, *Militant Nationalism: Between Movement and Party in Northern Ireland and the Basque Country* (Duluth: University of Minnesota Press, 1999).

41. Her Majesty's Government. "Frameworks for the Future" (Belfast: HMSO, 1995).

42. Sean Byrne and Loraleigh Keashly, "Working with Ethnopolitical Conflict: A Multi-Modal and Multi-Level Approach to Conflict Intervention," *International Peacekeeping* (forthcoming, 2000).

43. Ronda Paisley, "Framework Document Asks for the Impossible: Cheated Unionists Are Due a Place in the Sun," *Irish Times*, 24 February 1995, 16.

44. O'Leary and McGarry, *The Politics of Antagonism*; Whyte, *Interpreting Northern Ireland*.

45. Byrne and Keashly, "Working with Ethnopolitical Conflict"; Jackson and McHardy, "The Two Irelands."

46. Ed Cairns, "Intergroup Conflict in Northern Ireland," in *Social Identity and Intergroup Relations,* ed. Henri Tajfel (Cambridge: Cambridge University Press, 1982), 227-95; Whyte, "How Is the Boundary Maintained."

47. Byrne, *Growing Up*; Byrne, "Belfast Schoolchildrens' Images."

48. Whyte, *Interpreting Northern Ireland*.

49. Coles, *The Political Life*; Andrew Dawes, "The Effects of Political Violence on Children: A Consideration of South Africa and Related Studies," *International Journal of Psychology* 25, no. 1 (1990): 13-31; Gill Straker, *Faces in the Revolution: The Psychological Effects of Violence in Township Youth in South Africa* (Athens, Ohio: Ohio University Press, 1992).

50. Yogev Bilu, "The Other as a Nightmare: The Israeli-Arab Encounter as Reflected in Children's Dreams in Israel and the West Bank," *Journal of Political Psychology* 11, no. 2 (1990): 243-82; R. Miligram and N. A. Miligram, "The Effects of the Yom Kippur War on Anxiety Level in Israeli Children," *Journal of Psychology* 94, no. 1 (1976): 107-13; R. Punamaki and R. Suileman, "Predictors and Effectiveness of Coping with Political Violence among Palestinian Children," *British Journal of Social Psychology* 29, no. 1 (1990): 67-77; A. Yogev and N. S. Ben-Yehosshua, "Determinants of Readiness for Contact with Jewish Children among Young Arab Students in Israel," *Journal of Conflict Resolution* 35, no. 3 (1991): 547-62.

51. Byrne, *Growing Up*; Byrne, "Belfast Schoolchildrens' Images"; Ed Cairns, *Caught in a Crossfire: Children and the Northern Ireland Conflict* (Belfast: Appletree Press, 1987); Cairns, *Children and Politics*; Coles, *The Political Life*; Greer, "The Persistence of Religion."

52. Vamik Volkan, "The Need to Have Enemies and Allies: A Developmental Approach," *Journal of Political Psychology* 12, no. 2 (1991): 205-13; Vamik Volkan, *Blood Lines: From Ethnic Pride to Ethnic Terrorism* (Boulder, Colo.: Westview Press, 1998).

53. Donald H. Akenson, *Education and Enmity: The Control of Schooling in Northern Ireland, 1920-1950* (Newton and Abbot, UK: David and Charles, 1973); John Darby and Seamus Dunn, "Segregated Education: The Research Evidence," in *Education and Policy in Northern Ireland,* ed. R. D. Hepburn and R. L. Miller (Belfast: Queen's University and the University of Ulster Policy Institute, 1987), 45-64; Whyte, "How Is the Boundary Maintained."

54. Coles, *The Political Life.*

55. G. Jahoda and S. Harrison, "Belfast Children: Some Effects of a Conflict Environment," *Irish Journal of Psychology* 3, no. 1 (1975): 1-19; Domnic Murray, "Schools and Conflict," in *Northern Ireland: The Background to the Conflict,* ed. John Darby (Syracuse, N.Y.: Syracuse University Press, 1983), 136-51; Domnic Murray, *Worlds Apart: Segregated Schools in Northern Ireland* (Belfast: Appletree Press, 1985).

56. Murray, "Schools and Conflict"; Murray, *Worlds Apart.*

57. Chris Moffat, ed., *Education Together for a Change: Integrated Education and Community Relations in Northern Ireland* (Belfast: Fortnight Educational Trust, 1993).

58. Tony Gallagher, "Religious Divisions in Schools in Northern Ireland," paper presented at the British Educational Research Association Annual conference, Queen's University, Belfast, Northern Ireland, 28 August 1998, 1-15.

59. Sean Byrne, "Conflict Regulation or Conflict Resolution: Third Party Intervention in the Northern Ireland Conflict: Prospects for Peace," *Terrorism and Political Violence* 7, no. 2 (1995): 1-24; Joanne Hughes, "Prejudice and Identity in a Mixed Environment," and Colin Irwin, "The Myths of Segregation," in *New Perspectives on the Northern Ireland Conflict,* ed. Adrian Guelke (Aldershot: Avebury, 1994), 86-118; Colin Irwin, "Education and the Development of Social Interaction in Divided Societies," (Belfast: Queen's University, Department of Social Anthropology, 1991), 1-97; Chris Moffat, ed., *Education Together for a Change* (Belfast: Fortnight Educational Trust, 1993); Frank Wright, "Integrated Education and New Beginnings in Northern Ireland," Working Paper 6, (Coleraine: Center for the Study of Conflict, University of Ulster, 1991): 1-30.

60. Seamus Dunn, "Integrated Schools in Northern Ireland," *Oxford Review of Education* 25, no. 2 (1989): 121-28; Irwin, "Education and the Development"; Wright, "Integrated Education."

61. Alex McEwen, "Segregation and Integration in Northern Ireland's Education system," in *Schools under Scrutiny: The Case of Northern Ireland,* ed. L. Caul (London: Macmillan, 1990), 15-36; James Russell, "Sources of Conflict," *Northern Teacher* 11, no. 3 (1974): 3-11; John Salters, "Attitudes towards Society in Protestant and Roman Catholic School Children in Belfast," M.Ed. thesis, Queens' University, Belfast 1970, 1-58.

62. Byrne, *Growing Up*; Byrne, "Belfast Schoolchildrens' Images."

63. Byrne, *Growing Up*; Byrne, "Belfast Schoolchildrens' Images."

64. Fred I. Greenstein and Sidney Tarrow, *Political Orientations of Children: The Use of a Semi-Projective Technique in Three Nations* (California: Sage, 1970).

65. Margaret M. Braunguart and Richard G. Braunguart, "The Life Course Development of Left- and Right-Wing Youth Activist Leaders from the 1960s." *Journal of Political Psychology* 11, no. 2 (1990): 243-382; Jessica Senehi, "Getting a Handle on the Intangibles: Storytelling and Reconciliation in Intercommunal Conflict," in *Conflict and Peaceful Change in Divided Societies: Theories and Applications,* ed. Sean Byrne and Cynthia Irvin (West Hartford, Conn.: Kumarian Press, 2000); Straker, *Faces in the Revolution.*

66. Whyte, *Interpreting Northern Ireland*.

67. Dermot Keogh and Michael H. Haltzel, eds., *Northern Ireland and the Politics of Reconciliation* (Washington, D.C.: Woodrow Wilson Center Press, 1994); Moxon-Browne, *Nation, Class and Creed*.

68. Byrne, *Growing Up*; Byrne, "Belfast Schoolchildrens' Images."

69. Byrne, "Conflict Regulation or Conflict Resolution"; Byrne and Keashly, "Working with Ethnopolitical Conflict."

70. Bruce, *God Save Ulster*; Bruce, *The Red Hand*; Miller, *Queen's Rebels*.

71. Bruce, *God Save Ulster*; Bruce, *The Red Hand*; Whyte, *Interpreting Northern Ireland*.

72. Wallis, Bruce, and Taylor, "No Surrender!"

73. McGarry and O'Leary, *Explaining Northern Ireland*.

74. Dunn and Morgan, "Protestant Alienation."

75. Adrian Guelke, *Northern Ireland: The International Perspective* (Dublin: Gill and Macmillan, 1988).

76. Byrne, *Growing Up*.

77. Byrne, *Growing Up*; Byrne, "Belfast Schoolchildrens' Images"; Volkan, *Blood Lines*.

Part Two

Constructing Identities and Resolving Conflicts

Chapter Six

Who Do They Say We Are?

Framing Social Identity and Gender in Church Conflict

Celia Cook-Huffman

Identity and conflict emerged in the 1990s as central components of the discourse on violence. Whether the topic is ethnic conflict in Kosovo or spouse abuse, theorists and practitioners are examining the interrelationship between identity and conflict, trying to uncover links that could bring about lasting resolutions to difficult problems. The research presented in this chapter was motivated by a desire to further these goals. Using a qualitative research design I explored how social identities are conceptualized and imbued with meaning in conflicts among members of an urban church in the Northeast United States.

Social Identity Theory and Social Conflict

Two sets of literature explore the relationship between identity and conflict at the social level: Social identity theory (SIT)[1] and Social Conflict theory.[2] This literature has been critiqued and enhanced in recent years by contributions from researchers paying particular attention to issues of gender identity and culture.[3] I will briefly review the important contributions of each.

Identity refers to an individual's sense of self[4] that develops from and is realized in interactions, making life predictable and meaningful. It is a process of self-categorization formed in relationship with other people and the world, acquiring significance, meaning, and value within specific contexts and cultures.[5]

The level of identity focused on in this chapter is social identity:[6] "that part of an individual's self concept which derives from his [*sic*] knowledge of his membership [in] a social group (or groups) together with the value and emotional significance attached to that membership."[7] Social identity thus defined includes a sense of the "self in-relation-to-the-world"[8] and looks at "the individual defined in relation to the group."[9]

The basic tenet of social identity theory hypothesizes that individuals need a positive self-image and thus strive for positive social identity.[10] Achieving this goal requires that the groups in which one is a member be different and distinct from other groups in society in ways which are, or can be, evaluated positively.[11]

Tajfel theorized that social groups evaluate themselves and create social identity through intergroup comparison. In-groups compare with similar but distinct out-groups along comparable dimensions called *social categorizations*.[12] Social categorizations are consensual constructions that characterize and delineate boundaries of group membership. Social identity is the internalization of these social categories.[13]

This relationship between in-groups and out-groups is constructed within the context of the social system and the relative status of comparison groups. In most societies, all groups are not equal. Those groups in society which are dominant "have the power and status to impose the dominant value system and ideology which serves to legitimate and perpetuate the status quo."[14] As the social system divides into groups, perceptions, meanings, and behaviors are influenced by an interaction between the salience of particular social identities for individuals and the contexts which give them meaning. Thus, high-status groups within a system achieve high self-esteem from group memberships, and members of subordinate or low-status groups will derive less positive or perhaps negative social identity from membership. The ability of a group to achieve positive distinction vis-à-vis other groups and the strategies they use to do so are dependent on the larger social context. Moreover, "the erosion, preservation or creation of differentials [distinctions between various groups on important characteristics] has been . . . one of the fundamental features of some of the most acute social and industrial conflicts."[15]

SIT hypothesizes that social categorization results in intergroup competition by stimulating a self-evaluative social comparison process; intergroup competition and conflict are stimulated by the impact of social categorizations on social identity and self-perception. Thus, the theory suggests that social identity and the desire for positive group distinctiveness may be the cause of many intergroup conflicts.[16]

Social conflict theorists have also examined the role of social identity in social conflict. Kriesberg suggests "a group's self-awareness of being a collective entity in opposition to another group is formed and transformed in the course of a conflict."[17] Social identity aspects that evolve and change as a conflict moves in and out of various stages include: consciousness of a social identity, salience and solidification of the traits and symbols which accompany it, the meaning and centrality of a social identity for group members, and its importance for security and survival. Add to this picture other needs, along with an ever-changing context involving various levels of conflict, and one has immense complexity to sort through when trying to analyze the role of social identity in conflicts.

Conflict theorists offer two distinct conceptions of the relationship between intergroup conflict and social identity: conflicts emerge over realistic conflicts of interest which result in the development of in-groups, out-groups, and social identities, or conversely, social identity needs cause intergroup conflicts. While these theories assess the causes of intergroup conflict as based in either identity needs or allocation of goods and resources, the difficulty of clearly delineating this relationship is also recognized. Thus, the literature includes discussions about the interplay between social identity and access to goods and resources as the antecedents of social conflict.

Gender research offers several critiques and raises interesting theoretical questions. This work challenges the theoretical models of SIT, arguing that the assumption that groups compete for positive social identity via processes of differentiation and social comparison signifies a "preoccupation with a process of identity construction typically more important for males."[18] Williams defines "agentic identification" to be that which is based on competition and differentiation from others. She contrasts this with a process of "communal identification," associated with women, where positive social identity is developed via constructive relationships with other groups, as well as through intragroup relations.

One set of questions raised by this research is how, when, and if *Woman* operates as a social identity and how this categorization is important for understanding social conflict.[19] Social conflict theory is only beginning to address questions related to gendered identities and sex differences in intergroup behavior during conflict. For example, how do we explain gender differences in participation in large-scale social conflict, in experiences of and the use of violence, and in conflicts, etc.?

Sumner raised a question that continues to stimulate research: Do intergroup conflicts arise from a group's need for a "lesser" out-group to compare with, thus allowing them to feel both unique and superior, or do in-group/out-group behaviors develop once intergroup conflict has emerged?[20] Gender research has prompted a second question: Do groups need intergroup competition and conflict in order to define themselves? While social identity is acknowledged as an important component of conflicts,[21] systematic research into what social identity involves, how it is defined by group members, and how it influences social conflicts is lacking.[22] This chapter focuses on this last question, examining the interaction of social identity in intra and intergroup conflict.

Methodology

This research was designed to explore the relationship between social identity and conflict, and the interaction of gender, social identity, and social conflict. To this end, the research design involved a field study of a community-oriented group I call the Downtown Church.

Downtown was chosen as the data group for this study for several reasons. My reading of SIT and social conflict theories exploring the importance of social identity in conflict revealed several gaps which I wanted to explore. Primarily I was concerned with two things: (1) the almost exclusive focus of SIT research utilizing competitive contexts for exploring the relationship between social identity and conflict,[23] and (2) the lack of qualitative work examining participant understandings of identity outside of the research laboratory. Therefore, I sought a context which had conflicts and which also claimed to have cooperative interactions. The goal was to expand the understanding of how social identities are defined in cooperative and competitive situations. This context also offered an opportunity to study social identity in a setting in which overlapping and cross-cutting social identities were present.[24]

The study incorporated a qualitative research design using the theoretical framework of symbolic interactionism[25] to guide data collection, and analytical induction[26] as a methodology for data analysis. The research site and context are important for understanding the findings discussed below. Because the participants share an overarching social categorization[27]—membership in the church—the boundaries between groups shift, sometimes very rapidly. Thus, the nature of social categorization in this study gives insight into the implications of both cross-cutting identities and shifting salience for intergroup as well as intragroup conflict theory.[28]

Social Identity and the Construction of Social Conflict

The interaction of social identity and conflict as observed in this study demonstrates how social identities are fluid entities which both shift and change and paradoxically serve as static constructs at any given point in a conflict. They become salient and are defined within the conflict, while concurrently providing a context and the resources for understanding what is said or what happens.[29]

In order to understand this reflexive process, I first explore the illustrations of social identity operating as fixed constructs.[30] Then, I will return to the fluid movements of social identity in conflict and discuss how social identities are influenced by conflict. I discuss the dynamics of social identity in both intra- and intergroup conflicts.

Frames

I use the language of frames[31] to explore how social identities function as static constructs, defining and organizing events or occurrences in conflicts. In conflicts, social identities may act as frames that contextualize and influence people's perceptions and actions. A social identity serves as a "frame" when it implicitly or explicitly invokes the norms, rules, expectations, feelings, beliefs, or actions associated with a particular social identity or its symbolic representation. Social identities as frames act as boundaries that delineate and characterize the issues and/or the individuals or groups in the conflict. They focus perspectives, which color images and interpretations of both in-group and out-group members.

Social identities operate as frames in this study in one of two ways. First, a social identity can serve as a *contextual frame* for the perceiver in a particular conflict by providing a context in which the participants and their actions can be understood or given meaning. The social identity operates like a paradigm, serving to interpret the information in the given situation through the categorization of self, other, or both, as members of a particular group or groups.

The following example explores how social identities structure a context in a conflict. Here Ella speaks as a member of the church. She believes that the leaders of the church have assumed more power than they should, particularly given the church's denominational affiliation. Her membership in the church and her understanding of what it means to be part of the larger denomination operates as a contextual frame, a frame which places her in opposition to the staff in the church. The "spring experience" she discusses refers to an attempt to resolve a difference of opinion between the leadership of the church and the congregation over how to best expose children to the worship experience. During the spring they experimented with a new worship style for six months.[32]

> That's what the "spring experience" was. It was not from the congregation. That was them in a staff meeting deciding this would be good for us. "Now take your medicine. You will do this. And we will experiment with it and you will evaluate it, not just once, but twice, and three times. Then we'll have a meeting to vote on it. You didn't vote right. How could you do this? You're turning your back on change! You're not growing! You're not. . . ." Whoa! Whoa! Time out! Where is the flow here? This is a [names church denomination] background. This isn't a hierarchical power structure. We are one. We, you know, we work together. That's what boards are for. That's what dialogue is for.

Her identification as a member of the larger denomination to which this church belongs influences her expectations of how decisions should be made in the church: "we work together"; "this is not a hierarchical power structure"; expectations which she believes have been violated by the actions of the church staff "deciding this would be good for us."

Gender identity provides another example of a contextual frame. The conflict for Jane involves the pastor and issues of pastoral care. Jane believes her relationship with the pastor has shifted from one which was fairly close and supportive to one which is distant. She attributes this, in part, to her becoming a stronger woman, something with which she believes the pastor is not comfortable:

> I have become more of a proponent of women's rights as I've gotten into quilting more. I mean into quilting history, and teaching quilting as teaching women's history, as being women's first support groups and bonding efforts in this new world, as being a source of strength for women. I've gotten stronger in my statements and opinions on those subjects, and I've grown a lot in that way since we came here ten years ago. I think, as I've grown that way, the distance with [the pastor] has become more - I'm not as easily manageable as I was and not as awed by him. And, I think he feels that. And it's hard to be real close to someone when those dynamics are going on.

Jane understands this conflict in part from her perspective as a woman, and she believes that one of the reasons the conflict exists is because of the kind of woman she is: i.e., an increasingly strong proponent of women's rights. Once again the contextual frame, this time as identification with a gender social categorization, influences Jane's interpretation and understanding of what is happening in the conflict.

The second type of frame, what I call a *defining frame*, is manifest when salient social identities are used to limit the scope and range of conflict. In this case, a group character or a group standard is invoked as a way to try to impose certain norms, beliefs, or courses of action on the people or groups in conflict. Rather than serving to provide a general context of understanding, it focuses the lens more narrowly and specifically in a way congruent with a particular social identity. The specific meaning is used to create a standard or to justify an action or belief.

In the next example from a church council meeting, the pastor speaks as a pastor and a Christian about "Christian hospitality" as the reason for the suggested change in the worship schedule:

> Hospitality has been our thrust for the last 10 years . . . the main thrust, and I think this has been so disturbing because it is the first hospitality experience that has hit us in the gut. This hospitality is for young kids, the most important thing and it is always with us. I think it is so disturbing because we brought the hospitality home.

He interprets the Christian identity and presents it to other members of the council in a way which suggests that the current impetus for change is part of a larger plan and that people are resisting because it affects them so directly. Some of the listeners felt that implicit in his words was the suggestion that they are willing to be "hospitable" only when it doesn't hurt too much. This specific definition of what it means to be a Christian is used to persuade members to vote in a particular way: if you are a "good Christian" you are willing to be hospitable even when it hurts—vote yes.

In this study, social identities as contextual and defining frames create expectations and influence perceptions of conflicts within the in-group and between in-groups and out-groups. Clearly this distinction may be difficult to make in some instances. A powerful group identity may always serve as a defining frame, whether implicitly or explicitly invoked. Further study of this distinction is needed; however, it is clear that while all social identities operate to some extent as contextual frames, their use as defining frames suggests they become a central aspect of the conflict. This shift may lead them to have an even more direct impact on the process of the conflict. I explore how this happens below.

Substantive Issues

In conflicts in this study, when a social identity serves as a frame and structures a context or perspective, others may choose to accept or deny the frame and the social identity. If the frame is not accepted or shared by others, the result may be an attempt to negotiate meaning and understanding. Social identities then become substantive issues in the conflict in one of two ways: clashes over the definition of a group attribute, or clashes between two different social identities. They may contribute to intragroup conflict or serve as the basis by which two groups emerge and intergroup divisions become salient.

For example, assumptions and understandings about the meaning of mission are one source of conflict connected to social identity in the church. Many members talk about what they believe to be the mission work of the church. For some it includes the daily support of the day care and the food pantry. For others "mission" constitutes those projects defined as mission projects by the national offices of the church which Downtown gives monies to support. For others social action constitutes mission work. Thus "mission" takes the form of providing sanctuary for Central American refugees and working on housing for low-income families. Given the limited financial and human resources of the church, conflicts emerged over the issue a number of times.

Kay describes a conflict that exemplifies how different understandings of the group attribute "mission" can lead to conflict. This conflict concerns the question of "care" in relation to the mission of the church. Several years before the current pastor came to Downtown, Kay worked with the previous pastor to put on a Thanksgiving dinner for members of the church who do not regularly attend church functions. She understands this project to be an example of caring, Christian mission, which she defines as showing those most in need that they are cared for and appreciated members of the church. One way she ministers to them is by including them in the church's family Thanksgiving.

When the new pastor came, Kay's perception was that he wanted to turn it into a meal for street people, more of a charity project. This was the focus of his understanding of Christian mission and care. For Kay, this created several problems. First, charity to street people is not how she wanted to express her care on Thanksgiving. Her mission is to the isolated people of the church. Second, the dinner has always been one in which everyone helps with both the cooking and the clean-up; this is a dinner where people come together to eat and work together and in doing so, demonstrate their care and concern for one another. For her this is not a social service project, but she believes that is what the pastor wants it to be. After several years of struggling with the pastor over the purpose of the project she decided not to participate any more. She believes that the pastor never understood her reasons for quitting.

This conflict is not about how to organize a dinner or who to invite, but rather stems from different understandings and beliefs about what it means to care and minister to others as Christians. In this conflict, the pastor and Kay share a social identity—of membership in Downtown—which is operating as a contextual frame. They are both interested in operationalizing a component of this social identity, Christian mission that becomes a defining frame. Each has a different understanding of what this means and, in the experience of cooking the dinner, their understandings clash. Therefore, the social identity no longer operates as a contextual or defining frame which informs perceptions or define issues; rather, it becomes a substantive issue in the conflict as the pastor and Kay struggle to negotiate how "mission" will be operationalized.

A second way social identities as frames become substantive issues in contention in a conflict concerns the clash of two different social identities. During the conflict over the worship schedule ("spring experience"), several different social identities were clearly salient for the parties in the conflict: parents, worshippers, leaders, Christians, and the particular denomination. Each salient social identity carried different needs and expectations for appropriate action. Members of the church struggled in part because they did not understand that these different identities existed, and because they were not seen as equally legitimate identities for guiding choices. As people talked past and around each other, the conflicts often escalated. This example illustrates how social identities affected both the substance of conflicts and the conflict process.

The Conflict Process

Social identities as frames influenced the conflict process in other ways as well. As stated previously, frames may be accepted or rejected by the parties in the conflict, or they may remain invisible in that they cannot be named, yet they are felt or experienced. If group members (or a faction within the group) share a common frame, or if one member's frame is accepted by all, then a point of common ground is established and a shared understanding exists in the conflict. For example, one social identity attribute salient to many members was "community." Group members commented that sharing this frame allowed them to continue to work together after a controversial ending to one of the most explosive conflicts they faced: changing the worship schedule. Here the shared sense of who the group is contributed to an effective settlement process.

It should not be assumed, however, that a social identity frame is accepted because it is unchallenged, nor should one assume that an accepted frame is productive in terms of resolving a conflict. For example, the internalization of a dominant social identity frame may simply mean the status quo is unchanged and that a conflict remains latent. If the frame is openly challenged or covertly or even unconsciously resisted, the conflict may escalate and resolution may become less likely.[33] In these cases, social identity frames, whether they were unnamed, ignored, accepted by all, or not shared by anyone in the conflict, serve to delegitimize and silence parties to the conflict in a variety of ways.

Delegitimization occurs in both in-group and out-group relations and affects the person, the group, or the issue being advocated by the group or the person. In-group delegitimization occurs when a member of the group is held up to the group standard and found wanting, and is therefore delegitimized. For example, the pastor deviates from some member's expectations of a leader in this church denomination. Failure to act like the "pastor" should within this congregation, as defined by some members, lessens his credibility. Out-group delegitimization happens when a social categorization attributed to a person is used to stereotype them in such a way that they, or their issues, are dismissed. One of the out-groups in the worship schedule conflict was parents. Several members of the in-group labeled these parents as "dysfunctional" parents, dismissing their needs in the conflict as illegitimate and wrong.

In some instances, an ascribed rather than achieved social identity may delegitimize the group, group members, or certain issues important to group members. Women may be delegitimized simply by that fact that they are categorized as *women*. This is suggested in an example where Kay, a long-time member of the church, states that she believes the pastor does not want her daughter to lead in the church because "women are not leaders."

Gender may also become the dividing attribute for in-group/out-group membership. Women in the church discuss several conflicts in which they feel their gender plays a role in how they are treated. When the social identity of *women* operates as a defining frame, it may serve to delegitimize the needs, interests, and issues that the women of the church find important. This delegitimization may come from the perceiver or from the women themselves, if they have internalized that social identity frame.

One such conflict involved the use of a small kitchenette in the church. Seven groups used this space throughout the week, and often no one took responsibility for cleaning up. One woman took it upon herself to raise this issue. The response of the pastor was that rather than being a problem, the fact that this sharing occurred reasonably well was a "small miracle." For Maryanne, this response felt very dismissive of her concerns. She heard a message which said, "These concerns you have raised are petty." She began to feel that she was being petty, even though she still had a lot of anger about the issues she had raised.

One of the implications of these findings is that stereotypes of women in the U.S. culture are so strong and so pervasive that a standard of *truth* is implicitly invoked by the simple process of categorizing a person as *woman*. Simple categorization may create a defining frame which delegitimizes a person.[34]

This is problematic for two reasons. It is a social categorization that is difficult to exit, or to choose not to be a part of, and when it is salient for others, it may or may not be salient for the women themselves. In conflicts, this means that women may be judged according to a social categorization that is not salient for them or has different meanings for the women than for the perceiver. It is also probable that it is difficult for both the women and the perceiver to sort through the stereotypes and assumptions because they remain implicit and unarticulated.

These processes complicate the conflict because they may mask issues, needs, and perspectives of the parties in the conflict. When individuals or groups are delegitimized, their issues are often silenced as well. This process operates in both intra- and intergroup conflicts resulting in in-group/out-group stereotyping and misperception and may render invisible intragroup differences.

The Construction of Social Identity in Conflict

The second piece of the reflective process deals with the ways in which social identities are fluid constructs which are modified and sometimes transformed throughout the conflict process. The findings are important because they suggest that social identities are not monolithic constructs and that they may be constructed and reconstructed during conflicts.

Throughout the conflict involving the worship schedule, the meaning and salience of various group attributes were altered for people. For example, the staff had a sense of itself as a group. One of the attributes of this group was that it provided leadership in the church. The various members of the staff each had articulated the notion that one of the things leaders do is carry a vision for the church and this vision should have validity because they are the spiritual leaders of the group. After the vote to return to the previous worship schedule, essentially a "no" vote to the position of the staff in the conflict, the staff talked about what it means to be leaders in the church.

The conflict left them unsure of their vision and their role in the church. Their conversation demonstrated their uncertainty about their assumptions concerning how they think about themselves as a group, and this understanding of what it means to lead: what is the role of the staff, what do you do when the church body does not share your vision? As a group, they struggled to redefine themselves and find meaning as leaders in the church. They struggled to negotiate a new place for themselves in the larger body of the "post-worship schedule conflict" congregation.

The issue of salience suggests that the question of meaning is compounded by a question of emphasis. In the process of a conflict, the salience of various group characteristics would shift for the people involved. Also, specific conflicts made salient different group attributes and social identities. There were several conflicts which appeared to tap into different group attributes for different people. Ella, a long-time member of the church, talks about a conflict she has with the pastor in which she does not agree with the way he administers and directs the church. The salient group attribute is that of being a member in this particular denomination, and it influences her feelings about the worship schedule conflict. The salience of the denominational component of her social identity is evident in her discussion. She stresses the importance of this background for understanding how decision-making in the church should be handled.

Later, Ella talks about another conflict in which the mission work of the church is a central component. Here her understanding of mission is influenced by the salience of the "Christian" aspects of the group character. In both conflicts she is upset with the leadership of the church and the choices they have made. However, in each a different aspect of her social identity is most salient.

The following excerpt demonstrates the points made above. In the example, members of the church council are discussing the decision-making process to be used to determine the outcome of the spring experience.[35] We can see the conflict happening at two levels. At the first level, the argument concerns what it means to vote as Christians. Other members bring up other salient group attributes to support different perspectives on what is appropriate voting behavior. Different assumptions in this instance are associated with different group characteristics. The issue is further complicated as alternative social identities are brought into play, e.g., the family, the denomination, and the "American way."

> Fran: I think the [church] meeting should have an anonymous vote.
>
> Alex: Why would we do that? Sanctuary wasn't secret.
>
> Pat: We don't necessarily do that [secret ballot].
>
> Keri: I believe this issue is closer to the day-to-day realities of people.
>
> Fran: The sanctuary vote was secret ballot.
>
> Alex: You're right, it was secret, because of legal issues, we still have the ballots in the safe. I am very disturbed that you think people can't state decisions in front of each other. This is a family decision being made by a church. I am afraid of not being willing to vote in front of each other.
>
> Henry: That is not the reason for it at all. The reason is people shouldn't feel pressure not to vote their conscience. People, if they are not strong, shouldn't feel they have to vote in a contradictory atmosphere. People won't feel like voting their conscience, this choice has been presented all along as a pro-family, pro-child, pro-God and pro-religious exercise.
>
> Alex: This is not government, this is a Christian church.
>
> Henry: It is also [names the church denomination].
>
> Alex: But foremost it is a Christian church, and my understanding of that is that you do things in love, you agree and disagree and treat all opinions and people with respect. I think people can differ and feel strongly on both sides and vote what they believe and live with the consequences. That is part of the Christian commitment.
>
> Cheryl: I think that you are wrong in assuming that all people here are Christians. We're working towards it, but we're not there. We fall short.
>
> Alex: But we are, that is what we are about.
>
> Cheryl: We disagree on this. This is a family issue, people will take it personally, if they see a friend voting against it, they will be offended.
>
> Alex: I think the long-term problems come from secrecy.
>
> Cheryl: It is not secrecy. People are entitled to privacy in voting. We go into booths to vote for elections.
>
> Alex: But this is a Christian church, not the government.

Alex spoke as a Christian and described the inherent obligations that being a Christian implies in terms of worship. He argues that Christians should be willing to vote in front of one another, and he equates Christian community with the family, where members should be willing to speak their minds. Henry refocuses the discussion around another group attribute, the church denomination. He implies that the democratic process is an essential aspect of the church and voting in secret is certainly part of the democratic process. Cheryl takes the argument in a different direction, denies the validity of calling everyone Christians, and brings into the discussion another salient social identity, being Americans. "In

America we vote in secret all the time," she says "It is a right to be able to cast a private vote."

In this conversation, several things are happening. First, participants seem to negotiate the meaning of Christianity as it relates to decision-making procedures in the church. Second, at least two different salient group attributes are operative for different group members: being a Christian and being members of this particular denomination. Third, there are alternative salient social categorizations operating as well—that of Christians and U.S. citizens. Each new level adds to the complexity of the argument and the conflict as different meanings and social identities come into play.

Individuals use different group attributes and social categorizations to support their arguments and to influence the others in the conflict. These movements attest to the fluid nature of social identities in conflict. While they certainly serve as points of departure for creating meaning and understanding, they are reflexive and thus responsive in the conflict, shifting as the context and the conflict progresses.

Implications for Theory Building

Because the study was qualitative in design, the generalizability of the findings is very limited. However, they do begin to build understanding and theory relevant to this context and to contexts which are similar in character. The study serves as a beginning exploration of a new context which helps explain the phenomena of social identity and provides a rich basis for the testing of these findings in other contexts.

Both SIT and conflict theory seek to explicate in-group processes during social conflict. SIT suggests that the process of self-categorization leads to an accentuation of in-group similarities and out-group differences and creates assumptions about what are normative behaviors for in-group members.[36] Conflict theorists have also documented the tendency for groups in conflict to accentuate in-group similarity.[37] The evidence that social identities as frames serve to define what are "right" or "correct" behaviors or attitudes supports the hypothesis that social identities incorporate conceptualizations of normative behaviors.

Turner and Oakes further suggest that as shared consensual constructs, social identities are products of shared social realities and become a "mechanism whereby society forms the psychology of its members to pursue its goal and conflicts as with the examples of 'citizens,' 'Americans,' 'Irish Republicans,' 'conservatives,' 'socialists,' or 'Catholics.'"[38] While my study was conducted on a much smaller group, it supports Turner and Oakes's idea that social identities are used as defining frames to pursue certain goals. Group members in conflict use frames to try to persuade, perhaps coerce, other group members into accepting their perspective of the group identity, the meaning of this identity, and its implications for action.

In this process, people resist and oppose this group pressure to conform to a group standard, sometimes openly challenging it, and, thus, social identities contribute to intragroup conflict. This suggests an interesting line of research to pursue the question of how social identities are used to keep the in-group similar. Just as social identities create out-group dissimilarities where they do not exist,[39] perceived similarities among members of the in-group and among out-group members may come to be seen as realities, as social identities are invoked to establish and maintain in-group norms.

The use of defining frames to create in-group homogeneity reveals issues of power within the in-group. Much of the SIT research on power has examined the effects of status and power differentials on intergroup behavior.[40] The study addresses how power within the group affects social identity definition and how it is used in both intra- and intergroup conflict. Here, in intragroup conflicts power is an issue in terms of whose definitions of a social identity are accepted or carry weight in an argument and how social identities incorporate and influence power structures. Power is important in terms of who has more influence within the group. What makes this complex is that this study suggests that power and influence may be related to cross-cutting social categorizations, such as gender, that are attributed to group members and in some cases serve as the basis for out-group distinctions.

For example, the evidence in the study supports St. Claire's theory that gender as a social identity often operates as a "social handicap" for women.[41] The terminology I use is "delegitimization" and "marginalization." Identification of females as *women* served to delegitimize women's voices in conflict. The issues they raised were not taken seriously and their viewpoints were marginalized. Categorization as *women* also limited the roles they were allowed to play in the church, and the activities and responsibilities they did have were often devalued.

Some conflict theorists have suggested that one way to overcome intergroup hostilities is to create a super-ordinate identity.[42] However, if women's voices are marginalized, the question "Who gets to define the super-ordinate identity?" must be asked. Given the delegitimizing and silencing that results from some uses of defining frames, researchers need to be cautious about assuming in-group homogeneity, even if there is no visible conflict. Researchers must ask, whose meanings define the "homogeneous" aspects of the group and whose voices are lost and when do perceptions of in-group similarities begin to override perceptions of in-group difference? Further study is also needed to understand how gender identity as fluid construct changes in the conflict process. If gender stereotypes are constructed in a larger social context, how fluid are gender identities and what aspects of them shift?

In contexts of intergroup conflict, further research is needed to understand consequences of gender as a salient attribute in intergroup conflict, both in terms of how salience affects women's behaviors within the in-group and toward out-groups and how out-groups treat women within the in-group. For example, as we have seen, SIT studies often cite perceptions of in-group and out-group homogeneity as one type of intergroup behavior.[43] However, violence aimed specifically at *women* as the "out-group" (the systematic rape of Bosnian women for example) clearly shows that gender as a salient identification has implications for the treatment of out-group members, even in cases of highly escalated conflict where in-group/out-group boundaries seem very rigid. If perceptions of the homogeneity of the group are based on stereotyped group attributes, are there minority members within the group and, if so, what are the implications for our understanding of intergroup behavior? Concepts of rigid or stable intergroup distinctions must be rethought in light of the information in this study documenting the rapid shifts in people's salient social categorizations and possible cross-cutting categorizations such as gender.

In exploring how social categorizations respond to the social world, shifts in the meaning and significance of group attributes suggest that during conflict social identities are constantly being negotiated within groups. This information has implications for understanding how conflicts are waged and resolved. Burton contends that social identities are non-negotiable.[44] Certainly it is true that social identities cannot be negotiated away. However, this study suggests that within an overarching group identity, meanings of social identities may be negotiated. It is also possible that negotiations occur in terms of who is in the in-group and who is in the out-group. The variations in the salience of social identities and meanings, and the importance of group attributes, all exist as intra-group differences which became intergroup boundaries. The extent to which negotiability extends into conflicts characterized by rigid in-group/out-group distinctions needs further exploration. However, the evidence presented here clearly demonstrates that social identities are not simply static entities, but rather dynamic processes which interact with conflict.

Conclusion

This chapter explores how individual's perceptions, ideologies, beliefs, feelings, and actions in conflict are connected to social identities. In seeking to explicate the role of social identity in both intra- and intergroup conflict, this research affirms some of the theorizing about social identities and conflict done in SIT and conflict theory. It also challenges some of the assumptions theorists working in these fields have made. Social identities as frames do create and maintain boundaries that delegitimize the out-group and affirm the in-group. This chapter delves more deeply into this relationship, exploring the complexity found in both contexts.

It is critical, as we seek to better understand social conflict, that we look at both the role of the out-group in social identity formation and the role of social categorization within the in-group. The role of social identities in framing perspectives and behaviors in both instances challenges assumption about the static nature of social identities and concepts of homogeneity.

Examining the fluid nature of social identity in terms of salience and meaning offers insight into when social identities are sources of conflict and how they influence the conflict process, which further helps us understand both challenges in problem definition and resolution strategies.

When theorists assume within-group homogeneity, the true complexities of a conflict situation are lost. Assumptions of out-group homogeneity ignore cross-cutting social identities such as gender that may lead to subgroups within an out-group receiving differential treatment. Assumptions of in-group homogeneity render invisible the active role of social identities in creating homogeneity, conflicts which arise from these attempts, and the voices which are silenced in the process. Fundamentally, what this chapter pushes us to consider when seeking to understand the relationship between social identities and social conflict, is that the meanings and significance of social identities are intricately connected to, and constructed within, the conflict process.

Notes

1. For more information see: Henri Tajfel, *Differentiation between Social Groups* (New York: Academic Press, 1978); John Turner, *Rediscovering the Social Group* (Oxford: Basil Blackwell, 1987).

2. For more information see: Edward Azar and John Burton, *International Conflict Resolution* (Sussex: Wheatsheaf Books, 1986); John Burton, ed., *Conflict: Human Needs Theory* (New York: St. Martins, 1990); Morton Deutsch, *The Resolution of Conflict* (New Haven, Conn.: Yale University Press, 1973); Jerome Frank, *Sanity and Survival* (New York: Random House, 1967); LeVine and Campbell, *Ethnocentrism: Theories of Conflict, Ethnic Attitudes, and Group Behavior* (New York: Wiley, 1972); Ralph White, *Fearful Warriors* (New York: Free Press, 1984).

3. For further readings see: Carol Gilligan, Janie Victoria Ward, Jill Mclean Taylor, and Betty Bardige, eds., *Mapping the Moral Domain* (Cambridge, Mass.: Harvard University Press, 1988); Margaret Hall, *Women and Identity: Value Choices in a Changing World* (New York: Hemisphere Publishers, 1990); Jean Baker Miller, *Toward a New Psychology of Women* (Boston: Beacon Press, 1986); Suzanne Skevington and Deborah Baker, eds., *The Social Identity of Women* (London: Sage, 1989); Jane L. Surrey, "Self-in-Relation: A Theory of Women's Development," occasional paper series, Wellesley College, Wellesley, Mass., 1984; Sue Wilkinson, ed., *Feminist Social Psychology* (Philadelphia: Open University Press, 1986).

4. Self-concepts can be categorized on three basic levels: self as a member of the human species, self as a member of various groups, and self as an individual. Various self-concepts or "sub-identities" are both ascribed (sex, race) and achieved (soccer player, pianist).

5. For more resources see: Deutsch, *The Resolution of Conflict*; Ruthellen Josselson, *Finding Herself* (San Francisco: Jossey-Bass, 1987); Terrell Northrup, "The Dynamics of Identity in Personal and Social Conflict," in *Intractable Conflicts and Their Transformation*, ed. Louis Kriesberg, Terrell Northrup, and Stuart Thorson (Syracuse, N.Y.: Syracuse University Press, 1989), 55-82; Tajfel, *Differentiation*; Turner, *Rediscovering*; A. Weigert, J. Smith Teitge, and D. W. Teitge, *Society and Identity* (New York: Cambridge University Press, 1986).

6. Social identities play an essential role in helping people make sense of their world, allowing for the presence of some measure of predictability and control. "Identity" is seen to be a dynamic, ongoing process in which persons, alone and in groups, attempt "to establish, maintain, and protect a sense of self-meaning, predictability, and purpose" (Northrup, "The Dynamics of Identity," 63).

7. Henri Tajfel, ed., *Social Identity and Intergroup Relations* (New York: Cambridge University Press, 1982), 2.

8. Surrey, "Self-in-Relation."

9. Gerard Duveen and Barbara Lloyd, "The Significance of Social Identities," *British Journal of Social Psychology* 25 (1986): 220.

10. Tajfel, *Differentiation*; Tajfel, *Identity and Intergroup Relations*; Henri Tajfel and John Turner, "An Integrative Theory of Intergroup Conflict," in *The Social Psychology of Intergroup Relations*, ed. W. G. Austin and S. Worchel (Monterey, Calif.: Brooks/Cole, 1979), 33-53; J. Turner and Howard Giles, eds., *Intergroup Behavior* (Oxford: Basil Blackwell, 1981).

11. Henri Tajfel, "Social Stereotypes and Social Groups," in *Intergroup Behavior*, ed. J. Turner and Howard Giles (Oxford: Basil Blackwell, 1981): 144-67; Turner, *Rediscovering*.

12. *In-group* and *out-group* are terms used to describe the boundary distinctions (psychological, social, and physical) to distinguish who is "us" and who is "them," the emotions and values attached to these distinctions, and the behaviors which result from them.

13. Itesh Sachdev and Richard Bourhis, "Power and Status Differentials in Minority and Majority Group Relations," *European Journal of Social Psychology* 21 (1991): 1-24; Skevington and Baker, *Social Identity*.

14. Skevington and Baker, *Social Identity*, 2.

15. Henri Tajfel, *Human Groups and Social Categories* (New York: Cambridge University Press, 1981), 223.

16. Turner and Giles, *Intergroup Behavior*.

17. Louis Kriesberg, *Social Conflicts* (Englewood Cliffs, N.J.: Prentice-Hall, 1982), 66.

18. Jennifer Williams, "Gender and Intergroup Behavior: Towards an Integration," *British Journal of Social Psychology* 23 (1984): 313.

19. Skevington and Baker, *Social Identity*; Williams, "Gender and Intergroup Behavior."

20. William Graham Sumner, *Folkways* (New York: New American Library of World Literature, 1906).

21. Burton, *Conflict*.

22. Skevington and Baker, *Social Identity*; Williams, "Gender and Intergroup Behavior."

23. The work of Williams ("Gender and Intergroup Behavior") shows the possibility of at least two processes, agentic and communal, by which social identifications are structured. It seems to me that these two issues are related in that one might expect agentic processes of identification to occur in contexts that were highly competitive. Thus, the findings of agentic processes in much of the SIT research may be a product of the research design.

24. As I was also interested in gender, I sought a context in which women were active participants. Because my methodology was qualitative, I could not introduce gender as a topic of conversation. My hope was that, if women were actively participating in the life of the church, gender would be salient for them.

25. Herbert Blumer, *Symbolic Interactionism: Perspective and Method* (Englewood Cliffs, N.J.: Prentice-Hall, 1969).

26. W. S. Robinson, "The Logical Structure of Analytic Induction," in *Issues in Participant Observation: A Text and Reader*, ed. G. McCall and J. Simmons (Reading, Mass.: Addison-Wesely, 1969), 196-204; Florian Znaniecki, *The Method of Sociology*. (New York: Farrar and Rinehart, 1934).

27. *Social categorization* encompasses perceptions based on categorizations of the self by one's self and by others, and categorizations of others.

28. For the purposes of this study, *conflict* is defined as the perception, by at least one party, that there are incompatible goals or interests between two or more parties. Con-

flicts so defined may be correctly perceived or misperceived incompatibilities and exist as conflicts as long as one of the parties in the conflict has this perception. See Kriesberg, *Social Conflicts*; see also Dean Pruitt, Jeffrey Rubin, and Sung Hee Kim, *Social Conflict,* 2d ed (New York: Random House, 1994).

29. Charles Goodwin and M. H. Goodwin, "Interstitial Argument," in *Conflict Talk*, ed. Allen Grimshaw (Cambridge: Cambridge University Press, 1990), 85-117.

30. Some theorists argue that in extreme cases some characteristics of social identities become rigid: meanings become non-negotiable and the significance of the group membership plays a greater role in influencing perceptions and understandings. For further discussion of this topic, see Northrup, "The Dynamics of Identity."

31. This use of the term is consistent with that of Erving Goffman, *Frame Analysis* (New York: Harper and Row, 1974), and David Snow, "Frame Alignment Processes, Micromobilization and Movement Participation," *American Sociological Review* 51, no. 4 (1986).

32. The "spring experience" was an attempt by the leaders of Downtown to alter the worship practices of the congregation. In the traditional worship service, children participated with the adults through a children's story and then left for age-appropriate activities. The leadership of Downtown felt that the children were missing essential aspects of worship because they did not experience the whole service. Parents and other members of the church felt that the current practice was better for their worship needs and those of the children. The church experimented with the new worship style for six months during the spring. At the end of the trial period, a vote was taken to settle the issue. This issue led to a long and difficult conflict for members of the church.

33. Tajfel discusses these as issues of illegitimacy (*Differentiation*; *Identity and Intergroup Relations*).

34. This contention is supported by studies that suggest that dichotomizing men and women into separate groups has different consequences for each sex. "Men may continue to be viewed as individuals, and in terms of many social groupings, while women are viewed as Women." See Mary Crawford, "Agreeing to Differ: Feminist Epistemologies and Women's Ways of Knowing," in *Gender and Thought,* ed. M. Crawford and M. Gentry (New York: Spring Verlag, 1989), 14.

35. Possible outcomes included (1) return to the previous worship schedule, (2) continue with the new schedule permanently, and (3) continue with the new schedule for an extended trial period of six more weeks.

36. Michael Hogg and Dominic Abrams, *Social Identifications* (New York: Routledge, 1988).

37. Muzafer Sherif, et al., *The Robbers Cave Experiment* (Middletown, Conn.: Wesleyan University Press, 1988).

38. John Turner and P. J. Oakes, "The Significance of the Social Identity Concept for Social Psychology with Reference to Individual Interactions and Social Influence," *British Journal of Social Psychology* 25 (1986): 25.

39. Hogg and Abrams, *Social Identifications*.

40. Jean-Claude Deschamps, "Social Identity and Relations of Power between Groups," in Tajfel, *Social Identity and Intergroup Relations*, 85-97; Jean-Claude Deschamps and Willem Doise, "Crossed Category Memberships in Intergroup Relations," in Tajfel, *Differentiation*, 141-58; Sachdev and Bourhis. "Power and Status."

41. Lindsay St. Claire, "When Is Gender a Handicap? Towards Conceptualizing the Socially Constructed Disadvantages Experienced by Women," in Skevington and Baker, *Social Identity*, 130-151.

42. Muzafer Sherif, *In Common Predicament: The Social Psychology of Intergroup Conflict and Cooperation* (Boston: Houghton Mifflin, 1966).

43. Hogg and Abrams, *Social Identifications*; Tajfel, *Identity and Intergroup Relations*.
44. John Burton, *Resolving Deep-Rooted Conflicts* (New York: Lanham, 1987).

Chapter Seven

Fighting among Friends

The Quaker Separation of 1827

Verna M. Cavey

This is a study of the conflict which grew among Quakers in the early part of the nineteenth century and which was called by different names—schism, reformation, and revolution, among others—but which will be referred to here primarily as the Separation of 1827. This was a complicated, intense, intractable conflict, with multiple and emotional issues of religion, neighborhood, family, politics, class and power, which would keep Quakers throughout North America separated for more than a hundred years. It is not only the historical importance of this religious, social dispute and its impact upon the Quaker community that encouraged this research. Also important is the nature of the Quaker community itself, with its testimony of nonviolence and traditional conflict resolution techniques.

Using both qualitative and social-historical methods, nineteenth-century Quaker documents were examined and analyzed to determine Quaker perceptions and behaviors during the Separation and to understand why traditional Quaker conflict resolution mechanisms failed to prevent a schism. Examination of archival documents—especially those of the Hilles family of Wilmington, Delaware, respected and active members of the Quaker community—provided an excellent position from which to analyze the context, issues, stages, actors, and outcome of the conflict. The Hilles family's close connections to the central parties in the dispute, Hicksite and Orthodox leaders within the Philadelphia Yearly Meeting, facilitated scrutiny of how Quakers conceptualized and responded to the conflict.[1]

As a student of conflict resolution, I approached this research with several questions: How does such an intense, internal conflict emerge among a community of peacemakers? How did Quakers, members of the Religious Society of Friends, perceive and conceptualize conflict which resulted in a major schism? Is there anything peculiar in either the dynamics of this conflict or the methods utilized to regulate or resolve it? My expectations were that I would find in these documents some new approaches to conflict resolution that would be particularly instructive to practitioners of conflict resolution. However, it was often in the way that Quakers in 1827 chose *not* to utilize their tools of conflict resolution that important lessons were learned.

Bases of Conflict: Social Context

The first major finding of the research was that multiple, multifaceted, external and internal socioeconomic factors produced the Quaker conflict. That is, both social context and circumstances influenced how nineteenth-century Quakers conceptualized and defined the conflict not only at the emergence of the dispute but also during the escalation and various stages of the conflict. These contextual factors affected how Quakers shaped their collective identity, how they framed their rationale for fighting other Quakers, and how they altered their traditional techniques of conflict resolution.

In the early nineteenth century Quakers witnessed industrialization, urbanization and materialism, immigration, and the decline of Quaker influence in Pennsylvania. Quakers eventually grew separate from each other in their class, personal tastes and sensitivities, education, geographical boundaries, religious emphasis, political allegiance, kinship groupings, philosophy about issues of modernization, and belief about what were acceptable levels of power and intragroup conflict. A review of comparative studies demonstrated that many of these same socioeconomic factors influenced other nineteenth-century conflicts, some of them church related. The bases of conflict—political, economic, theological, geographical and kinship factors—were tightly interrelated. While they can be separated and studied individually, in the social reality of the nineteenth century, one affected the other and it is the whole that social scientists must examine. In the Separation of 1827, the interaction of these factors compounded the effect upon the Quaker population.

While it is very simplistic to separate Quakers into two groups, it is true that eventually two distinguishable groups, the Hicksites and the Orthodox, emerged in the dispute. Hicksites became associated with liberal political ideologies, were devoted to the mystical position of the Inner Light, and felt the Orthodox were distorting the basic tenets of their religion. Most Hicksites resided in rural areas; their leaders, however, notably the Wilmington group, were upwardly mobile but did not live at the level of Philadelphia luxury nor were included in the Philadelphia inner circle. The Orthodox, on the other hand, were well-placed and well-monied Philadelphia merchants with very strong evangelical feelings and were disturbed by those who called themselves liberals or rationalists (whether they were Quakers or Philadelphia laborers complaining about the status quo).

Two different sets of definitions of conflict and conflict resolution, both consistent with Quaker tradition, came out of each respective group's experiences with change and its concomitant sense of threat. The Hicksites emphasized the spiritual struggle within an individual person engaged in attending to concerns and conflict around them and to taking action. They wanted to balance power and to return to their nonhierarchical, decentralized system of meetings; to regain autonomy and an acceptance of all Quakers as legitimate participants in the decision-making process; and to make those responsible for injustice yield to the true way of Quakers.

The Orthodox emphasized the other traditional Quaker concept of resigning themselves to the will of God and the order of the Society and suffering for Christ in the company of other Quakers. Those Quakers who so badly wanted order in a time of accelerating social change valued this form of resignation, which was more consistent with their need to maintain a quiet peace without noise or dissension. The Orthodox vowed to protect the order and authority of the Society from what they perceived to be the backward, ranterish elements of the Hicksite group and were watchful for indications of deviance. One group was perceived as unsound and threatening in their anarchy, and the other group was perceived to be in sheepish conformity to unjust, arrogant, un-Quakerlike authority.

As with most religious schisms, one can point to a central dispute over religious belief that was the focus of the conflict. Such was the case in 1827 as Quakers polarized over their emphasis on either the scriptural or the mystical. However, data strongly indicate that, if this was the only point of disagreement between Quakers, the Separation of 1827 would never have occurred. The religious was in fact deeply intertwined with the political and economic context, and opposing leaders framed their religious discussions using the language of politics and economics. A more complex system of socioeconomic variables is correlated with the rise of Quaker dissatisfaction and their perception of incompatibility of values, goals, and solutions.

Threat to Quaker Identity

Quakers shared a cultural identity, a unique culture with its own history, language, system of meetings, religious testimonies, rules and sanctions. Even after more than one hundred years of separation, Quakers were able to preserve many aspects of these cultural foundations sacred to Quaker meaning. Their membership in the Quaker community or tribe was tied to their concept of self, which gave them a sense of order and meaning in the world. With such a shared identity, Quakers could feel secure in their mutual spiritual and social worlds. They understood who they were as Quakers, what they believed, and how they should behave. The second major finding of the research was that out of the previously mentioned social change and socioeconomic background of the early nineteenth century, Quakers came to redefine their social identities as separate and incompatible. Quakers were not alone in a century that shook the foundations of American government and religion. When people began to have separate, inconsistent definitions of what it meant to be Quaker, a serious threat to identity and unity came to exist. In turn, this threat to their identity resulted in various defen-

Table 7.1. Philadelphia Yearly Meeting Separation of 1827: A Chronology

1806 Philadelphia Yearly Meeting established that Friends should be disowned for denying the authenticity of Scripture. Quaker elder and traveling minister Elias Hicks, instead, emphasized that truth came primarily from inward searching and revelation.

1817 Philadelphia Yearly Meeting pushed for a uniform Quaker discipline which would standardize Quaker belief and behavior, limiting disagreement and discussion of important issues. A moratorium was used to calm tensions and manage the conflict. However, some Quakers, sensing a power imbalance and a threat to identity, spoke privately with similar or "particular" Friends, which eventually influenced separate Quaker entities.

1819 Philadelphia elder Jonathan Evans censored Elias Hicks for his teachings.

1820-1821 Quakers waged a written, religious debate with Presbyterians. However, as it played out, inconsistencies in Quaker belief became apparent. While at this stage Quakers did not see Scripture and the Inner Light as incompatible or mutually exclusive, the public debate further agitated conflict, and as conflict escalated, goals began to change.

1820s Philadelphia Quakers welcomed English traveling ministers of evangelical persuasion to their meetinghouses, while others meetings—including the Green Street Meeting in Philadelphia—welcomed Elias Hicks. The preaching polarized groups around separate beliefs and identities.

April 1927 Philadelphia Yearly Meeting's Orthodox leadership, after several heated sessions, retained control of the position of Clerk of Yearly Meeting. Hicksites withdrew to the Green Street Meeting for their own session. They signed an allegiance that declared Orthodox documents unsound and decided that Separation was necessary. They established their own Yearly Meeting and Clerk.

Post-1827 As the division and new identities were formalized, the separate Quaker meetings proceeded to disown dissenters. Fights over Quaker property, often in court, occurred as each group tried to prove its position as the true Quaker group. Quakers carried on their battle in print and sent correspondence and religious tracts to other meetings. Eventually the schism spread across the U.S. and into Canada. However, in the twentieth century, with still long-held, similar religious and cultural beliefs—and super-ordinate goals coming out of their humanitarian work in two world wars—Quakers reunited.

---

sive responses. Research findings emphasize the central role that the threat to Quaker identity played in encouraging conflict emergence and escalation.

Sociologists, psychologists, and social historians can agree that in a time of socioeconomic stressors, people may feel alienated, uncertain, isolated, and afraid and often under these circumstances conflict is more rampant. Conflict scholar Kriesberg has observed that rapid social change can foster chaos and even revolution between groups who previously shared backgrounds, values and beliefs and who were interdependent within a societal system.[2] Northrup noted that change and stressful events in society can lead to crises in personal and social identities, which will elicit defensive responses developed in order to protect but which can also lead to the introduction and escalation of conflict.[3] The two very different perceptions of what it was to be a legitimate Quaker moved the conflict from a latent to a manifest state and the first stages of the conflict process. Another related finding of this research is that it was not, as some historians have suggested, a depleted and tired sect which facilitated separation. The nineteenth-century Quaker sect had been experiencing a decline and a lack of clear vision but it was not a lethargic population who waged a heated dispute. Rather, it was a Society resuscitated by two respective beliefs, moving in two separate directions without consensus. Quakers were engaged and invested in active revivals. They were people who had found a renewed purpose which gave spiritual comfort and restored to them a strong social identity and sense of security and self-respect in uncertain times.

My findings regarding the Separation are consistent with comparative research. In Goen's study of the schisms between Northern and Southern churches during the Civil War period, he stated that groups disoriented by social change and out of touch with their religious foundations found a new common identity and emotional bond through revival which led to fragmentation in nineteenth-century religious circles.[4] The Lynds' study *Middletown* in 1929 found that revivals can expose latent conflict and promote an energy that has been compared to a "war spirit," and that enthusiastic church members can respond to a threat to their mission or group like "a body of shock troops."[5]

Frost, a Quaker historian, noted that evangelical Quakers had come to see Quaker mystical worship as undynamic in a modern city where their neighbors had more exciting forms of prayer and the Orthodox chose not to return to what they saw to be a vague, silent searching.[6] Instead Philadelphia Quakers found stability in the written authority of Scripture and a hierarchical church, which were attractive to people tossed about in new and confusing social patterns and roles. In Peter's comparative study[7] of another Anabaptist peace sect, he stated that Hutterites found a sense of relief in giving up the constant inner toil and uncertainty of a mystical-based religion and instead found greater security in a religion that embraced a community based on an economic system more in line with the modern world. Scholars of revival also suggest that the established nineteenth-century American population could even turn to the new evangelical force to control and moralize the large numbers of immigrants whom they feared. Miller in a comparative study of seventeenth-century Puritans stated that the "storm" or "disease" which the religious group believed arose because of lack of virtue and rise of worldiness was really a manifestation of inevitable social change.[8] Puritans, like the Orthodox Quakers, emphasized Order, Authority and Truth over self. Their leaders condemned the wrongs of others but neglected to note their own conspicuous pursuit of wealth and their obvious desertion of tradition.

Because of the correlation between geography and kinship groups, Quakers often were able to distance themselves from those carrying dissonant messages about their growing differences. When Philadelphia family members, however, did write to their more mystical, rural family of their pleasurable evangelical experiences with those more like themselves, the respondents in true Quaker fashion could find—for a time at least—some thread that they could agree upon, such as their antislavery work. Sharing traditional elements which they held in common, they could simply respond in a tender but avoiding manner. As con-

flict was ignored, avoided or suppressed, the illusion of peace was maintained
for a time. When latent conflict finally did become manifest, as it did when one
Quaker expressed a genuine concern for another Quaker's detraction and un-
soundness, members of each group had come to justify and rationalize their own
violations of Quaker ways and testimonies as Quakerlike and necessary for the
health and preservation of their Society.

Stages of the Conflict

For the first time, with this research, the Separation of 1827 is analyzed by utilizing the conflict-stage model and carefully examining each step of the conflict
process. Other researchers must be acknowledged for their contributions in
identifying causes, specific socioeconomic factors, attitudes and behaviors in the
conflict.[9] However, using both Kriesberg's and Northrup's theoretical explanations of conflict stages, the Separation of 1827 can be broken down into specific,
chronological stages which provide a framework for analyzing both the process
and dynamics of the Quaker conflict.[10]

Social psychologists inform us that one of the first defenses humans use
against a threat to identity is to try to block any new information that is incompatible with their positive perception of self and of the in-group—to deny or re-
ject the information or redefine it so that it is less emotionally troubling.[11] For
example, one can stifle messages that are cognitively and affectively dissonant
by simply dismissing the messengers; in the case of the Quakers, they often labeled out-group leadership (sometimes friends of the family) as drunk or de-
ranged rather than morally incorrigible. Coser says that conflict becomes dysfunctional in a social structure that is rigid and unresponsive.[12] Group rigidity
can come out of a fear of change and can block communications with others
who threaten their sense of identity and group survival. Rigidity suppresses dissent and allows hostility to increase until there is a major cleavage in the system.

One can turn again to social psychology and the concept of "groupthink" to
better understand Quakers who polarized into two in-groups with strong interpersonal attraction and empathy for each other.[13] The members of the in-group
at a time of low self-esteem and at a time of crisis or moral dilemma rely upon
each other for security and acceptance; they avoid conflict with in-group members, see themselves as correct, conform, and insulate themselves; they do not
allow information from the other side to come into the in-group without bias;
and they stereotype the out-group. Believing in their own inherent superiority
and morality, and censoring individual doubts about in-group beliefs or choices,
the group limits consideration of the full range of problem-solving alternatives
and potentially positive solutions. Members either sit and suffer together or whip
up a campaign with particular friends to achieve certain objectives. There is a
sense of urgency to reduce the conflict, which reduces needed time for decision-
making as well as encouraging withdrawal from the other group at the very time
when communication and possible negotiation is so crucial.

The characteristics of both groupthink and group rigidity are consistent with the characteristics of the breakdown in consensus-making which Quakers experienced at the beginning of the nineteenth century. Understanding the Quaker identity crisis in a time of threatening social upheaval helps to explain Sheeran's position that consensus disappeared in the early nineteenth century because Quakers as a whole were unable to endow themselves sufficiently with a "we feeling" but polarized instead within an in-group.[14] The most crucial elements of the unique process of Quaker consensus-making were missing: calm, sensitive listening, a spirit of worship, neutrality, open-mindedness, and trust. Orthodox and Hicksites each had an agenda and very specific goals in which they were deeply invested in achieving. Both sides saw themselves with too much to lose if they opened themselves up to the opinions of those whom they felt they could no longer trust. If the traditional problem-solving process of consensus-making was allowed to proceed unimpeded, their purpose would be blended into a sense of meeting which they now found undesirable. For example, Hicksites did not want to resign themselves to Quaker ways of peace, which would move them no closer to their goals of equal power, nor to the Quaker decision-making process, which they felt was being manipulated. Instead they utilized language of sarcasm and disrespect against the Philadelphians, their lifestyle and their theology. Nor did Philadelphia Orthodox acknowledge their arrogance and authoritarian rule as undemocratic or un-Quakerlike but rather grew even more determined to stop ideas which they saw to be antagonistic and dangerous heresy and which they feared would destroy their meetings.

Goen's findings regarding Southern and Northern ministers during the Civil War period support the above ideas, as well as the research finding that conflict escalated because of the behavior of Hicksite and Orthodox traveling ministers. Goen stated that religious leaders, rather than assist in problem-solving, facilitated division by increasing tensions through their preaching and publishing. While some merely urged silence in the hopes that the problems would go away, disunionists urged schism for the sake of freedom.[15] Both sides drew upon a common heritage and language to argue their respective causes. Leadership emerged only too willing to proselytize new guiding principles for the Society. Quaker traveling ministers, as well, restored followers in religion and identity, yet at the same time polarized them towards conflict. The preachers removed the ambiguity that plagued congregants and assured them that they could be comforted in the message of their legitimate, religious identity. For example, Hicksites revered the ancient and plain preacher Hicks, who gave back to young, rural Quakers the core belief in the Inner Light in a dynamic way and allowed them pride in their simplicity as well as recognition of their right to a legitimate role within the religious organization. At the same time, Wilmington Hicksites added a rationalistic and nationalistic twist with their rich, stirring language of freedom and inalienable rights. Both sides expressed hurt and offense as their beloved preachers were censored or mocked. At this stage of conflict escalation, the respective groups began to mobilize their resources. Each side possessed respected and determined leadership, good numbers, a good economic base, an excellent communication network, and pen and printing press, which were as essential to Quakers in religious war as cannons were to others. The attack and counterattack behavior of leadership eventually filtered down to rank-and-file Quakers who joined the fray.

Conflict Resolution

To summarize, social change and the threat to Quaker identity influenced behavioral responses which instigated separation. Humans do not fight easily those whom they like or those like themselves. When Quakers came to see each other as dissimilar in belief, behavior, and purpose, they grew uncomfortable and avoided each other. With similarities de-emphasized and differences accentuated, and hostility and suspicion increasing, they slowly created an enemy. Boundaries of acceptable behavior, which Quakers had guarded for centuries, were crossed when in-group members were influenced by rigidity, agenda, preaching, detraction and rumor, and when defensiveness made the Quaker process of calm reflection and deliberation in consensus-making impossible. Trust in the neutrality of weighty members who normally would act as advisers and mediators had dissipated. Factors within the social environment not only encouraged internal conflict but also altered the conflict resolution techniques which Quakers had traditionally counted on.

When Quakers could not get a satisfactory resolution of conflicts at the local meeting, they usually went through an appeal process and sought out neutral mediators of another venue. The appeal process moved upward through the system of meetings until it reached the weighty members of the yearly meeting. The difficulty in 1827 was that the conflict was moving downward as the dispute spread from the Philadelphia Yearly Meeting into local meetings. Quakers who sought the clear deliberation of elders could no longer find anyone still neutral. The failure of traditional conflict resolution methods added to their sense of helplessness and confusion about how to deal with an internal conflict. They waited for the inevitable "tornado" to hit and scatter them, and it did.

Northrup argues that the conflict struggle itself or the "rituals which sanctified their struggle" can become part of a group's identity.[16] If the conflict had been resolved, that would have destroyed a new secure identity. Instead, the conflict was maintained and became institutionalized into two separate yearly meetings. As Festinger has stated, in order to reduce dissonance in our lives, we sometimes learn to love the things we suffer for.[17] It enhances the attractiveness of our choice in a difficult time. Also, we cannot assume that conflict is always negative or destructive. The resolution of conflict is not always desirable for the healthy functioning of a group. Parties felt there was a need for change and were not motivated or willing to go to the table either to share power or to maintain low-power status. Conflict can be a vehicle for attaining justice and societal benefits. Social conflict which is caused by power imbalance will not result in justice until the inequities are removed. Coser states that conflict not only provides a healthy safety valve for tensions but promotes internal cohesion of members of a group and can balance power through creation of coalitions.[18]

With in-group cohesion, there is pride, commitment, and meaningful productivity; with schism, goals may be reached. Although Quakers did not consciously seek to separate at the beginning of the dispute, they did have goals which they wanted to achieve and the conflict provided definite rewards.

Goen noted in his study that when one side tried to preserve structures and behaviors that were inconsistent with traditional ethical beliefs, while the other side lacked the skills to rectify a rigid social system, actions only increased frustration so that all concerned came to believe that separation was the only alternative.[19] Northrup has stated that a low-power group which feels invalidated often splits off from the original society, giving itself a different name, meeting in a new location, revising norms, and construing the other party as negative while portraying the new group as noble and courageous in light of a terrible conflict.[20]

It is very clear from Quaker correspondence that they felt liberated at freeing themselves of their antagonists. What is so shocking to the researcher is that after carefully tracking patterns throughout the course of the dispute, it is observed that Quakers in their correspondence suddenly, lucidly, and very specifically spoke out about the causes of the Separation as if they were reading back the list of research categories: disruptive role of traveling ministers, distortions in Quaker language and traditional behaviors, detraction, private meetings among particular friends, political agendas, the threat of rationalistic ideology to some, the behavior of reformers, and the inability to go to meeting with the Quaker open mind, patience, and respect.

If in fact their evaluation of the causes was correct, was there any way to prevent the schism? Was there someone who early on could have been perceptive enough to recognize latent conflict and its potential? Who would have been sufficiently skilled, or trusted enough, or objective enough to be accepted by all parties? Who would have been willing to open the emotional and complicated Pandora's Box of conflict which Quakers feared? It's unknown whether some channel of dialogue or some emphasis on super-ordinate goals could have been tried. In an intractable, ideological, emotional conflict, problem-solving alone won't work. Traditions and shared experiences may not be enough. Only finding super-ordinate goals,[21] or the shared and mutually satisfactory goals which require cooperation and common effort, would have worked as a conflict resolution technique. However, as Kriesberg has noted, if constrained by history and multiple dimensions of a conflict, prevention of conflict would be very difficult.[22] Perhaps they would have resolved some issues for a time, but numerous, powerful factors relating to social change and group identity would have brought forward new issues to argue over. With rigid thinking and pressing agendas already in place, persons attending to the conflict are often not heard. Good mediation involves the balancing of power and offers each party an opportunity to speak and be heard. The terms of a moratorium or negotiated truce would probably be neither acceptable to parties nor manageable.

Researchers have studied the various typologies or approaches of conflict resolution.[23] Authoritarian rule and its negative sanctions, which can be effective in times of crisis, did not work in the day-to-day business of running a religious organization, especially one founded upon a nonhierarchical, decentralized system of meetings. Avoidance only exacerbated the problem, except in families; and societal conditions were such that collaborative measures failed.

When Quakers redefined and reaffirmed their purpose, identity, and legitimacy as heir to the Quakerism of their ancestors in separate religious meetings, they moved forward again in harmony. When each group remained firm in its respective position, separate meetings formalized the division and proceeded with disowning so that impurities might be sifted out and the true Order and Discipline of the Society preserved. Many Quakers were now released from guilt and went about their work of abolitionism and other social reforms with a new vigor.

However, it is critical that Quakers not be viewed narrowly, as sharing only a religious meetinghouse. Quakers found varying strategies for managing or resolving the conflict in three separate social compartments: the religious meeting, family and home life, and involvement in civic and secular activities. Quakers resolved conflict differently depending upon the circumstances, goals, and relationships applicable to each social arena.

In the second social area, the Quaker family itself acted as a super-ordinate goal, and after the Separation of 1827 families transformed an intractable conflict into a resolvable one. Conflict resolution is a process of communication and exchange which reestablishes social relationships. Although family life was closely intertwined with the meeting and this made resolution of differences somewhat difficult, resolution was essential to preserving a personal sense of order and meaning. While in the area of religious meeting there were rewards in separation, in the family sector the rewards came in maintaining unity. Further, Quakers knew they had an overriding spiritual mandate to continue ancestral connections and provide for family. If Quakers were to take on the world with their religious testimonies, such as their anti-slavery position, they needed an anchor in the deep emotional and supportive ties of family. Further, one's connection with family had important practical implications related to education, career, and one's place in society. The conflict style of avoidance was effective in preserving family relations, so that many Quakers used the techniques of silence, patience, and tenderness to avoid confrontation with separated kin. Conversations were kept to safe topics of weather, gardening and strawberry preserves, as Quakers struggled to find ways to communicate during an awkward period following separation. As a result, most familial ties were maintained, although it is acknowledged that in some cases Quakers did migrate away from meeting, neighborhood, and family tensions.

Finally, it is in the third area of secular activities in their communities that Quakers most fully and publicly interacted with their separatist Friends and readily resolved their conflict. Quakers of different stripe demonstrated to the outside world that they were still a peaceful people. While certainly some discomfort was felt by Quakers doing business with each other in the initial period of the separation, in the Wilmington community secular organizations and clubs did provide a haven where both Hicksites and Orthodox could share their similar interests. The Quakers continued in their mutual involvement and cooperation in business, social, scientific and educational concerns. Ironically, in civic organizations, which were not subject to the rules, sanctions, and problems of the religious meeting, many Quakers continued to attend to their religious testimonies together. We are witness to an early precursor to the shift of responsibility for humanitarian activity from the religious organization to the secular social agency. Before the schism, Quakers were already involved with those of different religious denominations in social reform and they saw no impediment in working with Quakers of a different perspective. They labored together as before on behalf of the poor, the sick, the uneducated, and the enslaved. Documents also bear witness to the fact that they worked together in the more secretive, often dangerous, labors of the Underground Railroad.

While this study is directly concerned with the Separation of 1827, the historical data give clear indications that additional schism occurred among both the Hicksites and Orthodox; however, the Orthodox, whose organization grew even more rigid after 1827, experienced more intensive and problematic disputes. The Likerts have noted that repetitive patterns of rigidity can become ritual and can lock a group into inflexibility.[24] Kriesberg has pointed out that at the end of a conflict a new cycle of conflict can begin if factors that helped bring about the initial conflict were not resolved.[25] However, by the end of the nineteenth century there was evidence of decreasing bitterness between the different branches of Quakers. In Wilmington, Quakers shared a meetinghouse for a time. Through the increased interaction and combined efforts of twentieth-century Quakers in the American Friends Service Committee they worked together on social action and reform, emphasizing their mutual backgrounds and purpose, especially the religious testimonies related to peace, education, race relations, international mediation and assistance to refugees. Cooperation and dialogue through two world wars displaced hurt feelings, and the religious groups reconciled in 1955.

Implications

Originally, I wanted to locate within the nineteenth-century Quaker culture techniques of conflict resolution that had been previously overlooked in the conflict literature and would be valuable to practitioners today. In fact, there is much to be learned from the Quaker form of consensus-making, queries, clearness and actively speaking to concerns, mediation, reconciliation, eldering, language choice, and the use of silence. In Quaker tradition, for example, much responsibility is taken for language as a peacekeeping device, so that aggressive expression does not distort meaning and create fear, anger, and even violence. Also, silence, an important tool, continues to be studied and any good mediator can explain its power and potential for conflict resolution. However, examination of methods will prove fruitless without examining the context within which these techniques exist. To ignore all social factors is to examine the problem in a vacuum, leaving incomplete answers and unsatisfactory findings. Kriesberg stated that conflict resolution techniques are more effective when they are congruent with converging factors.[26] One can argue that Quakers, like so many others in human conflicts, were guilty of detraction, lack of trust, humility, and other such virtues, but, without some explanation of why they were influenced to behave in certain ways, we are left at a dead end.

As a student of sociology, I found the conclusions emphasizing socioeconomic factors perfectly satisfactory. However, as a student of conflict, I wanted to believe that people equipped with conflict resolution techniques could make a difference even in a difficult situation. The truth continues to be that conflict may be manageable, but not always resolvable; and, further, given the particular circumstances of a situation, that perhaps it should not be resolved at all. As Coser stated, conflict can reaffirm the identity of a group and establish necessary boundaries.[27] The group is a basic change agent and the greater the attractiveness of the group to its members and the greater the need for change, the more it will exert influence towards that change. Conflict origins can be viewed in light of human need in time of change. Research findings showed that Quakers did a very good job of resolving the conflict in family and in secular environments, and, to the degree that they were able, managing the religious environment as well. The Separation, although many would prefer that it had not happened, was an intervention of sorts, a solution, a cease-fire, a settlement that prevented violence.

As for other research implications, I noted that it was only when I was knee-deep in research data that I realized how essential—in a very practical way—my conflict theory training was. Theory can be best learned backwards when it is applicable to a sticky problem at hand. We can unravel the mysteries with the help of both comparative studies and existing theory. Research cases act as laboratories, as excellent instructional forums where we can dispute, affirm, augment, qualify, and refine current conflict theory, as well as develop new theories altogether. For example, Northrup designated rigidification as the third stage in a conflict, at the point where there is an escalation of defensive responses and the group polarizes.[28] In the Quaker study, rigidification was a prerequisite to the conflict and was present throughout all of the stages of the conflict from latency to outcome. At the same time, elements of both the Kriesberg and Northrup conflict models (which related to multiple, contextual conditions and issues surrounding the conflict, threat to identity, conflict emergence, escalation and outcome, and distortion of language and mechanisms) are consistent with my findings and were critical in helping me understand a number of dilemmas posed by the research.[29] Practitioners can examine the relevancy and potential effectiveness of conflict resolution styles and theories to particular conditions and stages of a conflict. With more and more students of conflict coming from areas not only in international studies or political science but also from counseling, education, social work, the ministry, law, and management, theory can be helpful in solving everyday problems.

The last finding from this research is that the potential for retrieving valuable data about conflict from historical archives is immense and yet so many of these documents are left on shelves by social scientists who dismiss any use of them. Historical examples often go undiscussed, making little contribution to the discipline. Document research, like any research approach, has its limitations; but with care and knowledge of the methodology, findings from archival information can enhance our understanding of the social world. Document research allows us to examine the nature and social context of conflict, the issues of the dispute, the incompatible goals of opposing groups, the principles and resources at stake, power imbalances or inequities which may exist, the stages of the conflict, and the actors involved, their actions and their motivations. Observations about how these nineteenth-century subjects defined, described and judged the conflict tell us much about how the conflict was handled at the various conflict stages, as well as how participants on both sides framed their arguments and rationales. Certainly there are many advantages to studying conflicts in progress, but we need not travel halfway around the world or wait for social conflict to erupt in order to add to the literature.

In the field of conflict resolution today, in a very practical way, antagonists in international disputes have been brought together in a neutral setting to examine conflict cases.[30] Actors in conflict can benefit from the theoretical examination of past conflicts. Twentieth-century Friends have commented that Quakers experiencing difficulty in their monthly meeting feel less threatened studying a conflict from the nineteenth century, as there is sufficient historical distance to allow them to labor safely. Yet caution should be taken in generalizing the Wilmington situation to the rest of the Quaker world, and the nineteenth-century world to the twentieth. As for applicability to conflict situations in general and whether findings are instructive to practitioners in the field, any close study of the conflict process is of value. The more that people of various religious, political, educational, and other groups familiarize themselves with the nature, prerequisites and stages of conflict, the more able they are to recognize similar patterns in their own situations. In a theoretical workshop, people in a safe setting can learn conflict resolution strategies that will transform real feuds. Even considering elements of social context, there are also universal elements of human conflict, and techniques which worked for one group are at least worthy of examination and experimentation.

Upon beginning this research, which blended two methodologies and numerous disciplines, I was warned that it would be "messy." Only upon finishing and writing up the research could I fully appreciate the depth of the definition and the frustration which this messiness encompassed, even though my background in cross-disciplinary work did prepare me more than students raised in monodisciplines. However, as more students and scholars sit down to explain their language and methods to each other and guidelines are made available, much of this confusion which comes from lack of information can be eliminated. Numerous historians and sociologists today have given up the rigidity of the past and contribute to the creative development of their own disciplines by learning other methods, rather than fearing them and closing their minds to them, and utilize these valuable methodological tools in a sound and honest way. I believe the cross-disciplinary approach to be an excellent way to investigate and I found methods to be not only very compatible but often very similar, and differences often more related to semantics than to method. Corroboration and triangulated techniques as well as other measures can act as multiple, quality control checks which tighten up the research. I admit that it is a challenge to constantly be moving from history to sociology to religion, and again, to conflict resolution or social psychology, but there are advantages even in these mental gymnastics.

Finally, just as this chapter cannot give justice to all the intricacies and richness of Quaker belief and history, neither can it ask all of the other questions raised during the research regarding such areas as gender, marginality, or the impact of personal versus political constructions of the conflict. However, research provided not only answers about conflict in the nineteenth century but also offered questions for a new century when new social dilemmas will emerge and when boundaries between the personal, economic, political and religious will continue to blur.

Notes

1. Verna M. Cavey, "Fighting among Friends: The Quaker Separation of 1827 as a Study in Conflict Resolution," doctoral diss. Syracuse University, 1992.

2. Louis Kriesberg, *Social Conflicts* (Englewood Cliffs, N.J.: Prentice-Hall, 1982).

3. Terrell Northrup, "The Dynamics of Identity in Personal and Social Conflict," in *Intractable Conflicts and Their Transformation*, ed. Louis Kriesberg, et al. (Syracuse, N.Y.: Syracuse University Press, 1989).

4. C. C. Goen, *Broken Churches, Broken Nation: Denominational Schisms and the Coming of the American Civil War* (Macon, Ga.: Mercer University Press, 1985).

5. Robert S. Lynd and Helen M. Lynd, *Middletown: A Study in American Culture* (New York: Harcourt and Brace, 1929).

6. William J. Frost, "Years of Crisis and Separation: Philadelphia Yearly Meeting, 1790-1860," in *Friends in the Delaware Valley*, ed. John Moore (Haverford, Pa.: Friends Historical Association, 1981).

7. Karl Peter, *The Dynamics of Hutterite Society: An Analytical Approach* (Edmonton, Canada: University of Alberta Press, 1987).

8. Perry Miller, *Errand in the Wilderness* (Cambridge, Mass.: Harvard University Press, 1960).

9. Robert W. Doherty, *The Hicksite Separation: A Sociological Analysis of Religious Schism in Early Nineteenth-Century America* (New Brunswick, N.J.: Rutgers University Press, 1967); Frost, "Years of Crisis"; Larry H. Ingle, *Quakers in Conflict: The Hicksite Reformation* (Knoxville: University of Tennessee, 1986); David Holden, *Friends Divided: Conflict and Division in the Society of Friends* (Richmond, Ind.: Friends United Press, 1988).

10 Kriesberg, *Social Conflicts*; Louis Kriesberg, "Social Conflict Theories and Conflict Resolution," *Peace and Change* 8 (Summer 1982): 2-3; Northrup, "Dynamics of Identity."

11. Leon Festinger, *A Theory of Cognitive Dissonance* (Evanston, Il.: Row, Peterson, 1957).

12. Lewis Coser, *The Functions of Social Conflict* (New York: Free Press, 1956).

13. Irving L. Janis, *Victims of Groupthink* (Boston: Houghton Mifflin, 1972).

14. Michael J. Sheeran, S.J. *Beyond Majority Rule: Voteless Decisions in the Religious Society of Friends* (Philadelphia: Philadelphia Yearly Meeting, 1983).

15. Goen, *Broken Churches.*

16. Northrup, "Dynamics of Identity."

17. Festinger, *Cognitive Dissonance.*

18. Coser, *Social Conflict.*

19. Goen, *Broken Churches.*

20. Northrup, "Dynamics of Identity."

21. Muzafer Sherif, *In Common Predicament: Social Psychology of Intergroup Conflict and Cooperation* (Boston: Houghton Mifflin, 1966).

22 Kriesberg, *Social Conflicts*; Kriesberg, "Social Conflict Theories."

23. K. W. Thomas and R.H. Kilmann, *The Thomas-Kilmann Conflict Mode Instrument* (Tuxedo Park, N.Y.: Xicom, 1974); Alan C. Fillcy, *Interpersonal Conflict Resolution: Sources, Patterns and Consequences* (Glenview, Ill.: Scott, Foresman, 1975); Paul Wehr, Paul A. Hare, and Susan Carpenter. *Conflict Intervention* (New York: Pergamon Press, 1981).

24. Rensis Likert and Jane Likert, *New Ways of Managing Conflict* (New York: McGraw Hill, 1976).

25. Kriesberg, *Social Conflicts*; Kriesberg, "Social Conflict Theories."

26. Kriesberg, *Social Conflicts*; Kriesberg, "Social Conflict Theories."

27. Coser, *Social Conflict.*

28. Northrup, "Dynamics of Identity."

29. Kriesberg, *Social Conflicts*; Kriesberg, "Social Conflict Theories"; Northrup, "Dynamics of Identity."

30. Barbara Hill, "An Analysis of Conflict Resolution Techniques: From Problem Solving Workshops to Theory," *Journal of Conflict Resolution* 26, no. 1 (March 1982): 109.

Chapter Eight

Identity Politics and Environmental Conflict Dynamics

A Reexamination of the Negotiated Rulemaking Process

Brian Polkinghorn

This chapter focuses on the influence of group identity on conflict dynamics that occur during negotiations over the content of new environmental regulations. The host institution is the United States Environmental Protection Agency (EPA) and the decision-making process through which conflicts are managed is negotiated rulemaking or "reg-neg." We live in an age of identity politics where groups often actively seek higher strategic negotiating ground by laying claim to being victimized and blaming others for being the offenders. Attaching one's identity to tangible issues can contribute to conflict escalation in the form of labeling opponents and attributing ill will toward them. The influence of group identity is an important conceptual frame to adopt when examining environmental regulatory conflicts.

EPA is charged with the protection of human health and the environment. For descriptive purposes, the environment can be thought of as a combination of and interaction among social, biological and physical systems. Systems boundaries and functions are not always clearly defined nor are the cause-and-effect consequences of our actions. For example, people can live in just about any physical or biological environment and impact it in ways that those systems are not well suited to encounter. For this reason we should examine the environment as being more chaotic than ordered or homeostatic.

Environmental conflict is being examined here primarily from a social system perspective while delegating discussions of biological and physical systems to a secondary status. The reasoning for this is based on a number of assumptions that are designed to focus the reader's attention on the role of social identity in environmental conflict. The first is that the social system is the genesis of nearly all environmental conflict. When human activity produces (un)intentional, (non)linear, or (non)obvious consequences in the biological, physical or social environments these often become the basis for conflict. The second assumption posits that environmental conflicts are socially constructed events. In other words, the essential core issues and resultant dynamics of environmental conflict are a function of how groups choose to frame issues and relationships and not necessarily on how conditions exist within the larger natural environment. In addition, many environmental regulatory conflicts are anthropogenic in origin and thus focus on human habits and values.[1] The third assumption is that rational actor models that place a premium on logic and reason should be considered an ideal type that is rarely found within this study. Although focusing on stakeholders' rational thoughts may be useful in analyzing conflict, it is being nested conceptually within the dynamics of identity politics.

Together these assumptions focus the reader's attention on those human factors that include subjective and affective dimensions of identity. The reasons for this will become readily apparent later when, for instance, the focus shifts to examine how struggles develop over the distribution of benefits (e.g., affordable material goods, more efficient work processes or jobs, reduced risks) and the costs (e.g., location of industrial complexes, waste storage facilities, exposure to multiple forms of pollution or the disproportionate rate of cancer among groups) that accrue as a result of living in a post-industrial society.

Following a review of the relevant environmental literature and a brief discussion on social identity and its influence on the dynamics of environmental conflict, the focus of this chapter shifts to the research study of EPA's use of the negotiated rulemaking process. The data analysis and discussion are grouped into four areas that link social identity directly to environmental conflict dynamics. First, I focus on how groups often attack others by attaching derogatory labels to them in an attempt to destroy their credibility and legitimacy as rightful stakeholders. Second, I examine how engaging in conflict often functions to bind groups together, thus strengthening their identity. Objectified struggles can promote group cohesion and encourage a member to act as a representative rather than as an individual. This can increase radical positions as well as the intensity of the negotiation process. This section also examines how group identity and conflict can sometimes operate to bind antagonists.[2]

Third, I introduce the influence of conflict on constituent and representative relations and how this impacts in-group identity and resultant public images. In some groups an inverse relationship occurs whereby too much cooperation with an out-group actually serves to harm relations within the in-group. Yet, in order to gain desired results, cooperation with the perceived "enemy" is necessary. In other groups, too much antagonism and protracted conflict may actually do more to improve in-group relations while harming out-group relations.

Finally, I focus on the structural and systemic sources of discrimination.[3] Although regulatory negotiations go a long way to address problems found in the Administrative Procedures Act (APA) by reinforcing and encouraging the notion of participatory democracy, there are still problems of full involvement of minority groups in federal environmental decision-making.

Environmental Conflict Knowledge

Research and writing on environmental conflict falls into a number of categories. The first focuses on decision-making processes and how, if properly managed, they can alter the outcome of policy, regulatory or site-specific dilemmas.[4] This literature focuses largely on case studies, participant observation and other insights from interveners and stakeholders. There are three themes that are usually lacking in this category of literature. The first is that there is little analytical focus on the sources of conflict, or if there is more, it usually concentrates on how facilitated processes help people make decisions rather than on what information or knowledge bases they use to make decisions. Second, this area of the literature is largely anecdotal, descriptive and prescriptive and thus does not provide a framework for investigating what influences, *in situ*, environmental conflicts. Third, there is a clear need to focus on the analytical connection between sources of conflict and processes used to solve conflicts which is often missing in this type of literature.

There are disciplinary schools of thought that constitute another category that I call, for lack of a better label, "hard science knowledge." The generation of this type of knowledge allows it avoid much of the ambiguity that surrounds social knowledge but it is not completely free of it. Hard science knowledge is defined here as focusing primarily on cognitive frameworks that emphasize empirical research, positivism, the scientific method, and an insistence on the process of falsification. Areas of research concentrate on such things as human disease, toxicology, physiology, and various areas of geology, biology, physics, earth and environmental sciences.

Generally speaking, this category of knowledge can be divided into two areas. The first is literature written specifically by researchers for their colleagues and is therefore usually inaccessible to the majority of people involved in environmental conflicts. The second, more accessible, area clearly explains the role of science,[5] including its uncertainties[6] in environmental problem solving. Another closely related area focuses on the use of technology[7] or more specifically on the role of information technology in environmental decision making.[8] This category of the literature also encompasses a huge body of knowledge on environmental impact assessment[9] that emphasizes both the objective and subjective means of interpreting threats to health and the environment. The role of science and technology in the framing, assessment and final analysis of environmental conflicts is an extremely important and often highly contentious topic especially when it is used within the context of defining and defending the identity of groups in conflict.

Lee[10] and Ozawa[11] make good arguments in regard to the misperception that hard science knowledge is independent of a larger political context. They also make an excellent connection between how science can be effectively used to solve environmental problems. Basically, data that are generated from the "hard science knowledge" disciplines are interpreted through social lenses and can't be completely objective if we are to accept the second assumption discussed earlier that environmental conflict is socially constructed. For instance, one of the most troubling aspects of environmental conflict relates to how language is used and interpreted, especially when it comes to distinguishing between similar concepts such as risk and safety. Legislators and agencies often frame environmental protection statutes, policies and regulations on the calculated risks of exposure to pollution on human health and environmental protection. Deciding on acceptable and achievable levels is the essence of risk analysis. On the other hand, lay people have a tendency to frame and discuss pollution exposure issues with regard to safety, which is considered by most to be the absence of risk. Unfortunately, the threshold people call safe, as it is defined above, is rarely a realistic option for scientific and economic reasons.

A relevant area of research focuses directly on the generation of perceptions and estimations of risk[12] and on myths concerning environmental risks.[13] There is also a large body of literature on risks to the biological and physical environments,[14] as well as research on measurement and empirical analysis of risks.[15]

Another area of relevant literature emphasizes the human construction of knowledge through our experiences that teach us about the environment and ourselves. Research in this area focuses on such things as practical environmental politics,[16] philosophical schools,[17] applied environmental ethics,[18] legal history and statutory frameworks,[19] international environmental law,[20] global environmental problems,[21] and global environmental agreements.[22] These areas emphasize sources of conflict and the fact that in each context/situation, stakeholders are often forced to chose among competing ideologies, values, interests and needs. Such conflict can also be seen in policy formation[23] and the role of the courts in reviewing environmental regulatory language.[24]

Literature of this nature constitutes a foundation of knowledge that is useful for in-depth understanding of how we can engage others in addressing environmental conflict issues. Such knowledge also aids in establishing a history of environmental conflicts as well as the philosophy, ideology and political agendas that frame them. One problem with much of this literature is that although differences among people are assumed to exist, little attention is paid to how such differences influence the means and reasons by which they conflict rather than cooperate. In addition, much of this information and knowledge is of an intellectual or abstract nature and may not easily translate into how one practices environmental decision making.

Conflict, as a form of interaction, can also be seen as acting where drama and dialogue are used as a means to persuade others that one's idea, position or proposed solution is best. To this end, experienced negotiators know that the media are potent persuasive tools that, if manipulated correctly, can easily alter the dynamics and outcome of a negotiation. Social scientists continually examine the role of the media as a means of influencing the collective conscious and public opinion with regard to how we socially construct the environment.[25] This type of research is actually quite useful because it analyzes the context in which decisions are made and implemented. For example, in 1987 an EPA work group issued a list of what it considered the most important environmental hazards to human health, while environmentalists issued a distinctly different list. This demonstrates not only a lack of agreement but also that the very nature by which issues are framed can influence how groups identify with issues.

Up to this point the literature has tended to focus on numerous areas of knowledge and research that encompass environmental conflict studies. What is largely absent from this discussion is a set of studies that focus completely on people and how they relate to one another and the environment. It was not until the mid-1980s that this important body of work came into full development in the form of the environmental justice movement, which is a loosely constructed coalition composed of people and organizations that represent the environmental and health interests and needs of minorities and the poor. The literature is both activist and academic.[26] As one senior member of EPA's Office of Environmental Justice stated in a private interview: "What environmental justice is attempting to do is put people back into the environmental protection equation. Up to this point [late 1996] we have formulae that focus on economics, environmental systems and earth sciences but we have forgotten the people part of the equation."

There are two major sociological contributions that the environmental justice movement is making to the development of environmental conflict and decision making. The first is that social identity is directly injected into environmental conflict debates with such charges as environmental racism.[27] There are also studies that focus on the unfair locations of environmental hazards and facilities with regard to Native Americans[28] and women.[29] Although some of the assertions surrounding the evidence of environmental racism have been brought into question, the implications on environmental policy could be enormous.[30] The field data from these past studies have been used to bolster the legal theory of disproportionate impact wherein an inequitable number of Locally Unwanted Land Uses (LULUs) are located in and around minority communities, which ultimately increases the exposure of residents to environmental hazards. These experiences increase the sense of being oppressed, which solidifies the collective identity of such groups.

The second major sociological contribution of the environmental justice movement focuses directly on the demand for the fulfillment of basic human needs. Lee expresses this in terms of areas of equity.[31] The first area is procedural equity, which relates to the development of policies and regulations in which participatory democracy becomes the dominant thinking.[32] The second area is geographic equity wherein there is the realization that certain neighborhoods and communities are disproportionately burdened by hazardous waste facilities. And third, social equity follows from the second issue in that there are demographic variables such as race, class, ethnicity and culture that partially explain the geographical inequity that must therefore become a part of all environmental decision making.

Social identity and the fulfillment or blocking of basic human needs or other related goals provides a unique framework to explore the dynamics of environmental conflict. Environmental sociologists have attempted to do this but have largely left out of their discussions how particular decision-making processes are influenced by social identity. The rest of this chapter focuses precisely on this topic.

Social Identity

Identity is how people see themselves in comparison to others. It is a fluid continuous construction process that is negotiated at the personal and group levels. Social interaction influences how identities are shaped and as such are altered from time to time. Rothman suggests that below each tangible source of conflict, identity becomes a defining factor.[33] Although this may sound somewhat deterministic, there are numerous instances in the present study where identity is a factor in how participants interact. Various forms of identity have been studied and categorized by social scientists such as Goffman, who distinguishes between personal and social identities, or by Cooley, whose notion of the "looking glass self" points to inward and outward sources of peoples' sense of self.[34] Arguably people possess numerous identities that are nested within one another, where some are fleeting and less salient while others are more rooted in how individuals perceive themselves. The sense of self is an important component in social interaction and especially in conflict.

What is most important to focus on here is the power that identity plays in developing conflict strategies. For instance, if one party is capable of placing labels on others, it can effectively control them. In other words, at the symbolic level, stakeholders often attempt to attribute labels as a means of having power over others (attribution theory and labeling theory go into greater detail on this). Labeling others or creating images that allow stakeholders to blame "the other" is a common psychological maneuver. Likewise, stakeholders often undertake impression management techniques in an attempt to claim more desirable identities and labels. Suffice it to say that identity is a key factor in how stakeholders interact and align themselves when maintaining or building relationships (most notably coalitions) with other stakeholders.

Group identity can be a fluid or static and impermeable phenomenon. In this study, when conflict occurs, identities tend to lose their fluidity. In struggling over scarce resources relating to needs fulfillment or other related goals, groups often create exclusive and rigid identities. By producing images of others as unworthy of reward or by creating distinctive characteristics for those deemed eligible to receive benefits, a group's identity becomes a prime means of protecting themselves or attacking others. In essence, nurturing social identity is a process that involves things such as needs acquisition or goal attainment. For analytical purposes social identity is being framed here as a basic human need and given dynamic meaning much like the concept discussed by Burton as well as emulated, categorized and modeled by others.[35] In other words, social identity is a common means by which people demarcate themselves or others while engaging in struggles over more tangible resources.

There are critics of basic human needs theory that tend to find weakness in the universal nature of needs or find that there are other more powerful variables or factors by which to analyze conflict. Granted, other means of conflict analysis are available. The focus on the fulfillment of basic human needs as a means of conflicting is of particular utility when stakeholders describe their behavior as revolving around needs for clean air, water, soil, food supplies, a healthy economy and the ability to conduct business a freely as possible from government interference. When "the other" attempts to block the attainment of these needs or goals, then conflict, as participants' state, is likely to arise. The only contradiction to Maslow's hierarchy of needs that is present in this study is that people sometimes deliberately focus on the issue of identity when more basic needs are not secured. By doing so, many stakeholders are declaring that identity is perhaps the most important means by which to perceive environmental conflict.

The Research Setting

In 1982 the EPA undertook a pilot project to test the feasibility of negotiating the content of new environmental regulations with primary stakeholders. The effort still exists and has slowly developed into an institutional alternative to the conventional rulemaking process that is governed under the Administrative Procedures Act (APA). The APA is intended to ensure that citizens and organizations have fair access and ability to participate in rulemaking endeavors conducted by all federal agencies. However, in the effort to be open the APA is prone to efficiency problems, described by stakeholders involved in this study as overly complicated, as lacking a sense of consistency or control, and generally as a "joke," a "black box," or "the black hole of Calcutta."[36]

A total of twelve rulemaking efforts constitute the cases for this study. Within this group, six efforts utilize the reg-neg process and six do not. The primary data were collected via personal face-to-face interviews with EPA administrators, rule writers, reg-neg support staff, environmentalists, citizen activists, members of the environmental justice community, labor leaders, business representatives, EPA and corporate lawyers, state regulators, government and industry scientists, members of both the Bush and Clinton administrations, a vice president, a U.S. senator, a federal judge, five reg-neg facilitators and six academics directly involved in reg-neg research. Secondary data include internal EPA memos, information housed in EPA's public dockets, and personal negotiation notes.

The interview data were electronically transcribed and much of the secondary data were electronically scanned and loaded onto a mainframe qualitative program (QUALOG). The data were manipulated at the coding level into categories that were then compared in hypothesis testing procedures. From these data manipulation procedures, the following findings were made.

Attacking Others by Creating Negative Images

Coming primarily from the transcribed interviews the following findings focus on identity conflicts that are expressed in terms of legitimacy, credibility and
authority. Within the data are a number of strong patterns. A few categories of
data originally labeled "emotional outbursts," "personal attacks" and "respect"
were combined and re-examined with a focus on the use of social identity in labeling others or framing others outside the substantive scope of the negotiation.
It is apparent from this re-examination that symbolic challenges to others' legitimacy, credibility and rightful authority to be a stakeholder are evident.

From a symbolic interactionist perspective many stakeholders clearly engage
in a covert process of testing others. Although when asked to clarify what their
statements aimed at others mean, most tend to focus on their agenda and not on
the creation of images of an out-group. One way to view this is to see it as part
of a larger strategy of capturing a sense of credibility and legitimacy for themselves at the expense of others. A prime example comes from a scientist that
represents a large sector of organized labor that is demanding strong environmental protection regulations:

> Participant: The biggest problem with them [industry] is their slav-
> ishness toward profits at all costs and their masters are these invisible
> shareholders. [sigh] How can anyone act responsibly when they put
> profit in front of protection? What type of Neanderthal mentality is
> that? I can't figure out how anyone who has enough brains to make a
> billion dollars can't see these glaring contradictions, that is, unless
> they are really stupid. Come to think of it I don't know any intelligent
> business people at all.

> Interviewer: I see, so industry has an unusual way of viewing humans
> and . . .

> Participant: Unusual is not the word. Their thinking is of the lowest
> level and even when they are forced to comply with minimal stan-
> dards they still find ways to get around them. It makes it difficult to
> have to work with people like that knowing that their lawyers are
> searching, as we speak, to find loopholes.

> Interviewer: Is this a trust factor?

> Participant: Yes, because they can not be trusted. They say one thing
> and do the opposite. In California and Texas we have been fighting
> for basic protection standards and they fight over everything! They
> didn't want to give workers water stations or portable toilets! . . . So
> it makes me a little sick seeing some of these characters at the table.

The speaker believes that there are legitimate and illegitimate ways to weigh
protection of human health and the environment. One of the perceived threshold
characteristics to negotiating is to be trustworthy and this scientist says industry
stakeholders are not. Environmentalists, industry and even state regulators have

a tendency to mention why others' perspectives are "unbalanced," "catering to special interests" or "nonsense"—all implying that there is something wrong with the others' thought processes and ability to see the correct order of priorities.

Most might agree that each stakeholder brings a unique perspective, information and knowledge to the interaction that when viewed from a distance or larger perspective helps everyone understand the overall situation more fully. This is, in theory, the essence of education and there is a pattern not only within the interview data but also the archival documents that tend to support this notion. However, upon closer examination of the properties of controlled conflict (negotiating) there is another pattern that focuses directly on how education can be used to partially de-legitimize an opponent. In one of the best examples, a scientist expresses frustration over environmentalists' ignorance of science and technology and concludes that such people do not belong at the table or need someone else to represent and negotiate for them to make up for their lack of credentials:

> I was very frustrated when we went through hours and hours of discussions on what I feel were on elementary technical items to educate people. In fact, one of the meetings we had was a meeting in—where was it—I think it was in Houston, Texas. And we went through a core lab facility because these people didn't know anything about how cores were taken and how they test cores for permeability and porosity and things of this nature. And we had to take a trip down there. It was very costly just so they could get an idea what these people do and how it is done. To me, I thought it was utterly ridiculous.

For this participant there were specific identities necessary in order to sit at the table:

> Number one, I think that particular groups who want to participate should have [someone] available as their representative to participate, especially when you are dealing with areas of technical concern or technical matter. You know policy is maybe a different issue. But [for] technical matters they should have a person sitting at the table who is technically qualified to take part in it. Otherwise the process is extended and becomes more educational and it's just part education. You can't take a person who knows nothing about injection wells and make him into an injection well expert in eighteen months. There's no way at all.

Later he elaborates on this issue of legitimacy and knowledge:

> And this particular person spent thirty to forty minutes stating that the packer should be placed at a different position than it is now placed pursuant to the regulations. And we kept asking questions. Ya know, "Why do you feel that way?" Ya know, it didn't make any sense to us technically. So, finally, I talked to a fellow from Texas . . . and I said

to him, "I wonder if she even knows what a packer is?" So he asked
the question. He says, "Do you know what a packer is?" She says,
"Well, no, I don't." Well, how in the hell can anybody argue about
where a packer should be placed if they don't even know what it is?

In this category most stakeholder statements focus on actively challenging
others' credibility and legitimacy, usually through credentials and qualifications
revolving around various forms of knowledge to participate and represent others. Taking on the identity of an "expert" or of someone who possesses the right
type of knowledge and attempting to label others as "ignorant" is a prime means
of manipulating the negotiation dynamics.

Another participant provides a more pointed and derogatory example that
demonstrates that, no matter what anyone says, an arbitrary threshold of acceptance is set by a stakeholder:

> I don't really care if they talk science and technology as long as it is
> clear that first principles are not being violated. Whatever business
> says or states say has to be examined for first principles because they
> cooperate with each other and can not be trusted. What it all boils
> down to is, will this process potentially harm drinking water? Will it
> pollute aquifers? The answer is yes even though they have gone on
> record saying no. They have used technical language to make the
> truth less accessible and to intimidate people and to squeeze us out of
> the decision making, which makes them not only bullies but also li-
> ars.

The data demonstrate that people use information and labels to establish
credibility, legitimacy and even trustworthiness for themselves and perhaps
something else for others. By negotiating with specific language and knowledge,
stakeholders are labeling others as lacking proper credentials and undermining
their identity as a competitive or competent stakeholder. If differing forms of
knowledge can be used as the threshold of acceptance, then only certain types of
people would be allowed to make decisions. As absurd as it seems this is exactly
what many stakeholders believe is to their advantage to establish.

In one way or another stakeholders construct themselves as different from
other stakeholders. Even in cases where the interaction is less intense and negotiations are productive, many stakeholders still find ways to categorize themselves and others.

So even in cases where stakeholders cooperate and find ways to solve problems, differences based on roles and other forms of identity come into play.
More importantly, the interaction within the negotiation helps create a sense of
their own and the others' identity, much like Cooley's idea of the looking-glass
self.[37] Likewise, building relationships is partially a function of negotiating images and identities. It is instructive to examine more cases where negotiations
did not proceed well or did not produce an agreement to see if identity issues
play a larger role in stakeholder statements than in cases where agreements are
reached. This appears to be the case in this study and this is a prime question for
further research.

Engaging in Conflict Strengthens Identity

In cases where stakeholders see themselves in a situation of incompatible positions pitted against one another, the idea that engaging in conflict serves to bind individuals or groups together becomes readily apparent. For example, in one case environmentalists realized late in a negotiation that the potential outcome ranges were not going to decidedly support their agenda and so their priority shifted to concentrate on building group cohesion and the seeking of allies. In this case environmentalists did two things. The first was to publicly scrutinize EPA's and other stakeholders' actions in an effort to bring attention to their alleged misdeeds so as to create the image of them as offenders. The second, related activity was to begin the process of claiming sole possession of the identity of victim. This serves as another means of manipulating identity to control others. One stakeholder goes to great lengths to make this point clear:

> Participant: When EPA began to slowly make its data clear through our insistence—"come on EPA, show us the data; come on EPA, show us the numbers"—did it become clear to us that they ignored our concerns and our data. They [EPA] have a special relationship with business and as outsiders we have to fight to get the same consideration and respect. So when it became clear that EPA was not dealing with us in the same way as industry insiders we did the correct thing and withdrew from the negotiation.

> Interviewer: How did that go over with the other participants?

> Participant: Some of them were mad as hell because they almost got away with it. Others who weren't as involved in the dealings probably weren't happy either but we [all the environmentalists] decided unanimously as a group to walk out of this farce.

> Interviewer: I see. Did this do anything to how you relate to those at the table?

> Participant: Well, it did help the environmental groups get its priorities straight. We tend to let one group take the lead on certain issues, and in this case we were the lead and it wasn't until we realized that we were about to get a bad deal that we all met and got our act together. As for the rest I don't really see this as a personal thing but more as a professional thing. So they ought to know that we were the ones being reasonable and they were the ones who weren't. If they were in our shoes, they would have done the same thing. . . . I will be cautious with some of them in the future, though.

In this instance environmentalists coalesced when an outside threat emerged from others in the negotiation. Even though some environmentalists privately see this situation differently and went so far as to write letters to EPA explaining that they had no choice but to go along with the others so as not to break ranks, it did serve at least to make the collective environmental agenda more pronounced as well as to construct a story where environmentalists were victimized by industry. This particular passage also points to the insider and outsider identities that are often held by competing groups. Other stakeholders hold similar feelings, as one industry representative describes EPA's relationship with environmentalists as "a concerted effort to nail business every chance it gets."

These images of victims and offenders forces the question, does conflict cause representatives to become more radical? In this study, only in cases where conflict was actively expressed did stakeholders discuss how hard they negotiated. One participant states:

> I know I am going to come out looking like the bad guy but when people push too far you have to push back. I usually restrain myself but these people were being so unreasonable and so unbelievable that I felt I had to be aggressive and bring the discussion back to reality because what they were proposing was downright laughable. I wasn't going to get walked over by them and I had to fight their efforts to do so. If I took that back to [his trade association] I would have lost my job. So I was forced to go against my nature and get a little pushy.

This tendency to engage in radical behavior as one plays the role of a representative rather than an individual is hard to detect but there may be a few reasons for this. The first is that the identity as "representative" encourages the person to take a hard line.

However, there is also a data pattern that, although weak, may be instructive to this discussion. There are just a few instances where stakeholders produced unsolicited comments concerning the distinction between personal and professional roles. These comments come almost exclusively from stakeholders who took part in low-intensity conflict negotiations. One industry representative states:

> Participant: We may have gone in there as adversaries but we all came out friends. In fact we had a party after we finished it.
>
> Interviewer: How was your relationship with those people after the negotiations?
>
> Participant: Well, I always had a good relationship personally, socially, but it comes down then to the issues at stake because there are always differences of opinion between industry and the environmental community or whomever it may be with regard [to] pesticides [which] is a very controversial issue. And so what the point of it is, I was always taught that you can disagree but don't be disagreeable and so I think the opportunity for a neg-reg is to disagree without being disagreeable.

It appears that the perceived level of conflict can influence the role one plays. In the reg-neg context, as conflict escalates, the professional role may become more apparent. A related point that is not discussed here is that it is also apparent that the outcome of the negotiations is linked to how people perceive each other. If the negotiations fail, people are suspicious and typically see others as having been unreasonable. If they succeed in reaching an agreement, then perceptions of others are generally better.

The Pubic Image of Working with the Enemy

Social identity impacts environmental conflict in that many groups have preconceived relationships and firm ideas of what to expect from conflict resolution processes like reg-neg. One of the bases for these relationships relies on a non-obvious factor, namely, environmentalists often appeal to donors for funding and in exchange they act as their "watch dogs" over largely "unregulated" industrial polluters as well as "incompetent" or "easily swayable" federal regulatory agencies. Many environmentalists therefore have a tricky public relations task to perform when they are asked to negotiate environmental regulations. While some of their funding sources require them to be aggressive, even adversarial, many also see the utility of negotiating, though it may cause a withdrawal of support from constituencies. One environmentalist says:

> Participant: There's an incredible risk to negotiating because even though we will use the carrot, the stick or whatever to get EPA and industry to clean up their act we have to be conscious of our constituents. We don't want to lose sight of our mission nor do we want donors feeling as though we are not doing our job.
>
> Interviewer: Almost like shareholders?
>
> Participant: Yes, well, no, not in the sense like industry. People don't own stock in [the environmental group she works for] but support us because we have a common agenda of aggressively protecting human health and cleaning up the environment.

On the other hand, industry stakeholders almost universally adore negotiated rulemaking. Industry stakeholders praise the concept because that is exactly how they are used to working with others. Negotiated agreements are common events in the business world. One industry stakeholder says it best: "This is how things have been and ought to be done. Agree to something, shake hands and do what you say you are goin' to do and don't back out."

Many industry stakeholders see the delicate public relations that are needed to encourage environmentalists to come to the table and some have gone as far as to privately orchestrate face-saving deals so that in-group identity problems do not splinter an environmental group. Although there are no data specifically focusing on why some industry stakeholders want environmental groups to remain cohesive, one can speculate that by having an intact adversary one knows what to expect as well as allowing this arrangement to act as a binding mechanism among antagonists. In other words, if environmental groups begin to splinter, industry is faced with perhaps more opposition groups, which makes the ability to negotiate even less likely. By helping to preserve or at least encourage their counterparts to remain viable, a future relationship based on recognition and perhaps cooperation may arise. Without an intact adversary, environmental conflict can become more chaotic.

How do environmentalists come to the table? In some instances they have been able to get past the initial in-group struggle by demonstrating success through negotiating; this is seen by some as a gamble, though. In others they have worked out conditions that attend to the problem of "negotiating with the enemy." A paradox exists that requires a delicate balance between having too much cooperation with industry stakeholders while maintaining a high enough level of antagonism, because a change in either one can harm in-group cohesion. Antagonistic relationships often help in-group cohesion because of the existence of an out-group enemy. As negotiated rulemaking is now an institutionalized form of decision making, the initial concern about cooperating with the enemy may be less threatening. Continuing research in this area is needed.

The Invisible People and the Power of Identity

Although negotiated rulemaking goes a long way in solving many environmental management concerns associated with the Administrative Procedures Act (APA) by getting the best and brightest minds to work together early in the construction of new regulations, it still faces the structural and systemic problem. Environmental justice participants flatly state that the APA and reg-neg do not adequately attend to the needs of minority and poor communities. While initially conducting the first three phases of this study it became readily apparent that people who take part in negotiated rulemaking endeavors often represent governments, large dues-paying trade associations, environmental groups or other voluntary organizations. However, groups that represent people based on their primary social identity such as race, gender and lower socioeconomic status are largely absent from these negotiations. During the study, EPA convened the National Environmental Justice Advisory Committee (NEJAC) and formed the Office of Environmental Justice to bring the issues and concerns of minority groups to EPA decision making, thus at least giving an organizational outlet for the study of the relationship between group affiliation and protection from pollutants.

What frustrates some EPA personnel is the obvious lack of minority participation and the efforts the agency goes to in helping representatives of such groups. It is not until the decision making is complete and the regulation is being enforced that many minority groups—the invisible people—make themselves known and by then it is too late. However, as one EPA person put it, there are a number of concerns that are politically sensitive that no one wants to talk about:

> Over the last few years there's been a lot of talk about [the] effect of poverty and race on how and where industry locates. There is anecdotal evidence and firsthand testimony from people around the coun-

try who say their family's health problems resulted from some company plant. Regardless if it is true or not you can't help but feel for them. I mean, kids with cancer and healthy adults dying at young ages from rare diseases can't help but register. The agency has been studying this and other things such as brownstones and urban environments and whatnot to see how different populations are affected by pollution. It is interesting work, but the problem is getting past anecdotal information, which no one wants to dare say for fear of looking insensitive or worse racist but we need to know how these things happen. We need to get minority representatives and minority communities more involved. That's our challenge and as it stands reg-neg hasn't done a good job of that.

Toward the end of this study a number of environmental justice activists decided to take part. Their initial reluctance to participate was twofold. First they did not trust an academic claiming to have unintentionally discovered their existence because of a glaring omission in who participated in reg-negs. Second, many environmental justice activists seem tired of being studied. As one put it, "We're not some exotic tribe. We're Americans like everyone else. Subtle racism is still racism." One leading academic and activist had this to say:

> Participant: Look, how hard is it to ask for clean water? How hard is it to ask that lead isn't in your water, your land and in the air or the fish or the playground? If this were Beverly Hills there would be no problem, but it's Beaumont and other small African-American towns throughout the South. What we want is what everybody wants but what happens is industry moves in, gets a tax break, promises jobs and heaven on earth and then proceeds to hire people from outside the community and then poisons us! Look, I know [the associate director of the Office of Environmental Justice] and I know you two are friends and if you don't believe me I know he'll tell you the same thing. Race matters, period. If you want to find a minority community in a large city all you have to do is look for the dumps or the factories or the bus stations or any of the other facilities that pollute, and there we are.

> Interviewer: How can minority voices be heard?

> Participant: Well you have to put people first. . . . Create laws that force industry to take social issues and people into account and to make sure that the costs of civilization are distributed equally.

> Interviewer: How about the benefits of civilization too?

> Participant: Ha, now you're dreaming. Nah, I'm kidding.

> Interviewer: Doesn't any of the environmental groups attend to these things?

> Participant: Oh God! Don't get me started. Environmentalists don't know us and they try and represent us and it winds up being patron-

izing. Not only that they use us to get money by putting little brown,
black, and yellow faces on their glossy brochures but the money
never gets to them.

What EPA and the environmental justice community are saying collectively
is that there are problems not only with the processes through which decisions
are made but also with how decisions are framed in terms of what values are
most important. Social identity plays a role not only in how people negotiate and
conflict but also in how the benefits and costs of regulation are distributed.

Conclusion

Social identity can influence how environmental conflict dynamics develop and
vice versa. When conflict intensifies, identity-based issues become more pronounced and stakeholders attempt to use such differences to shape the context of
the negotiation and their relationships to other stakeholders. By framing issues
using specific language and ideas, people hope to be seen as the expert, capturing the highest levels of legitimacy, credibility and authority within the negotiating group. This tactic is essentially a form of social control. Stakeholders have
also engaged in deliberate attempts to attribute negative qualities to other
stakeholders, which is another means of social control.

Conflict can increase group cohesion by emphasizing differences based on
social identity. In addition, social identity boundaries can be flexible, allowing
in allies and shutting out others. The results of this study suggest that, when conflict escalates, people with similar or overlapping identities attempt to put aside
differences in order to collectively face external forces. The outcome of regulatory negotiations also influences identity, labels and attribution. When there is
success, people tend to use positive labels for themselves and others, but when
the negotiation fails, people tend to use negative labels for others.

Personal and professional identities are seen in these negotiations. When
events escalate, professional identities appear to be more prevalent. Stakeholders
are more willing to take tough stances in the name of their cause but later are
able to discuss the negotiation from a personal point of view and see things differently. This idea of various identities emerging at certain times during conflict
is not all that unusual.

Finally, the environmental justice community is perhaps the best case example where political identity overtly, as expressed by professional and personal
roles, drives environmental conflict dynamics. Everything else comes second.
The environmental justice community engages in intergroup struggle in this
fashion because it may be the only means for minorities and the poor to have
any chance of getting their points addressed and having their needs met.

In this day and age of identity politics many conflicts, whether for good or bad,
are framed around who is engaged in the conflict as much as by the content of the
conflict itself. In the end, focusing on social identity as the prime factor in how
environmental conflicts are shaped and carried out is an excellent alternative to
the overwhelming approach in the "hard science knowledge" and "rational" deci-

sion-making literature. And although a systems approach is a logical and mechanical way of describing and approaching environmental conflicts, we must recognize that differences among groups that are based largely on social identity are prime sources in explaining the sources and dynamics of environmental conflict.

Notes

1. C. Brannon Anderson and Brian Polkinghorn, "Geology as a Science: Addressing the Complexity of Human Habitats and Values in Water Quality Conflicts," *Geological Society America Today* 6, no. 4 (April 1996): 36-38.

2. Lewis A. Coser, *The Functions of Social Conflict* (New York: Free Press, 1996).

3. Johan Galtung, *Peace by Peaceful Means: Peace and Conflict Development and Civilization* (London: Sage, 1996).

4. Gail Bingham, *Resolving Environmental Disputes: A Decade of Experience* (Washington, D.C.: Conservation Foundation, 1986); James E. Crowfoot and Julia M. Wondolleck, *Environmental Disputes: Community Involvement in Conflict Resolution* (Washington, D.C.: Island Press, 1990); Cornelius M. Kerwin, *Rulemaking: How Government Agencies Write Law and Make Policy* (Washington, D.C.: Congressional Quarterly Press, 1994); Chris Maser, *Resolving Environmental Conflict: Towards Sustainable Community Development* (Delray Beach, Fla.: St. Lucie Press, 1996); Scott Mernitz, *Mediation of Environmental Disputes: A Sourcebook* (New York: Praeger Publishers, 1980).

5. S. C. Zehr, "The Centrality of Scientists and the Translation of Interests in the U.S. Acid Rain Controversy," *Canadian Review of Sociology and Anthropology* 31, no. 3 (1994): 325-53.

6. John Lemons, *Scientific Uncertainty and the Environmental Problem Solving* (Oxon, England: Blackwell Science, 1996).

7. W. R. Freudenberg and S. Pastor, "Public Responses to Technical Risks: Towards a Sociological Perspective," *The Sociology Quarterly* 33, no. 3 (1992): 389-412.

8. James K. Lein, *Environmental Decision Making: An Information Technology Approach* (Oxon, England: Blackwell Science, 1997).

9. Christopher Wood, *Environmental Impact Assessment: A Comparative Review* (London: Longman Scientific and Technical, 1995).

10. Kai N. Lee, *Compass and Gyroscope: Integrating Science and Politics for the Environment* (Washington, D.C.: Island Press, 1993).

11. Connie Ozawa, *Recasting Sciences: Consensual Procedures in Public Policy Making* (Boulder, Colo.: Westview Press, 1991).

12. Carol Heimer, "Social Structure, Psychology and the Estimation of Risk," *Annual Review of Sociology* 14 (1998): 491-519.

13. J. W. Spencer and E. Triche, "Media Constructions of Risk and Safety: Differential Framings of Hazard Events," *Sociological Inquiry* 64, no. 2 (1994), 199-213.

14. Derek Ellis, *Environments at Risk: Case Histories of Impact Assessment* (London: Springer-Verlag, 1989).

15. Joseph V. Rodricks, *Calculated Risk: The Toxicity and Human Health Risks of Chemicals in Our Environment* (Washington, D.C.: U.S. Environmental Protection Agency, 1992).

16. Douglas J. Amy, *The Politics of Environmental Mediation* (New York: Columbia University Press, 1987); Thomas Princen and Matthias Finger, *Environmental NGOs in World Politics: Linking the Local and the Global* (London: Routledge, 1994); Walter A. Rosenbaum, *Environmental Politics and Policy,* 2d ed. (Washington, D.C.: Congressional Quarterly Press, 1991).

17. William T. Blackstone, *Philosophy and Environmental Crisis* (Athens: University of Georgia, 1974); J. Baird Callicott, *In Defense of a Land Ethic: Essays in Environmental Philosophy* (Albany: State University of New York Press, 1989); Neil Evernden, *The Natural Alien* (Toronto: University of Toronto Press, 1985); Arran E. Gare, *Postmodernism and the Environmental Crisis* (London: Routledge, 1995); Enrique Leff, *Green Production: Toward an Environmental Rationality* (New York: Guilford Press, 1995); Roderick Nash, *Wilderness and the American Mind* (New Haven, Conn.: Yale University Press, 1982).

18. Eugene C. Hargrove, *Foundation of Environmental Ethics* (Englewood Cliffs, N.J: Prentice-Hall, 1989; F. Herbert Borman and Stephen R. Kellert, *Ecology, Economics, Ethics: The Broken Circle* (New Haven, Conn.: Yale University Press, 1994).

19. Nancy Kubasek and Gary S. Silverman, *Environmental Law,* 2d ed. (Englewood Cliffs, N.J.: Prentice-Hall, 1997).

20. Lynne M Jurgielewicz, *Global Environmental Change and International Law: Prospects for Progress in the Legal Order* (Lanham, Md.: University Press of America, 1996).

21. Jeffrey H. Leonard, *Environment and the Poor: Development Strategies for a Common Agenda* (New Brunswick, N.J.: Transaction Books, 1989); Charles H. Southwick, *Global Ecology in Human Perspective* (Oxford: Oxford University Press, 1996).

22. Ford C. Runge, Francois Orttalo-Magne, and Philip Vande Kamp, *Free Trade, Protected Environment: Balancing Trade Liberalization and Environmental Issues* (New York: Council on Foreign Relations Press, 1994); Lawrence E. Susskind, *Environmental Diplomacy: Negotiating More Effective Global Agreements* (Oxford: Oxford University Press, 1994).

23. Robyn Eckersley, *Environmentalism and Political Theory: Toward an Ecocentric Approach* (Albany: State University of New York Press, 1992); Rosemeary O'Leary, Robert F. Durant, Daniel J. Fiorino, and Paul S. Weiland, *Management for the Environment: Understanding the Legal, Organizational, and Policy Challenges* (San Francisco: Jossey-Bass, 1999); John O'Neill, *Ecology, Policy and Politics: Human Well-Being and the Natural World* (London: Routledge, 1993).

24. Rosemary O'Leary, *Environmental Change: Federal Courts and the EPA.* (Philadelphia: Temple University Press, 1993).

25. Riley E. Dunlap, "Public Opinion on the Environment in the Reagan Era: Polls, Pollution and Politics." *Environment* 29, no. 6 (1987): 6-11, 31-37; Anders Hansen, "The Media and the Social Construction of the Environment," *Media, Culture and Society* 13 (1991): 443-58; George D. Lowe, Thomas Pinhey, and Michael D. Grimes, "Public Support for Environmental Protection: New Evidence from National Surveys," *Pacific Sociological Review* 23, no. 4 (October 1980): 423-45.

26. Robert D. Bullard, *Confronting Environmental Racism: Voices from the Grassroots* (Boston: South End Press, 1993); Robert Bullard, *Dumping in Dixie: Race, Class and Environmental Quality* (Boulder, Colo.: Westview Press, 1990); Ward Churchill and Winona LaDuke, "Native America: The Political Economy of Radioactive Colonialism," *Insurgent Sociologist* 13 (Spring 1986), 51-68; Paul Mohai, "Black Environmentalism," *Social Science Quarterly* 71 (April 1990): 744-65.

27. Bullard, *Dumping in Dixie*; Bullard, *Confronting Environmental Racism*; Churchill and LaDuke, "Native America"; Mohai, "Black Environmentalism"; Bunyan Bryant, and Paul Mohai, *Race and the Incidence of Environmental Hazards: A Time for Discourse* (Boulder, Colo.: Westview Press, 1992); Richard Hofrichter, *Toxic Struggles: The Theory and Practice of Environmental Justice* (Philadelphia: New Society, 1993).

28. Churchill and LaDuke, "Native America."

29. Celene Krauss, "Women and Toxic Waste Protests," *Qualitative Sociology* 16, no. 3 (1993): 247-62; Mary Pardo, "Mexican-American Women Grassroots Community Activists: Mothers of East Los Angeles," *Frontiers: A Journal of Women's Studies* 11 (January 1990): 1-16.

30. Christopher H. Foreman, Jr., *The Promise and Peril of Environmental Justice* (Washington, D.C.: Brookings Institute, 1998).

31. C. Lee, *Proceedings, First National People of Color Environmental Leadership Summit* (New York: United Church of Christ Commission for Racial Justice, 1992).

32. Brian Polkinghorn, *The Influence of Regulatory Negotiations on the U.S. Environmental Protection Agency*, Ph.D. diss. The Maxwell School of Citizenship and Public Affairs, Syracuse University, 1994; Brian Polkinghorn and C. Brannon Andersen, "Expanding the Role and Responsibility of Geoscientists to Environmental Justice Communities: Aiding in the Management and Prevention of Environmental Hazards," *Geological Society of America Abstracts and Publications* 27, no. 5 (October 1995).

33. Jay Rothman, *Resolving Identity-Based Conflict in Nations, Organizations and Communities* (San Francisco: Jossey-Bass, 1997).

34. Erving Goffman, *Stigma: Notes on the Management of Spoiled Identity* (Englewood Cliffs, N.J.: Prentice-Hall, 1963); Charles H. Cooley, *Human Nature and Social Order* (New York: Scribner, 1962).

35. John W. Burton, *Conflict: Human Needs Theory* (New York: St. Martins, 1990); John W. Burton, *Resolving Deep-Rooted Conflict: A Handbook* (Lanham, Md.: University Press of America, 1987).

36. Polkinghorn, *Influence of Regulatory Negotiations*; Brian Polkinghorn, "Further Findings on the Use of Negotiated Rulemaking at the United States Environmental Protection Agency," *Journal of Practical Dispute Resolution* 1, no. 2 (1999): 33-45.

37. Cooley, *Human Nature*.

Chapter Nine

Rediscovering Memorial Day

Politics, Patriotism, and Gender

Christine Wagner

> Ah, what stories there are still to tell—
> about who we might be and what we might be doing
> to one another, ourselves and our world.
>   —John Shotter and Josephine Logan

This story is about Memorial Day—its meanings, its history, its rituals, its symbols, and its participants, both those who celebrate and those who mourn. The story is told by looking at a specific event, a Memorial Day parade, which over many years had come to embody, for individuals and for the community in which it was held, the meaning and utility, or futility, of war. The subtexts of the story, though, reveal deep insights into the management of human relationships.

Memorial Day is a United States national holiday officially commemorated each year on the fourth Monday of May. Originally, it was a day set aside to acknowledge the suffering and loss of life resulting from the Civil War, and it is generally marked in different parts of the country according to the regions' historical involvement with that war. In most of the Northeast it is a major event, warranting a weekend's worth of activities; in some places in the South it is ignored, or the "spirit of the day" is noted at another time; in the West the day may hold only perfunctory events.

The locus of this story is a mid-size city in the Northeast with a traditionally strong loyalty to the idea of Memorial Day. In 1983, 117 years after the first Memorial Day, a group of citizens believed that they had a perspective on the meaning of the day different from that of the veterans who traditionally planned the holiday events. They asked the veterans for permission to participate in the Memorial Day parade in order to share with the community their vision about honoring the dead by actively working for peace—in contrast to what they perceived as the militant message of the veterans. The veterans balked at the notion that year and every year after, believing that the parade and sorrow was theirs, not the community's, and that, somehow, the memories of the dead would be dishonored by the presence of a peace contingent. Nevertheless, through persistence, and the use of mediation and the courts, the alternative contingent participated in the 1983 parade and subsequent parades for twelve years.[1] The conflict of interests and values between veterans and "peace people" fueled annual debate in the community on the meaning of patriotism, the nature of national security, and the pervasiveness of militarism. But conflicts are usually more complex than they appear and this story is no exception. Probing the day-to-day dynamics of this conflict reveals subtle subplots about gender roles, sexual orientation, freedom of speech, and struggle over which strategies preserve life and which threaten it.

The variety of topics hints at the cultural significance of these events that go beyond that of a simple parade. The long-term, public interaction among individuals and groups over a variety of complex issues is symbolic of the struggle in which all communities are engaged. This chapter will explore what this community event reveals about the meaning of war, war memorials and Memorial Day, how conflicts need to be "unpacked" to understand their complexity and how gender and sexuality issues serve as major but often hidden stumbling blocks to communication and conflict resolution.

Surprising Intimacy: Collecting the Story

The study was limited to the first nine years of the controversy, from 1983 to 1992. Because of the large number of individuals and groups involved, as well as government agencies and the media, a variety of sources were available for research and corroboration. Newspaper clippings, meeting minutes, pictures, videotapes, personal and organizational files and records were all enthusiastically offered as components of the study.

The main body of information, though, came from parade participants. Twelve veterans and twelve peace coalition members were interviewed over a two-year period in sessions of at least two hours. The veterans were all male and white, and they represented World War II, Vietnam and noncombatant experiences. The peace coalition members were male and female, white, twenty to sixty years old, and they represented the variety of focus groups which comprised the coalition.

I was stunned at the openness, emotion, and urgency with which the interviewees spoke of even the previously most hidden events, meetings and feelings. This held true for both the veterans' community with which I had no connection and the peace coalition of which I had been a part. This openness alone impressed on me the importance given the event; the participants wanted the story—in all aspects—to be told.

An acute awareness was necessary during data gathering and analysis because of my familiarity with many of the peace coalition organizers. Two observations regarding researcher orientation bear mentioning. First, a researcher, particularly in a familiar milieu, must be obsessive about examining assumptions. Common language must be analyzed for accurate meaning, slang and acronyms must be clarified, common experiences must be probed for meaning from the interviewees point of view. A researcher can be dangerously blind and narrow-minded in a familiar setting.

Second, that same familiarity can be turned to advantage. In this instance, I realized that my base of knowledge of the peace community was extensive. With that knowledge I was able to articulate the facets of that database and map out a plan for learning the same information about the veterans' community. I was then able to do an analysis of both communities on a relatively even footing.

As an analytic perspective, symbolic interactionism focuses on the construction of meaning through the routine interaction of individuals. I used an interactionist approach in the analysis of this data, seeing a match between its appreciation for the ways in which cultural meanings are continually constructed through our daily lives, and the dynamic and often rapid-fire unfolding of meaning within the context of the Memorial Day parade events. In this particular instance, it was not only the normal activity of interpretation and interaction that was presented, but the purposeful engagement with a specific set of symbols and meanings. Those who chose to get involved in these events publicly declared the importance of their experiences and the meanings attached to them and willingly engaged in debate on these meanings.

In preliminary analysis of the written Memorial Day parade documents and from my initial coding of interviews, I identified three areas where there was active challenging (conscious and unconscious) of meanings, stereotypes, traditions and practices: the first involved the meanings attached to Memorial Day, the second focused on uncovering and then managing conflict between and within groups, and the third involved gender roles and sexuality issues. As the issues became more sensitive, the respondents became less open in their discussion. The meaning of Memorial Day events and symbols seemed relatively easy to identify in the text. Issues of conflict between coalitions were more easily discussed than conflict within coalitions and groups, an area where I found interview conversations more guarded and protective. Finally, issues of gender or sexuality were often either ignored or denied, or questionable behavior or decisions that seemed related to gender and sexuality issues were justified on some other pretext when challenged.

Not Just a Simple Parade

A parade is generally considered a fun but rather inconsequential event. Parades are a time for the community to gather and celebrate. Everyone is there—poor to middle-class to rich; black, white, Native American, Asian and Hispanic; highly to minimally educated; homeless and home proud; those who know no one marching in the parade and those who have come to support their soldier or spouse or trumpet player in the parade. At parades men, women and children

stand shoulder to shoulder at the curb to watch some of us walk in front of others of us, with that mix changing for each parade according to the occasion—St.
Patrick's Day, July 4th, New Year's Day, and so on. Rarely is there meaning
much beyond celebration attached to the parade.

When we look closely at Memorial Day, though, we find an exception to the
rule. Even though Memorial Day parades have taken on the "entertaining" quality of other parades, they maintain a sense of their original purpose of honoring
dead veterans, especially victims of war. This, in its essence, is a political motivation and sets a Memorial Day parade or commemoration apart from other
community events, warranting attention to its place and meaning in the community.

The history of Memorial Day, its rituals, meaning and purpose within the
culture, has evolved in close relationship to the international history of the
United States. Communities ritualize what they have lived. Memorial Day is officially recognized by the U.S. Congress as having started in Waterloo, New
York, in 1866. The first commemorations of Memorial Day were solemn gath-
erings of the community, more akin to a contemporary memorial service than a
parade. Following is a description of Memorial Day in 1868 in Waterloo from
the local newspaper, the *Seneca Observer.*

> The ladies assembled at Towsley Hall in the afternoon, and soon,
> with evergreens and the most beautiful flowers, manufactured a large
> number of crosses, wreaths and bouquets—all arranged with the taste
> and skill which might be expected from fair hands guided by inspira-
> tions of the highest patriotism and love.
>   At five o'clock a procession was formed of ladies, veteran soldiers
> and citizens generally, who bore the floral offerings and evergreen
> crosses and . . . took up the line of march for the cemeteries.
>   The procession came to a halt in the old burial ground, where Rev.
> Dr. Gridley made a few appropriate and eloquent remarks, after
> which the graves for the soldiers here interred were visited in rotation
> and suitable decorations placed on each.[2]

Memorial Day began as the simple gesture of decorating the graves of Civil
War soldiers, both Union and Confederate, "with a touch impartially tender."[3]
For many years, "Decoration Day," as it was originally called, was marked by
members of the community gathering at cemeteries or at memorial sites to sol-
emnly remember and mourn all those who had died in war. This community
gathering was also intended as a gesture of reconciliation, recognition of the
need, in a communal way, to heal the divisions caused by the war.

War touches everyone. Individuals play various roles in the waging of war,
and every generation has its own story, but much of the experience and emotion
is common human ground; the grief of life lost, the pain of defeat or the exhila-
ration of victory, the questioning of the cost, the sacrifice of a normal life routine, the uncertainty of the future and relief at war's end. War insinuates itself
into every crack and corner of life, leaving nothing untouched, from relationships to the routines of eating and working and thinking. War extends itself by
having both immediate and long-term effects. In the immediate, the actual expe-

Table 9.1. The Memorial Day Parade Conflict: A Chronology (1982-1991)

May 1866 The birth of Memorial Day in Waterloo, New York.

1982 A"Women's Encampment" is established adjacent to Seneca Army Depot in Romulus, N.Y., 50 miles from Rochester, N.Y.. The depot was thought to be a nuclear weapons storage and transport facility.

May 1983 Representatives of a Presbyterian Church committee and other related social groups request and eventually receive permission from the veterans organizing committee to participate in the Memorial Day parade. Their participation is received with hostility by the veterans.

February 1984 Organizers of the Women's Encampment take up the challenge presented by the veterans in 1983 and apply for a parade permit for Memorial Day, 1984. This request is denied, while the veterans' request for a permit was approved pro forma.

March-May 1984 Activists continue negotiating with the city and veterans and simultaneously devise alternative participation plans if negotiation fails.

May 16, 1984 Pre-Vietnam era veterans announce plans to cancel the Memorial Day parade if the now-forming peace coalition is allowed to march.

May 17–19, 1984 City-mandated mediation sessions reach no compromise. Veterans hold fast to decision to cancel the parade.

May 20–28, 1984 The city issues a parade permit for the peace coalition for Memorial Day. Death threats are received by parade organizers. Vietnam veterans break ranks and participate in parade with peace coalition; they also receive threats. This action marks a coming of age of the Vietnam veterans and a reconciliation in the relationship between Vietnam them and some activists who had protested the war in the 1960s and 1970s.

June 1984 A city-sponsored sesquicentennial parade peacefully includes all segments of community.

October 1984 A formal coalition of thirty-five groups is formed to begin planning 1985 parade.

December 1984 Veterans organization releases statement that all groups are welcome, following certain general guidelines, in 1985 parade.

May 27, 1985 Veterans accuse peace coalition of violating guidelines in the morning parade.

September 1985–May 1986 Negotiations fail and veterans deny coalition access to parade under their permit. City issues peace coalition its own permit for parade immediately following veterans'.

September 1986–May 1987 Both groups apply for 1986 parade permits. City denies both, insisting on mediation. Guidelines for participation by both parties are reached.

1988–1991 Both contingents continue to march and the controversy slips into a status quo for the community.

---

rience of war is often pivotal in defining the character and course of an individual's life and in shaping values held and decisions made. In the long term, the profound experiences of war can produce intense, life-long memories of the events, emotions and sacrifices that war demands—memories of pain, fear, pride, despair, and grief.

There is another equally important dimension to the experience of war: war is an extensively communal event, as well as an intensely intimate and personal one. Individuals experience war on a communal level and a personal level at the same time.

Community is defined here not by number of individuals, nor by consensus of political views, but by the fact of having the experience of war in common—not necessarily a common experience, but living through the same event.[4] The key factors here are relationship in community and relationship enhanced or threatened through a mutual experience.

A human community, like an individual, manifests the collective effects of war—the extraordinary living required by war and the profound changes which irrevocably alter its future. The community also possesses the same intensity of memory as an individual—and these memories have a long-lasting impact on the community as its members reflect on its experiences and arrive at diverse conclusions, meanings and commitments.

The change in the emphasis of Memorial Day from commemoration to today's celebration was slow and unplanned. Especially since World War I, each new military conflict has added layers of meaning to the commemoration so that today the original intent may seem quite obscure at times. The additional layers of meaning, which celebrate patriotism, national security, and military strength, were introduced gradually as the United States extended its history of war, increased its population of veterans, and added to its military influence in the world. The evolution of the meaning and purpose of Memorial Day and the communal memory of war is significantly influenced by these historic events.

Interwoven and essential in the history of war and the creation of community memory are the lives of veterans and the formation of veterans' organizations, with the latter a particularly significant element in the changing meaning of Memorial Day. While the Memorial Day parade is reflective of public sentiment on war, its presentation is mediated through the groups which facilitate its happening. Veterans' organizations in the United States have gradually assumed responsibility within their communities for staging Memorial Day events. Changes in Memorial Day have been strongly influenced by changes in these organizations; as their priorities and self-image have kept pace with public sentiment about war and the military, so too has the character of the commemorative events. How and why does a community maintain its memory of war? How does a community reflect on its experience of war and what are the results of this reflection?

Building Community Memory

The manifestation of a community memory of war is evident. Americans have worked hard to acknowledge the reality of the experience of war and to create reminders of that experience, including deliberate spaces, symbols and events that occupy public arenas and keep the memory of war constantly present. Signs of communal memory-making abound in monuments, buildings and bridges; in art work, drama and literature; in oral and written histories; and in anniversaries, ceremonies and ritual. Memories of war are publicly erected and preserved to serve as reminders of times and places and ways of thinking that completely absorbed and altered the community at the time, and they continue as influences on actions and decision making today.

The veterans continually asserted that war memorials were for the purpose of honoring and remembering those who lost their lives in the service of their country. I suggest two additional reasons for maintaining tangible community memories of war. First, they are tools, albeit unconscious ones, in a continuing process of reconciling participation in war; second, they can be perceived as an attempt to prevent future wars through the illustration of the price of war in the past. It is in this context that the peace contingent sought to be a part of the communal symbol of the Memorial Day parade.

War presents essential questions of life and death and related questions concerning justification of actions to individuals and to communities. Long after a war's official end, communities continue to live through its unfolding consequences and obstinate and difficult questions remain and reverberate with a nagging persistence. What is worth dying for? What is worth killing for? Who has the right to make those decisions? Was the action justified? What is the true cost of war? Who are the victims? The memorials created do not represent consensus on the answers to these questions, nor do they represent a common understanding of war and the experience of war.

What the memorials do represent is the common and ongoing struggle to justify, integrate and reconcile participation in war no matter what role was played. For some, the memorials may appease a conscience; for others they may justify deeds or provide encouragement; for yet others they are a source of pain and produce a sense of loss; and for still others they represent the dark side of human nature and grave social mistakes. These memorials serve as reminders of our continuing need to come to terms with and discover the meaning of the fatal and violent discord of the past.

A second reason to maintain community memories of war is in the profound hope that sober memorials of war will serve to prevent another. Opinions about the utility and necessity of war vary greatly, but rarely is there disagreement on the fact that the experience of war is devastating, costly in many ways, and to be avoided if possible. The monuments, anniversaries and rituals keep repeating the message: whatever was deemed gained or lost was paid for with great cost, war was an unfortunate last resort, do everything to avoid it in the future.

Memorial Day events in the United States are one example of a public ritual or memorial that demonstrates the concept of community memory of war and its dynamic, changing nature. Such is the case with the Memorial Day community parade event in this study. The event has for over 125 years reflected how one community and its various subgroupings remembers its war experience, and it has mirrored national changes in the meaning of and sentiment about war. It is both evidence of and part of the change in the meaning of war in the United States in the late twentieth century. In exploring the meaning of Memorial Day and of this parade in particular, the process by which a community integrates and accommodates itself to its experience of war can be seen, i.e., how the community memory functions.

The historical moment of the 1983 Memorial Day parade brought together complex and diverse ideas about the meaning and purpose of the event, diverse ideas about who held the right to define the meaning and purpose, and individual and group feelings about these issues strong enough to break through the silence and routine of many years to produce public debate and challenge. The Memorial Day parades from 1983 to 1998 are attempts by community members, using a storehouse of symbols, rules, negotiations, language and behavior, to redefine, reclaim and clarify the meaning of this public memorial of war.

Both the veterans and the peace coalition attempted to infuse the Memorial Day parade with all the diverse feelings, experiences, memories, questions, politics and visions that surrounded their musings about war and peace. The community memory of war is not a settled state of mind, but an arena in which all, to some degree, grapple with life and death, and moral and ethical issues. Contrary to one veteran who repeatedly stated that "honoring the dead is all it [the parade] amounts to," I believe it is impossible to identify all the individual layers in this event.

Public Debates/Private Wars: Gender Dimensions of the Conflict

The intent of the non-veteran groups that sought permission to participate in the parade was to make a public statement about alternatives to militarism, and to attempt to instigate some thought or dialogue along those lines in the wider community. The strength and scope of the veterans' resistance to the presence and message of the peace coalition, as well as the media coverage of the events, raised the profile of the controversy in the community and created both public and private debate on a wider range of issues than was originally intended by the peace coalition.

The public debate grew to include significant political questions of rights and responsibilities in participative government. What does it mean to be patriotic? What does freedom of speech guarantee to a citizen and require of a citizen? What relationship does political and economic oppression have to war and militarism? Who "owns" and therefore controls Memorial Day? What makes a country more secure—preparing for war or for peace? Who are the victims of war? Who and what should we mourn?

The public debate on these issues was conducted on both formal and informal levels, was of both a courteous and a crude nature, and extended itself beyond the parade participants. Discussion took place over a mediation table, in the offices of City Hall, and in formal phone conversations and correspondence. In less formal ways ideas were expressed in letters to the editor, editorials, radio talk shows and television interviews. There were also people who chose to make threatening phone calls to veterans and non-veterans alike and to heckle from the sidelines. The debate was joined by the general population, the media, church and civic bodies, and public institutions such as city government and the police. The vigor and emotion with which opinions were stated and the extent of the community response indicate the importance and strength of the meaning embedded in the idea of Memorial Day.

However, the panoply of issues was not wholly encompassed within the public debate. As the Memorial Day conflict was analyzed more deeply, a different set of sensitive, emotional and more personal issues began to emerge within the veteran and non-veteran groups and between these groups. Discomfort and conflict about diverse expressions of loyalty to a group or principle, what was a "real" war and who was a "real" soldier, appropriate gender roles, and perceived homophobia were some of the private wars being fought.

Some examples will illustrate the more personal and private pain experienced in these years. In 1984 when the traditional Memorial Day parade was canceled by veterans to protest the presence of the peace contingent, the Vietnam veterans voted to march with the peace groups in order to honor the dead, but not as an affront to other veterans groups. The Vietnam veterans received accolades from the community for their decision. All veterans were subsequently brought face-to-face with an animosity that existed between those who had fought in the World Wars and those who had served in Vietnam. They were forced to grapple with diverse meanings and experiences of war, with often vastly different political stances, and with organizational philosophies leading in opposite directions.

Within the peace coalition, as the magnitude and intensity of the situation increased, disagreements over territoriality, authority, and decision-making strategies became painful. Individuals, many of them old friends, and groups who believed in and preached consensus, collaboration, non-violence and acceptance of diversity found their values tested and come up wanting. Some friendships did not survive, some groups disbanded. In the face of these internal and emotionally draining issues, each group, veteran and non-veteran found it a struggle to maintain a unified and strong public presence.

The most far-reaching and pervasive issues to influence both the public and private debate, though, were those of gender and, by extension, sexuality. The impact of gender and sexuality issues was multidimensional, manifesting historical, political, social and personal aspects. Women and men entered this conflict with a historical and emotional heritage tied to Memorial Day and to the overall history of war in the United States. They entered this conflict with strongly internalized ideas about appropriate social and political status and roles for themselves and others. The meeting of this collection of individual histories and social expectations produced profound upheaval. Individuals found their memories disturbed, their status challenged, their expectations disrupted, and their assumptions often false. Examination of these issues in their historical and social context not only illuminates this particular study but also gives insight into the dynamic quality and social force of gender and sexual roles.

Women: At War and Peace

It is generally believed that it was women who began the tradition of visiting the graves of Civil War soldiers of the North and South to mourn their deaths and the war itself. John Bodnar, a scholar who writes on patriotic symbols and commemorations states:

> It [Memorial Day] was one of the first public ceremonies in which women played a prominent part, mourning was deemed to be in a women's realm, it was a natural.[5]

This observation is important in two ways. First, it demonstrates that women's participation in a public ceremony was unusual in the mid-1800s, implying that women's proper place was in the private sphere of the home and that only special occasions placed women in the public eye. Second, it shows women assigned to the task of mourning, which required emotion, sentiment, moral reflection on the causes and effects of the war, and a display of the community members' (read *women's*) dependence on and indebtedness to the men who provided their security and stood in their defense. Mourning tasks were seen by men as worthy but "naturally" feminine, not of primary importance in the order of male priorities and easily and properly relegated to women. Men participated as honorees and heroes, the fortunate and brave survivors, held in esteem by the community for the service they had provided. This arrangement of proper male and female roles for the Memorial Day commemoration was consistent with a culture that provided strict gender guidelines for all facets of life, prescribing a separation between public (male) and private (female) spheres.[6]

Memorial Day continues to hold strictly delineated roles for members of the community: specifically, the role and behavior expected of women has remained the same over the course of 125 years, i.e., as those who mourn and honor from a supportive, secondary arena. Despite constant efforts to dismantle, or at least alter, a cultural framework that prescribes appropriate gender roles, Memorial Day remains a reflection of a pervasive standard of limiting, value-ranked, cultural proprieties for women and men. For those involved in the parade organization and negotiation, the presence of gender issues was structural and concrete and also symbolic.

Structural Conflict

The women organizers of the peace coalition and the men who were ideologically aligned with them were continually frustrated at the struggle necessary to gain access to resources, people and bureaucratic considerations at the city level that were readily available to the veterans and to men within their own coalition. They found that the presence of men legitimized and expedited their work with veterans, the press and municipal authorities. They had no access to the networking system within the bureaucracy (usually known as the "old boys' club") that is commonly used to smooth negotiations. Indeed, this networking system operated to their detriment, and the veterans' privilege in this system was strengthened by financial resources unavailable to the peace coalition.

Jane, a peace coalition organizer, described how the women often felt as though they "didn't know how to play the game:"

> The whole year was spent just trying to get into the parade. Really that's all that committee has ever done is attempt to find out what are the rules this year and how do we make sure that we can walk in the parade.[7]

The peace coalition was organized mostly by women—the first year by choice and in subsequent years by necessity because few men in the coalition chose to take a committee position. The women organizers quickly learned that not being taken seriously in the political arena was a major problem to be overcome and that the largest source of that problem was that they were women. They often found themselves in a position of trying to gain power within a system designed to keep them powerless. They were involved in a difficult double bind, committed to advancing the objectives of the peace coalition and to gaining recognition as legitimate negotiators. In several painful instances they felt forced to choose between these goals—either strengthen the parade movement by relying on accepted power brokers in negotiations, thereby diminishing their own role, or compromise on parade achievements but retain their role as negotiators.

One such incident involved a male lawyer from the American Civil Liberties Union (ACLU) who had been retained to properly secure the legal rights of the peace contingent to march in the parade. His method of securing their presence involved behind-the-scenes deals which the organizers could neither rely on nor duplicate the next year.

> The lawyer who worked for us one year . . . He had a lot of problems working, I think, with lesbians, and with women, and he didn't do what we asked him to do. He defined the job he wanted to get done and he did it. He defined it as getting us into the parade. He didn't care, he really quite honestly didn't care how he did it as long as he did it. And he did it through the old boys' system . . . and what happened then is that the next year it created problems for us because we had nothing in writing.[8]

Another instance of the old boys' club seen as the logical and acceptable norm demonstrates how gender-oriented models of decision making were in conflict. The peace coalition was committed to a feminist model of consensus building and shared authority. The veterans operated on a model of delegated decision making and hierarchy. While professing a belief in the model of consensus and the importance of public debate on the issues of militarism, one male peace coalition organizer saw no incongruence in his proposal to get the men from each side together over lunch and settle the conflict once and for all.

> There was one time . . . I fancied a luncheon at the office dining room, with my three-piece suit and a couple of others who were counterparts from the veterans community, in which we could try and

talk about this issue, but somehow when it got into the real activist in the thing—media, third party interventions, threatening behavior—it became so polarized that that didn't seem to make any sense, but I had a fleeting moment of thought about trying big on having lunch, doing lunch over this thing other than a big confrontational thing.[9]

The structural conflicts—lack of access and communication, failure to be seen and recognized as legitimate agents, negotiations circumvented, discrimination at multiple levels of the controversy—plagued and frustrated the peace coalition women and their allies throughout the conflict. These concrete instances of gender bias point to the even more pervasive instances of symbolic gender conflict.

Symbolic Conflict

Goffman cites sexism as the most "fundamental inequality" in society and connects all other structures and interactions to this basic hierarchical premise.[10] Eisler names our Western social order a "culture of dominance" which is founded on the "ranking of one half of humanity over the other."[11] Through centuries this ranking has developed into a system of dominance and control over anyone who is perceived as the weaker "other," but is still primarily based on male control over women. Eisler lists the basic tools of dominance as force or the threat of force, alienation or disregard for relationship, and the promotion of competition.[12] The list is long of those who join Goffman and Eisler in identifying sexism as the basis for structural oppression.[13]

It is in this cultural model of sexism and other forms of dominance that Memorial Day is situated, and it is within this model that the parade and all of the participants operated and displayed gender as a specific axis of conflict. The peace activists (with mostly female leadership) and the veterans (with exclusively male leadership) worked with great fervor toward changing or preserving the meaning of the parade and the interpretation of peace, but they did so within an intransigent, sexist, hierarchical world view that ultimately defined the resources available to each side and limited the possible outcomes to those that would preserve the dominant culture.

The Memorial Day parade conflict is an example of the culture controlling and rewarding the status quo so it essentially stays the same. Adherence to roles within the hierarchy of dominance is so disciplined that conflicts, whether on an individual, group, national or global level, are resolved, almost without exception, within the boundaries of this world view. In a perverse twist of logic, these boundaries even include war and coercion in order to maintain the status quo, but not the possibility of equal partnership or new ways of relating among all persons. There is little, if any, tolerance for a discussion of radical social change or moving from a dominance to a partnership model of relationship.[14]

Despite its pervasive and controlling nature, however, the boundaries of this culture of dominance are being probed and challenged to an ever-increasing degree. Clear and essential questions are being asked, especially from the feminist/womanist movement: questions about the relationships between women and structural violence,[15] women and economic oppression,[16] women and political power,[17] and women and sexuality.[18] The Memorial Day parade conflict is a part of this clarifying activity, for even though the controversy was not seen nor undertaken as primarily a challenge to sexism, it presented to the public, in real and symbolic conflict, two archetypes essential to the existence of sexism and the culture of dominance: the warrior/protector and the peacemaker/nurturer.

Public demonstrations of these symbolic images were manifest in dress and ritual, in parade presentation and in management styles. For all negotiation meetings veterans appeared in military dress and decoration and observed the rituals of saluting. The veterans' dress and actions were interpreted as posturing and efforts at intimidation by the peace coalition negotiators, who had no such dress or ritual available to them. In the parades themselves, veterans' contingents marched in formation, uniformed, with an array of flags, martial music and drills. The peace contingent was made up of men, women and children, many walking as families, pushing strollers. They carried U.S. flags and identifying banners and signs and, at times, sang well-known peace and religious songs. They interacted with parade watchers, in contrast to the veterans who did not overtly acknowledge an audience presence. This contrast in engagement with the watching community is an expression of the differing attitudes about the appropriate status and role for members of the community in relation to war, definition of victim status, who mourns legitimately and ownership of the memories of war.

The manner in which the warrior/veteran and the nurturer/peacemaker each managed the conflict demonstrated their beliefs in how resolution occurs. Offers of mediation were met with threats of court action and, at times, bodily harm. Discussion and consensus building were countered with secret votes. Faith in law, tradition, and the rights of ownership met belief in negotiation, tests of long-held assumptions, and claiming the rights of the community.

Public conflict between the symbolic images of the warrior and the peacemaker, i.e., the veterans and the peace groups, did two things. First, the myth of male dominance was made suspect. The culture of dominance relies on the myth that man is naturally superior and by virtue of this fact dominates and "protects" all those who are inferior, particularly women. Women, as inferior and vulnerable, are assumed to be naturally suited to those less-valued roles of peacemaker and care-giver. But, here, on the main street of this community, contrary to the "natural way of things," peacemakers were challenging warriors, the need or desire for a fighting protector was debated, the scheme of male superiority and female inferiority was disputed, and the traditional acceptance of social roles was not adhered to. Male dominance was publicly subverted and made vulnerable to question.

Second, the issue of sexism was made conspicuous despite its being concealed within many peripheral issues. The parade debate focused on a murky brew of concerns and sexism was kept in obscurity. As the veterans and the peace activists came to embody the classic roles of warrior and peacemaker, the sexism underlying other issues in debate became increasingly conspicuous as the root problem in the controversy.

Some of the organizers realized, to different degrees, that sexism and the resulting gender and sexuality concerns were at the heart of the dispute. Pam, an organizer of the explosive 1984 parade noted:

> It became so obvious right from the very first minute that this was a gender issue, it had nothing to do with peace or war or anything else. It had to do with women who got *out of their place*.[19]

And John, a veteran, working in the peace coalition said:

> The thing is, the veterans don't mind nurturers as long as they know their place, they just don't like uppity nurturers. . . . They like feminine women and when they become feminists and get out there and . . . vie for political power then they don't want any part of that.[20]

Other peace coalition organizers saw the sexism and were very sensitive to the designation of the peace contingent as the "women's parade," recognizing it as implied degradation.

> We resented, or recognized what was happening with this being called the "women's parade."[21]

> One of the things that we often had trouble with was that we were referred to as "the women" rather than as the peace community. . . . It certainly went through the years that we were working. . . . Who did it? . . . I'm not sure if the city did it . . . but I know that the veterans did it and that, uh, I'm fairly certain that the press did it.[22]

No veteran acknowledged that sexism was an underlying problem in the conflict, but their implied understanding of sexism as a social issue showed in their language:

> . . . and then they have their own reviewing stand, the women or the peace group or whatever you call it.

> At the end of the veterans' parade they [the veterans] basically leave and the women's group, it's no longer a really women's group, it's like all sorts of groups. . . .

> . . . and this is what I think some of the women's group, or peace group, perceived.[23]

Other participants walked right into the middle of the fray and rejected the connections between sexism and war, but not without a nod of acknowledgment and some trepidation. What follows is a section of an interview with a couple who worked in the peace coalition, spearheaded a separate, somewhat conservative faction within the peace contingent, and eventually left the parade effort.

N: Well, I guess a lot of it was tied into feminism too. It was like I even, I happen to feel that the Women's Peace Encampment set us back, which was very sad.

R: Even though you went down and helped organize a service there and were very supportive of it, it's just that it became a feminist issue, not a peace issue.

N: I tried you tried so hard, I mean you really didn't say this to anybody that wasn't, you know, you were very careful not to say this, give other people ammunition but I, I felt that very strongly that it really was, it became, I didn't think they really cared as much about, um, the nuclear arms issue as they did about feminism.[24]

Making connections between dominance, sexism and war was seen by some in the peace coalition as diluting and detracting from the core issue of disarmament and peace, rather than contributing to the debate. But the evidence of sexism as an integral part of a dominance mentality was mounting as the controversy continued; the public symbolic conflict between these two classic types of warrior and peacemaker helped facilitate the issue of sexism coming to the fore.

Outcomes: The Community, the Coalitions, the People

This Memorial Day parade conflict has lost its fire and the public's interest, but the impact of the events and challenges beginning in 1983 left their mark on the city community, on groups and organizations, and on individuals.

After more than a decade, a veteran contingent and a social action contingent (there is no longer a peace coalition) still march in the city parade each year. And now it is the norm rather than a conflict. City policies on parades were rewritten as a result of the controversy. The city issued parade permits on a first come, first served basis—a policy which spurred veteran and non-veteran groups to compete for first-place status in the beginning years of conflict. Now in cases of a long-standing history of organizing, as with the veterans, the traditional group has a right of first refusal, but loses this priority status if they do not organize a parade for three years in a row. A permit is then granted to any first applicant. The permit also stipulates that for events of widespread community interest, such as Memorial Day, any community group that meets reasonable criteria cannot be excluded. There has been no controversy over any other parade.

Traditionally, the city had granted monies to the veterans for parade expenses, including paying marching bands. When the city was approached by the peace coalition for equal funding, "equal" translated into discontinuing the veterans' grants. Without this money, the veterans could not pay for professional music, even on a high school level. They resorted to grammar school bands and children's dance studios for entertainment to augment the military band.

The city parade began to become smaller and possibly irrelevant during the very late 1980s and early 1990s. Suburban towns were growing quickly and began having their own holiday parades, celebrations and services. The demand for marching groups and parade participants of all kinds to enhance these parades grew and, consequently, drained the available pool. Coupled with the lack of funds and the conflict linked with the city parade, many groups, veteran and non-veteran, opted for noncontroversial, hometown events.

A major controversy during the parade years, both with the veterans and within the peace coalition, was the overt presence of gay and lesbian antinuclear groups. (In their public stance, they highlighted the fact that gay and lesbian people had been a target Holocaust group and the continuing oppression of homophobia.) The publicness of this sensitive debate in the parade context coincided with the growing nationwide militancy of gay and lesbian rights groups. Though no direct link can be forged between the parade and future city policies on sexual orientation, it is interesting to note that this community has been in the forefront of initiating legislation protecting gay and lesbian rights and extending family benefits to domestic partnerships.

The Memorial Day parade conflict played a role in leading many community groups and organizations to some essential change. Some were strengthened. Some changed focus. Some were sustained beyond what their life may have been without this public rallying point, but have now gone out of existence. Some were born because of the controversy, seeing an opportunity for publicity, and have since died.

The 1984 parade was a watershed year for the Vietnam veterans. Their decision to march with the peace coalition proved to be a healing time for them. Within one year, their membership had swelled threefold to more than five hundred. Veterans struggling in private with their experiences found comfort and support in the association. The community applauded them for the agony of the time and circumstances they bore; with this support, many were now able to feel pride in their personal accomplishments even though they still struggled with the politics. The Vietnam veterans, as a group, also realized a legitimacy within the total veteran community. They now enjoy solid community support. Interestingly, they were instrumental in assisting Desert Storm veterans through the transition from active duty, wanting to help avoid a repeat of their own alienating homecoming experience.

Groups devoted to peace activism are now virtually gone from the community. Increased anti-nuclear sentiment in the 1980s had spurred the growth of many groups and coalitions nationwide. This community was no exception, and the groups that formed saw in the parade a powerful tactic for engaging public debate. The end of the Cold War, the successful negotiation of nuclear treaties and the waning threat of nuclear war forced groups formed around that agenda to either change focus or disband. Most did the latter. Of the groups that changed focus, the predominant new interests were nonviolence, post-Cold War international relations, systemic change of human service policies, and gay and lesbian rights.

A startling and disturbing awareness for many of the peace coalition organizers was the discord that erupted among peace groups and their individual members. Prior to the parade controversy, the groups had worked in easy collaboration, in sympathy with each other's foci on diverse social issues (anti-nuclear, Central America, sanctuary, environment, and so forth). Boundaries, methods, and tactics were defined and individuals gravitated towards their own "issue and action of choice." The intense collaboration required for organizing the parade placed groups and individuals in a position of having to choose among these diverse issues and methodologies to determine the best front to present to the public. When the coalition was forced to choose a public face, the tolerant acceptance of difference disintegrated into discord and struggle over means and message.

The basic choice lay between a coalition-wide anti-nuclear/pro-peace message with individual groups suppressing their own agendas, or each group displaying its own focus and tying it to the peace issue, thereby demonstrating the widespread oppressiveness of war. The "one-front" faction believed simplicity was appropriate in the parade context—that a diverse presentation would be confusing to the public. The "multiple-issue" faction believed this was a teachable moment and that the pervasiveness of a war mentality should be demonstrated. Groups working on more-sensitive issues such as abortion and gay and lesbian rights believed a latent function of the "one-front" argument was to submerge their presence and avoid public discussion or appearance of alignment with these controversial issues. In the end, some groups joined together as an anti-nuclear/pro-peace group, others chose to represent themselves. Consensus was not reached. Discord between groups and individuals persisted. There was no peace in the peace coalition.

The veterans struggled among themselves with issues such as parade ownership and decision-making styles, but the issue of how to present themselves publicly was never in question. They were the norm. They knew what to wear, how to march, and what the audience expected. Their public persona was solid and not questioned; they easily maintained the unified presence that the peace coalition could not achieve.

Beyond the impact on group dynamics lies the effect of the parade on the individuals involved, especially those in leadership positions on both sides. The parade conflict influenced participants in some intense personal ways as they struggled with a range of emotions, changes in relationships, and challenges to abilities, assumptions, beliefs and values. The conflict forced many into a process of self-examination that was uncomfortable, with sometimes rewarding, sometimes surprising results.

The veterans, especially those with war experience, view Memorial Day with great somberness. For many, their memories of war and death are vivid, and war experiences have remained pivotal in their life choices. These memories are life-altering for the veterans and were shared by them with great seriousness and only after a sense of trust and compassion had been established.

Many older veterans viewed the peace coalition efforts as an intrusion, not just on a parade but on their lives and memories. For some, this was a personal attack on who they were as men, on the defining moments of their lives, and on the value of the patriotic duty they had performed. They would fight again, just as fiercely, to defend this parade territory because it was a symbol of their lives.

Many younger veterans, especially of the Vietnam era, more easily discriminated between their experience and the politics of the war and the parade. Their memories were just as sacred and experiences just as life-impacting, but Vietnam itself was not a symbol of patriotic duty or unity and was not territory to be defended as vigorously.

Many of the peace coalition leaders, especially the women, were personally stretched far beyond what they thought were their talents and abilities. The successful organizing of a major public event was the catalyst for some to view their capabilities in a new light. They were proud, felt empowered, and faced fears about themselves and others that had previously immobilized them. Many reassessed who they were and examined goals and life decisions, based at least partially on this experience. Consequently, some people moved, changed jobs, made or broke relationships, and joined or left group affiliations.

The most poignant moments during the interviews—the times when tears came—occurred when individuals described the self-reflection that the parade experience led them to. Public confrontation seemed to be the mirror image of personal interior conflict, questioning and apprehension over what, for many, had been solid and stable ways of looking at the world. Looking at Memorial Day is like unpacking an old trunk in an attic. There are long-forgotten items in the trunk that bring a surge of memories, some with pain, some with delight, some with pride. They are taken out, turned to the light and examined. Some get packed away again; some are let go. But, most times before we even get to the trunk, there is an accumulation of other pieces of our life that have gathered around and we are forced to pick them up at the same time. This searching can be a complicated process, mixing emotions, history, memory and meaning. For those involved in the Memorial Day conflict, their private lives, the things in the trunk, became entangled with the realities of their lives now and the public world around them. The task became making sense of the past and present, a task to be done as individuals and as a community.

Notes

1. Veterans belonging to the American Legion and the Veterans of Foreign Wars (VFW), mostly older men, threatened to cancel the 1984 parade if the peace coalition, referred to by them as "the women," were allowed to march. The coalition was granted a parade permit by the city and the veterans refused to march, breaking a 116-year tradition. The Vietnam veterans, though, believed the symbol of the parade and memorializing their comrades were of greater importance and marched with the peace coalition. These decisions had great ramifications within all veterans organizations.

2. Mary Hedglon, editorial, *Democrate and Chronicle*, 12 May 1991, 1(A).

3. This quote is from a poem entitled "The Blue and the Gray," written shortly after the Civil War by Francis Miles Finch. In the poem he describes the sentiment of decorating the graves of both Confederate and Union soldiers as both healing and reconciling in a spirit that transcends national differences. The verse with this quote reads:

> So with an equal splendor
> The morning sun rays fall,
> With a touch impartially tender,

On the blossoms blooming for all;
Under the sod and the dew,
Waiting the judgment day;
Bordered with gold, the Blue;
Mellowed with gold, the Gray.

4. I refer to the distinction made in chapter one of my dissertation between the word *community*, meant to define a geographic locale or convenient grouping of individuals, and the concept of community, meaning the real, though intangible relationships between people. This essential connectedness is discussed by: R. Bellah, et al., *Habits of the Heart* (Berkeley: University of California Press, 1985); G. Tinder, *Community: Reflections on a Tragic Ideal* (Baton Rouge: Louisiana State University Press, 1980); J. Bernard, *The Sociology of Community* (Glenview, Ill.: Scott, Foresman, 1973); C. Heyward, *Our Passion for Justice* (New York: Pilgrim Press, 1984), D. W. Minar and S. Greer, eds., *The Concept of Community: Readings with Interpretations* (Chicago: Aldine, 1969), M. M. Gergen, *Feminist Thought and the Structure of Knowledge* (New York: New York University Press, 1989).

Each addresses the need to find the ground between profound individualism and the sense of mutual interdependence which preserves our individual selves while recognizing our necessary communion. The depth of this communion or community is enhanced with every experience the group holds in common—the group is creating its past and its stories—building its community of memory (Bellah, *Habits of the Heart*) out of which it acts and through which it is affected.

5. Hedglon, *Democrat and Chronicle*, 1(A).

6. J. Bernard, *The Female World* (New York: Free Press, 1981); S. M. Rothman, *Woman's Proper Place* (New York: Basic Books, 1978).

7. Christine Wagner, *Rediscovering Memorial Day: Politics, Patriotism and Gender*, Ph.D. diss., Syracuse University, 1992, 158.

8. Wagner, *Rediscovering*, 162.

9. Wagner, *Rediscovering*, 168.

10. Erving Goffman, "The Arrangement between the Sexes" *Theory and Society* 4 (Fall 1977): 301.

11. Riane Eisler, *The Chalice and the Blade* (San Francisco: Harper and Row, 1988): xvii.

12. Current or more specific terminology for these tools would be militarization, or quasi-militarization; individualism, including the separatist structures of racism, classism, etc.; and capitalism.

13. D. Adcock, "Fear of 'Other': The Common Root of Sexism and Militarism," in *Reweaving the Web of Life: Feminism and Non-Violence*, ed. P. McAllister (Philadelphia: New Society, 1982); S. deBeauvoir, *The Second Sex* (New York: Alfred A. Knopf, 1952); C. F. Epstein, "Women and Power: The Roles of Women in Politics in the United States," in *Feminist Frontiers: Rethinking Sex, Gender and Society*, ed. L. Richardson and V. Taylor (New York: Random House, 1983); A. Lorde, *Sister Outsider* (Freedom, Calif.: Crossing Press, 1984); R. Morgan, *Sisterhood Is Powerful* (New York: Vintage Books, 1970); B. A. Reardon, *Sexism and the War System* (New York: Teachers College Press, 1985); A. Rich, "Compulsory Heterosexuality and Lesbian Existence," in *Feminist Frontiers*, ed. Richardson and Taylor; D. Warnock, "Patriarchy Is a Killer: What People Concerned about Peace Should Know," in *Reweaving the Web of Life*, ed. McAllister; B. Zanotti, "Patriarchy, a State of War," in *Reweaving the Web of Life*, ed. McAllister.

14. Eisler, *Chalice and the Blade*.

15. J. Stiehm, *Arms and the Enlisted Woman* (Philadelphia: Temple University Press, 1989); B. A. Reardon, *Sexism and the War System*; B. Brock-Utne, *Educating for Peace: A Feminist Perspective* (New York: Pergamon Press, 1985).

16. A. Bookman and S. Morgen, *Women and the Politics of Empowerment* (Philadelphia: Temple University Press, 1988).

17. C. MacKinnon, *Feminism Unmodified: Discourses on Life and Law* (Cambridge Mass.: Harvard University Press, 1987); M. J. Deegan, *American Ritual Dramas: Social Rule and Cultural Meanings* (New York: Greenwood Press, 1989); Bookman and Morgen, *Women and the Politics of Empowerment*.

18. C. Heyward, *Our Passion for Justice* (New York: Pilgrim Press, 1984); S. Welch, *Communities of Resistance and Solidarity* (Maryknoll, N.Y: Orbis Press, 1985); b. hooks, *Feminist Theory: From Margin to Center* (Boston: South End Press, 1984); Lorde, *Sister Outsider*.

19. Wagner, *Rediscovering*, 155.

20. Wagner, *Rediscovering*, 156.

21. Wagner, *Rediscovering*, 156.

22. Wagner *Rediscovering*, 156.

23. Wagner *Rediscovering*, 156.

24. Wagner *Rediscovering*, 157.

Chapter Ten

Swimming against the Tide

Peace Movement Recruitment in an Abeyance Environment

Richard Kendrick

For social conflicts to emerge, Kriesberg argues that individuals must form a sense of themselves as a collective entity in opposition to another group, have a grievance, and believe that taking action will, at least to some extent, redress their grievance.[1] Individuals form a sense of group identity in interaction with others within a specific social context. As they mobilize to pursue conflict goals, they seek to persuade others that there is a problem and that they, too, should take action against it. More and more, researchers are paying attention to these processes of identity formation and extension by individuals acting in concert with one another. Stoecker labels the work of those who have been studying this process as the collective identity approach. He includes in this group the work of Snow, Rochford, Worden, and Benford, who were instrumental in applying frame analysis to the recruitment process. Their work demonstrated how the identities formed by individuals in their interactions as members of social movement organizations (SMOs) are extended to those outside of the SMO for the purpose of obtaining their support and participation.[2]

It is just as important to understand that these interactions occur in specific social and political contexts. Sometimes the environment in which groups are trying to organize is favorable and sometimes it isn't. Favorable environments facilitate communication between those who are organizing for change and those who are targets of recruitment by publicizing the grievance and bringing organizers and potential participants into contact with one another. An important question, though, is how do individuals recruit others for participation in social conflict when the social context in which the recruitment occurs is *not* conducive to recruitment appeals? More specifically, how do SMO members find ways to have contact with those who might become SMO participants, and how do they align their identities with those of the potential participants? This chapter focuses on recruitment processes in peace movement organizations (PMOs) in an abeyance climate to answer these questions. In addition, it sheds light on a problem social movement participants attempt to solve: as people in PMOs attempt to recruit others via their established social networks, what happens when their networks become saturated and limit the ability of PMO members to recruit new participants?

The data for the analysis comes from participant observation and interviews with members of two peace movement organizations in Syracuse, N.Y.: a group affiliated with SANE/Freeze (now called Peace Action), and a group affiliated with Physicians for Social Responsibility (PSR). SANE/Freeze was fairly active during the period of the study (1988-1990), but PSR was much less active. Both groups were attempting to maintain their organizations during a period of relative dormancy for the peace movement.

Background

Participation in the peace movement in the United States "declined" after a peak of activity in 1982,[3] but not all peace movement organizations became inactive. Peace movement cadre participants still tried to recruit participants for their organizations—new cadre participants and new workers—and they attempted to develop new constituents and new adherents.[4] Verta Taylor's work on the "trough" periods of SMO activity calls attention to abeyance structures—those forms of social movement organization that "sustain [movements] in nonreceptive political environments and provide continuity from one stage of mobilization to another."[5]

What is it about the political and social climate that influences the success or failure of SMO activities? Tarrow suggests that SMOs can offer their own interpretations for events, whereas Taylor maintains they need a supportive social and political climate in order to have their interpretations communicated and accepted.[6] Issues become prominent not only as a result of the claims of SMO participants but also through the actions of others who are external to SMOs. McCrea and Markle wrote, "Historical contingencies are extremely important in shaping the evaluation of a claim. Randall Forsberg [who put forth the 'Call to Halt the Nuclear Arms Race' in 1980, which was the rallying document of the Nuclear Weapons Freeze Campaign] may have been brilliant, but she was also in the right place at the right time."[7] But even during abeyance periods, organizations can continue to mount new challenges, new people join, and long-time cadre participants leave.

The recruitment process is complex, and it is particularly difficult for organizations in abeyance. Their potential to recruit is limited by the number of adherents in their recruitment environment. Ordinarily, PMOs could count on external sources, such as the media, for support in developing an adherent pool. In an abeyance context, these sources are less available. Consequently, the recruitment task includes developing the pool of adherents from which recruitment is possible, as well as attempting to contact those who are already sympathetic to the goals of the movement, with little help from other organizations or social institutions.

The Problems of Recruiting in an Abeyance Climate

The social movement literature to date has identified two primary tracks for recruitment: (1) via the social networks of which participants are a part and (2) block recruitment from organizations that are sympathetic to the goals of a social movement organization. As the literature points out, those most likely to become participants in an SMO are individuals well-integrated into society (meaning they have a variety of ties to other people via friendships, family, jobs, and/or community activities).[8] McAdam concluded, "If there is anything approximating a consistent finding in the empirical literature, it is that movement participants are recruited along established lines of interaction."[9]

Lines of interaction can include the personal networks of movement participants or organizations in which participants are involved. In fact, Fireman and Gamson believe that an individual's membership in a group becomes a vehicle for recruitment: "Our argument, then, is that the relationships [of individuals with groups] . . . generate solidarity and that this solidarity becomes an important basis for mobilization."[10]

Being limited to one's own network of individuals and organizations poses a problem for social movement participants. If they recruit others by appealing to those individuals and groups in their own social networks who are likely to be sympathetic to the goals of the SMO, what happens when those networks are exhausted? According to a PSR participant interviewed in my study, this is what happened in Syracuse following their mobilization in the early 1980s:

> The mission of PSR, for the first several years, was educational. It was to alert people to the flawed thinking up there. And that met with, you know, dramatic responses—people interested in hearing it—it was a scary, dramatic message, people were ready to hear it, and it got a lot of coverage and opened a lot of people's eyes, and you could do that for several years. And then people had heard it. And continuing to do it beyond 1985-86 had less and less purpose to take the same old line of a scary message of how dangerous nuclear war is.

How do SMO participants try to overcome this saturation?[11] Do these attempts succeed at recruiting new members in abeyance environments?

There are few descriptions of recruitment processes and techniques or how SMO participants create contexts for recruitment.[12] Most of what has been written takes the point of view of the individual, describing the ways individuals become participants in SMOs.[13] More recently, attention has focused on what transpires between individuals and the SMO participants who are trying to recruit them.

Frame alignment is a particularly compelling way to view SMO participants' attempts to align their "interpretive orientations" with the orientations of others, and Stoecker has situated frame alignment within the larger context of collective identity formation.[14] "Frames are narrow depictions of meaning. Collective identity is much broader and more encompassing—it is the universe of frames that are often linked together."[15] Frame alignment is the process by which SMO members attempt to align their sense of identity with that of others. To the extent they are successful, others are more likely to participate in the work of the SMO. "The [collective identity] approach argues that individuals join social movement action because movement organizers frame issues to match or change recruits' frames."[16] However, this convergence may not be complete. Individual identities are complex and multi-layered, and frame alignment may take place with regards to some aspect(s) of individuals' identities but not others.

Convergence cannot occur at all unless SMO members have contact with potential participants. What has been neglected in the social movement literature to date is how social movement organizations create contexts in which these interactions can take place, contexts which enable SMO participants to connect with individuals outside of their own social networks.[17] Staggenborg began to correct this deficiency with her work on pro- and anti-abortion movement organizations, arguing that SMO participants devise strategies to take advantage of "organizational interaction sites," those institutions and organizations in which SMO adherents are likely to be found.[18] For example, SMO participants may come up with strategies for gaining entry into organizations composed of people who might share movement interests. Peace movement participants may make contact with people who advocate for the homeless to demonstrate how working for peace (reducing military budgets) might provide more resources to spend on fighting homelessness.

In addition to those strategies, however, we also need to pay attention to how SMOs *create* interaction sites—contexts (Rochford's term)—in order to recruit participants.[19] Rochford maintains, "Movement organizations devise strategies by which their adherents can make contact with those people who might be generally sympathetic to the movement's goals and ideology."[20] Movement participants organize their own events and projects to attract adherents and constituents for the purpose of making appeals based to some extent on identity.

At least theoretically, these contexts should improve an organization's opportunities for recruitment. McAdam and Paulsen extend their analysis of the role of social ties in recruitment to the Freedom Summer project to suggest that "the ultimate network structure for a movement would be one in which dense networks of weak bridging ties linked numerous local groups bound together by means of strong interpersonal bonds."[21] The contribution my research makes is to describe those strategies for making contact and to find out if they work.

I conclude that PMO participants develop a variety of contexts for recruitment aimed at breaking out of the boundaries of their own social networks in order to connect with other networks of which they would not normally be a part. These recruitment efforts center around the activities of transitory teams—people working together on specific projects—which provide the organization's cadre participants and workers with a pretext for contacting individuals and organizations with which they might not otherwise have contact. While these strategies work to recruit participants for transitory teams working on these projects, they do not generally succeed in recruiting new cadre participants for the PMOs.

Creating Contexts for Recruitment: The Role of Projects

Observations of SANE/Freeze events and interviews with both SANE/Freeze and PSR participants revealed a process of recruitment by which participants try to tap into various networks of individuals and organizations to which they would not normally have access.[22] There are four goals of these recruitment attempts: (1) to increase the mobilizing potential of the movement by winning new adherents; (2) to identify adherents of the movement; (3) to recruit new supporters for the movement organization; and (4) to recruit new workers and cadre participants. While the term "recruitment" may be too loosely applied to the PMO participants' attempts to build their adherent pool and identify its members, the recruitment *process* for PMOs clearly includes activities designed to win new adherents. PMO participants recognize, as do social movement theorists, that individuals move through levels of participation, and they create projects for the purpose of developing adherent pools, recruiting workers from those pools, and identifying potential cadre participants from among the workers.

There are three types of contexts which SANE/Freeze and PSR participants create: programs, coalition-building activities, and projects. *Programs* are the periodic (monthly in the case of SANE/Freeze) meetings that PMO participants put on, *coalition-building activities* are events designed to bring together participants from a variety of SMOs, and *projects* are tasks of limited duration carried out by transitory teams largely for the purpose of making contact with individuals outside the established networks of social movement participants. All three are important processes for enabling cadre participants to make contact with those outside of their own organization. I will concentrate on the role of projects, because as one SANE/Freeze cadre participant pointed out, they are "the heart of our work." Later, the same person was asked something like, "How is membership tied to projects?" The answer: "[We] scoop people in through the projects." Projects may culminate in one event or a series of events. Projects may be what Marwell and Oliver refer to as "mixed actions" or they may be "cadre actions," projects created and organized by cadre participants to involve others in some limited way as workers on transitory teams.[23] Sometimes projects become institutionalized—develop into their own independent organizations—and thereby form new contexts for cadre participation.

There were two major projects in which SANE/Freeze was engaged while I was doing my research.[24] One project, the Food Arsenal Project, fell into the mixed action category. It was an educational project with the goal of collecting 30,000 cans of food—one can for every weapon in the United States nuclear arsenal—for distribution to Syracuse area food banks. Project participants presented a slide show, designed to demonstrate the link between military spending and hunger, to various groups in the community.

The second project, the Peace Child project, fell into the cadre action category. It involved a theatrical presentation in Syracuse by a group of children from around the world, including the Soviet Union. The show involved local area children in the chorus. Eventually, this project developed into an independent organization of Syracuse area children and their parents. After the major event in August 1989, the children continued to rehearse and sing at other events in the Syracuse area.

How do projects work for recruiting adherents, developing adherents, and winning new supporters?[25] In order to increase the pool of adherents and to recruit supporters, projects create opportunities for PMO participants to influence how people think about the nuclear arms race—people with whom PMO participants would not normally have contact. This goal of projects is typified by a comment heard at a meeting of SANE/Freeze, "We need to try to get in touch and have an honest dialogue with people who are not where we are." When SANE/Freeze was trying to decide whether or not to sponsor the Peace Child project, one of the selling points was that it would be "a wonderful outreach to get people we don't usually get very excited."

As McAdam and Paulsen point out, the recruitment process involves several steps, the first of which is to create "a positive association between the movement and a highly salient identity."[26] This is one of the functions of project work: PMO participants attempt to align their own beliefs with those of potential adherents. Snow et al. refer to these processes as *frame bridging*, which involves the alignment of movement ideologies with those of other individuals and groups who might be presumed to share the movement's interests; *frame amplification*, which involves the "clarification" of values and beliefs by movement participants to increase the salience of the movement's values for potential participants; *frame extension*, which involves linking movement ideologies to seemingly unrelated interests of potential participants in order to tie the movement to the paramount values and beliefs of those to which it is making its appeals; and *frame transformation*, which involves the creation of new understandings among potential participants.[27]

The Food Arsenal and Peace Child projects enabled SANE/Freeze participants to make contact with a variety of other groups in the community, such as church groups and school groups, with which they might not otherwise have contact or to which they might not have an opportunity to make their appeals, using weak ties to form bridges to other organizations. SANE/Freeze participants referred to this as not just "singing to the choir." One example is the way the Peace Child project got off the ground, as described by a SANE/Freeze cadre participant: "So I got some people interested initially just through phone calls, and, you know, asking around who people thought would be interested. . . . I started with people that I knew or knew of . . . and then those people gave me, you know, more names."

Projects provide pretexts for participants to contact individuals about SANE/Freeze issues, people they would otherwise have no reason to contact. While I was interviewing one of the Peace Child organizers, she received a telephone call. When she hung up the telephone, she said something like, "There's an example of someone I wouldn't usually talk to—I've never talked to my son's principal before. But I can talk to him about something like this."

Projects have a good chance of bringing people in, according to PMO participants, because they appeal to a multiplicity of interests. In collective identity terms, PMO participants are engaged in identity convergence through the process of frame alignment. They attempt to make connections between their own identities and those of others by using frame bridging, "the linkage of two or more ideologically congruent but structurally unconnected frames," and frame extension, "attempting to enlarge [one's] adherent pool by portraying [one's] objectives or activities as being congruent with the values or interests of potential adherents."[28] In McAdam and Paulsen's terms, the attempt is made to connect movement interests with individual identities—often at a very abstract level practically devoid of the particulars of movement ideology.[29]

In this respect, the movement takes on the characteristics of a consensus-building movement. As defined by Lofland, consensus-building movements "espouse versions of 'nonpartisanship' and phrase their aims and programs. . . in ways that achieve a facade of consensus."[30] The function of the "facade" is to bring people closer to the movement organization and give the PMO cadre a chance to build bridges between their beliefs with the goal of developing convergent identities. Each of the projects took a different approach to building these ties.

The Food Arsenal Project took a frame-bridging approach, attempting to use what the SANE/Freeze cadre perceived as potentially "connectable" or congruent beliefs, to develop adherents. The bridge connected increases in military spending with reductions in social programs. In the words of a SANE/Freeze cadre participant, "I've always realized if you're spending money one place you can't spend it some other place. If you're making weapons, you can't be feeding the hungry." Other SANE/Freeze cadre participants agreed:

> The Food Arsenal Project has been really exciting because it makes a new tie. . . . It's also making a lot of connections with other people. We've been working together with people who advocate for the hungry, you know, the religious organizations and so on, beyond what we've done in the past so that . . . it's really spreading the word, strengthening our bonds with other parts of the community, and, therefore, strengthening the whole movement.

> You know, there have been people from a lot of different organizations who have not been involved in peace work before who always understood the link between military spending and cuts in social services and all that kind of stuff. And . . . a lot of those people have been very active in the Food Arsenal Project.

The Peace Child project engaged largely in frame extension, connecting potential participants' interests in music, theater, and family with the movement's seemingly unrelated interest in promoting understanding between the United States and the former Soviet Union. The Peace Child project, which involved families interested in theater and music in a show promoting world peace (even though at an abstract level), linked interests which had previously not been connected. And, at this broad level, who could object? As one of the cadre participants told me:

The other thing about Peace Child that's so exciting is that it's . . . really very noncontroversial. I don't think there's anybody . . . that would say O.K., "well, that's a bad idea," because it's just a matter of saying that people can be friends. . . . So it throws things wide open and at the same time it gets people thinking about how people can be friends when their governments are supposed to be enemies. . . . No one is trying to make people think a certain way about peace, but we just want people to start to think about it. The songs have a message, but the play itself doesn't come with any message.

Appeals (or the "pitches," as the participants call them) to potential participants are geared towards the perceived interests of the recruitment targets:

RK: How did you pitch this to the folks that you were calling?

SANE/Freeze cadre participant: I think I focused on the fact that it was an international youth exchange between the United States and the Soviet Union. I told them who I was, that I was from [SANE/Freeze], but I didn't emphasize the Freeze per se. And again, it depended on who I was talking to. People who are peace activists . . . I talked about how I thought it would bring in more people. . . . People who were involved in music I talked about the music . . . and that the music is very appealing to kids. And the people that I knew were most interested in U.S.-Soviet relations, I talked about that aspect. There's a lot to sink your teeth into in a lot of different ways.

Do Projects Work?

It is clear that projects allow PMO participants to appeal to a large number of people, and once having made contact, appeal to many aspects of the social identities of the individuals to whom they are making their "pitches." For example, in promoting the Food Arsenal and Peace Child projects, there were general meetings, auditions, and fund-raising events to which the public was invited. Sign-up sheets were passed around, and the PMO participants got a look at people who may have been interested in participating. One event was described by one of the organizers this way:

[There was] a big [Peace Child] meeting, a couple hundred people. Part of it was a choir of fifty, sixty kids. I think it was fifty. . . . We got a fair number of names from the . . . program. But to some extent we missed a little bit of opportunity in that the clipboard went around, but it didn't get all the way around before the kids and their parents left.

Projects serve to build the pool of adherents and recruit supporters in another way. They usually involve events to which the public is invited and for which the movement hopes to get media attention. The following passage is drawn from field notes:

> [Participant] mentioned that the [Peace Child] project was also ena-
> bling the development of relationships with the media. [Participant]
> mentioned that the some of the children were going to be on a radio
> show and that one of the TV stations was running public service an-
> nouncements for the Peace Child show. Finally, [participant] said that
> [two local stores] were going to sponsor the event. [Participant] said
> that the Peace Child project has enabled, "a whole lot of outreach."

PMO participants succeeded in making news with two projects: the Peace Child program[31] and an appearance by the national SANE/Freeze president, William Sloan Coffin, at a dinner to honor a local PSR participant with a long history of cadre participation in the organization.[32] The projects themselves bring people with whom they might not otherwise interact close to the organization and sometimes generate media attention which gives the PMO exposure to even more people.

Although it is through projects that SANE/Freeze and PSR participants attempt to recruit new participants, the question remains, do they succeed at turning them into supporters, workers, or cadre participants? The evidence indicates that, on the one hand, projects are successful at creating new contexts (and new audiences) for disseminating peace movement participants' views for mobilizing workers into transitory (project) teams. In the case of Peace Child, the project resulted in the creation of a new organization, too. On the other hand, projects don't seem to create fertile soil for recruitment of new cadre participants for the sponsoring organization. One cadre participant commented on the success of mobilizing SANE/Freeze workers for various activities: "One of the advantages [to project work] is that people can get fired up and put in a lot of energy over a short term that they couldn't sustain over a longer period. But . . . that's both an advantage and a disadvantage, I suppose. Maybe instead of trying to activate people at that level, we should be activating people at a level that they could sustain."

The Food Arsenal Project mobilized a number of workers to the project planning team, but it seemed most successful at mobilizing supporters—people who would donate their names, some money, or some food to the canned food drive. According to the SANE/Freeze newsletter a variety of organizations sponsored the project at the outset (ten altogether)—some traditional PMOs (such as PSR and Pax Christi, an affiliate of a national and international Catholic peace movement organization) and other not-so-traditional PMO supporters (like businesses and professional organizations).[33] Over one hundred people attended its kickoff event, a rally in downtown Syracuse, and the project eventually listed thirty-one sponsors, including a number of churches.[34]

Peace Child was successful at mobilizing supporters, too, as a variety of businesses and "other leaders in religion, education, the arts and politics" lent their names and money to the project.[35] In addition, Peace Child was more successful than the Food Arsenal Project at mobilizing workers—both from the ranks of inactive SANE/Freeze members and from among the untapped pool of SANE/Freeze adherents.

The reason seems to be that the cadre's frame extension aligned well with the values of members of their target audiences. One Peace Child participant, an inactive SANE/Freeze member, commented that she became involved because "I saw the SANE/Freeze newsletter piece [about Peace Child], and I gave it to my daughter who loves singing. . . . [The project is] worthwhile. It's fun. The kids are having a good time. [Improving] U.S.-U.S.S.R. relations is a good idea."

Others, for whom participation in Peace Child was their first involvement with a PMO, bought the frame extension and became involved because the project provided a connection between their interests in peace and their emphasis on family and children:

> I saw an ad [about the auditions] in a small newsletter. . . . My son has been identified as musically gifted, so I'm on the lookout for opportunities for him. With a peace theme it's even more exciting.

> My daughter's music teacher recommended that she audition, and she auditioned and was accepted. . . . My daughter watches TV and worries about war. She asks [my husband], "Are you going to have to go off to war?" So, I'm happy to be involved. I'd do anything for peace.

Altogether, the Peace Child project drew 180 children to auditions, of which 147 were selected for the chorus, representing twelve school districts in a four-county area of Central New York.[36] According to one of the organizers of the project, seventy-eight people joined the Peace Child organization as paid members.

Eventually, the Peace Child project became an organization of its own, sponsoring events in the community and changing its name to Creative Response.[37] As such, it has its own requirements for cadre participants, workers, and supporters. In some ways, the new organization could be seen as competing with SANE/Freeze for participants. To the extent that it is, projects which lead to new organizations may be hampering, rather than facilitating, the recruitment efforts of the sponsoring *organization*. On the other hand, if one views the net increase in participants in the *movement* as the goal of the project, then it appears that well-designed projects with broad-based appeal can be vehicles for drawing in people who might not otherwise participate.

Project participation did not feed into recruitment to cadre participation in the sponsoring organization. PMO participants hope that participation in projects will feed into the process by which they recruit cadre participants—recruitment brainstorming. Recruitment brainstorming involves coming up with names of people who might be willing to become cadre participants—people who have participated in the PMO's projects, people who work with PMO participants, people from other organizations that are known to be sympathetic to the PMO's goals, people who have left the PMO but who might be drawn back in, and people who are on the membership list. PMO participants' social networks seem to be most important for recruitment to this specific type of participation—cadre participation. Potential cadre participants are identified in a number of different contexts: board meetings, committee meetings, probably even as a solitary member tries to think of someone to call to serve on the PMO board or a committee. Projects, at least in theory, are supposed to extend the network of individuals upon which PMO cadre participants can call for participation.

In reality, I found very few examples in which cadre participants—defined as participants on the board of SANE/Freeze—were drawn from the ranks of project cadre participants or workers. An analysis of the nominees to the SANE/Freeze board for the period 1989 to 1994 revealed that only one of the thirty-six nominees was drawn from the ranks of those recruited for either the Food Arsenal Project or the Peace Child project.[38] The personal networks of participants seemed more important for recruiting cadre participants than project participation. For example, five of the thirty-six board nominees were recruited from the ranks of a single social service organization that employed several SANE/Freeze participants. It is interesting that three of the nominees were first recruited as workers in the SANE/Freeze campaign against the Persian Gulf War. I explore the reasons why projects may have failed at cadre recruitment in the conclusion.

Conclusion

I began with the questions, how do PMO participants in abeyance organizations attempt to recruit people for participation in peace movement organizations? and how do they break out of the confines of their own social networks to expand the pool of potential recruits? I found that PMO participants create contexts for recruitment through projects—the work of transitory teams. In this way, they come into contact with people and organizations with which they would not ordinarily have contact, and they create the contexts for interaction which make frame alignment possible. In addition, they attempt to make contact with people who might become participants. Projects provide vehicles by which PMO participants can tap into social networks outside of their own.

PMO participants hope they will build the pool of adherents from which they can recruit participants, identify their adherents, recruit new supporters, and recruit new workers and cadre participants. I was not able to evaluate the extent to which the projects created new adherents. Perhaps future research could focus on this question alone. PMO participants were somewhat successful, particularly with the Peace Child project, at *identifying* adherents to at least the most abstract principles of the movement (building a peaceful world). In the case of the Food Arsenal Project, they recruited some workers to participate on the project (transitory) team, and they recruited others for minimal levels of participation as supporters. The Peace Child project, on the other hand, produced a number of new supporters, workers, and cadre participants for the project itself. Together, the projects produced only one cadre participant in the SANE/Freeze organization itself.

Why is this so? The collective identity approach provides some insight into what might be going on. While the SANE/Freeze cadre seemed successful at building ties between their own identities as movement participants and the identities of others, it seemed to be happening at a very abstract level. In collective identity terms, there may not have been very much convergence between the identities of PMO cadre participants and those they recruited as workers to transitory teams. According to Stoecker, it is SMO cadre participants who have the most congruent sense of their own identities in relation to the collective identity of the SMO. "Since SMO involvement requires greater commitment of time, risk, and energy, goals are most focused and identity most developed at this level."[39] In order for workers to become cadre, it may be that the process of identity convergence needs to continue. If it does, then one might hypothesize that the greater the degree of congruence between an individual's identity and that of the collective identity of a movement organization, the more likely it is that the individual will become a cadre participant. Longitudinal data on the development of movement identities might help understand how this process unfolds and how some individuals develop identities that are entirely congruent with the collective identity of a movement organization while others do not. It may also help us to understand the process by which individuals' identities, once congruent, begin to diverge from that of movement organizations, too.

Projects should not be judged solely on their success or failure at recruitment, though. Apart from the stated goal of project development as a vehicle for having contact and making appeals to individuals outside of the PMO, another function might be to provide vehicles for action and the expression of identity for those who are participating in the abeyance organization. If it is true, as Hunt and Benford suggest, that "identities are constructed, reinforced, and transformed by the interactions between and among movement participants and outsiders,"[40] then it follows that activists may need to create vehicles for interaction for the purpose of identity construction, reinforcement, and change. In abeyance climates, this task is made more difficult because the environment does not facilitate communication between organizers of conflict activities and those who might participate in them. Consequently, conflict organizers must create their own contexts for interaction with potential participants.

Furthermore, project participation may very well be what the movement has to offer cadre participants to sustain them in abeyance environments, a platform for the reinforcement and expression of identity. Through project participation, cadre can involve themselves in what Hunt and Benford term "identity talk," stories activists tell which serve several important functions for the PMO and its participants.

> [They] concretize activists' perceptions of a social movement drama . . . , demonstrate activists' extant perceptions of their own personal identities and, at times, their biographies . . . , impute collective identities to the peace movement as a whole and to specific SMOs . . . , demonstrate to the speakers and others that their personal identities are aligned with the collective identities imputed to the

movement or specific SMOs . . . [and accomplish] micromobilization tasks (e.g., recruitment, resource mobilization, commitment).[41]

In sum, projects create opportunities for PMO participants to have contact with those outside of their own networks, and they may be an important means by which PMO cadre maintain a sense of momentum, even in an abeyance environment. The evidence shows that projects help PMO cadre continue to attract supporters and workers, because they are able to create some degree of identity convergence through the frame alignment processes of frame bridging and frame extension. However, the identity convergence achieved appears to be incomplete. Consequently, the project activities of the PMO cadre are less successful at attracting new cadre participants. However, projects may help organizations in abeyance environments by serving as vehicles for sustaining the sense of collective identity so important for engaging in conflict activities and surviving environments that are not particularly hospitable to a movement organization's existence.

Notes

1. L. Kriesberg, *Social Conflicts* (Englewood Cliffs, N.J.: Prentice-Hall, 1982).

2. R. Stoecker, "Community, Movement, Organization: The Problem of Identity Convergence in Collective Action," *Sociological Quarterly* 36 (1995): 111-30; D. A. Snow, E. B. Rochford, Jr., S. K. Worden, and R. D. Benford, "Frame Alignment Processes, Micromobilization, and Movement Participation," *American Sociological Review* 51 (1986): 464-81.

3. F. B. McCrea and G. Markle, *Minutes to Midnight: Nuclear Weapons Protest in America* (Newbury Park, Calif.: Sage, 1989); D. C. Waller, *Congress and the Nuclear Freeze* (Amherst: University of Massachusetts Press, 1987).

4. I use McCarthy and Zald's terms and definitions to categorize participants, constituents, and adherents. *Cadre participants* are people who involve themselves in the decision-making processes of the movement organization and devote significant amounts of their time to it. *Workers* are people who participate from time to time in various activities of the organization, usually as members of transitory teams. *Transitory teams* are groups of workers who devote themselves to completion of a specific task or project. *Constituents* are people who support the organization with time, money, or other contributions of resources. Time commitments of constituents are limited to participation in specific events, such as attending a demonstration or organization fund-raiser. Marullo calls people who support the organization in these limited ways "weak supporters." *Adherents* are people who believe in the goals of the social movement organization. See J. D. McCarthy and M. N. Zald, "Resource Mobilization and Social Movements: A Partial Theory" *American Journal of Sociology* 82 (1977): 1221-27; S. Marullo, "Patterns of Peacemaking in the Local Freeze Campaign," in *Peace Action in the Eighties: Social Science Perspectives*, ed. S. Marullo and J. Lofland (New Brunswick, N.J.: Rutgers University Press, 1990).

5. V. Taylor, "Social Movement Continuity: The Women's Movement in Abeyance," *American Sociological Review* 54 (1989): 761.

6. S. Tarrow, *Struggle, Politics, and Reform: Collective Action, Social Movements, and Cycles of Protest,* Western Societies Program Occasional Paper No. 21 (Ithaca, N.Y.:

Center for International Studies, Cornell University, 1989). See also Taylor, "Social Movement Continuity."

7. McCrea, and Markle, *Minutes to Midnight*, 153.

8. B. Fireman and W. Gamson, "Utilitarian Logic in the Resource Mobilization Perspective," in *The Dynamics of Social Movements*, ed. M. N. Zald and J. D. McCarthy. (Cambridge, Mass.: Winthrop Publishers, 1979), 8-44; L. P. Gerlach and V. H. Hine, *People, Power, Change: Movements of Social Transformation* (New York: Bobbs-Merrill, 1970); G. T. Marx and J. L. Wood, "Strands of Theory and Research in Collective Behavior," in *Annual Review of Sociology,* vol. 1, ed. A. Inkeles, J. Coleman, and J. Smelser (Palo Alto, Calif.: Annual Reviews, 1975), 362-428; A. Oberschall, *Social Conflict and Social Movements* (Englewood Cliffs, N.J.: Prentice-Hall, 1973); F. F. Piven and R. A. Cloward, *Poor People's Movements: Why They Succeed, How They Fail* (New York: Vintage Books, 1977); D. A. Snow, L. A. Zurcher, Jr., and S. Ekland-Olson, "Social Networks and Social Movements: A Microstructural Approach to Differential Recruitment," *American Sociological Review* 45 (1980): 787-801; B. Useem, "Solidarity Model, Breakdown Model, and the Boston Anti-busing Movement," *American Sociological Review* 45 (1980): 357-69; J. L. Wood and W. C. Ng, "Socialization and Student Activism: Examination of a Relationship," in *Research in Social Movements, Conflicts and Change,* vol. 3, ed. L. Kriesberg (Greenwich, Conn.: JAI Press, 1980), 21-43.

9. D. McAdam, *Political Processes and the Development of Black Insurgency* (Chicago: University of Chicago Press, 1982), 44.

10. Fireman and Gamson, "Utilitarian Logic," 22. In addition, as some scholars emphasize, people need to be available for participation. Individuals cannot be so consumed with matters of family, work, friends, and other volunteer commitments that they are not able to participate in social movement organizations. See J. C. Jenkins, "Resource Mobilization Theory and the Study of Social Movements," in *Annual Review of Sociology,* vol. 9, ed. R. H. Turner and J. F. Short, Jr. (Palo Alto, Calif.: Annual Reviews, 1983), 527-53; D. McAdam, "Recruitment to High-Risk Activism: The Case of Freedom Summer," *American Journal of Sociology* 92 (1986): 64-90; Snow, Zurcher, and Ekland-Olson, "Social Networks and Social Movements"; Wood and Ng, "Socialization and Student Activism."

11. Snow et al. also use this term to refer to this phenomenon. See Snow, Rochford, Worden, and Benford. "Frame Alignment Processes."

12. Staggenborg points out that the study of "organizational-level processes" in SMOs has been "neglected." There are, however, analyses of the recruitment appeals of religious movement organizations, but as Lofland points out, "Little that is said [about recruitment to religious movement organizations] can be generalized to workaday, interest group, violent organizations, ad hoc 'organizations,' or even *political* or *ego* movement organizations . . . without exceeding care or caution." My contribution is to examine recruitment processes of a particular kind of SMO, the political movement organization. See S. Staggenborg, "Life-style Preferences and Social Movement Recruitment: Illustrations from the Abortion Conflict," *Social Science Quarterly* 68 (1987): 780; J. Lofland, *Protest* (New Brunswick, N.J.: Transaction Books, 1985), 16.

13. Bromley and Shupe, describing recruitment to the "Moonies," suggest a process of contact by an organization, followed by initial involvement, active involvement, and, eventually, commitment. Like Bromley and Shupe, McAdam outlined a process by which individuals move through various levels of participation, from initial "low risk" involvement, through integration into activist networks ideological socialization, and into "high risk" activism. Toch outlines a process by which Quakers became involved in the Fellowship of Reconciliation (FOR). In that process, Toch claimed that self-identification as a pacifist "of the FOR variety" was important for participation, but the process by which the FOR became integrated into the community of Quakers was not addressed. This work

on recruitment processes emphasizes the social psychological, structural, and relational factors at work in the life of an individual. See D. G. Bromley and A. D. Shupe, Jr. *"Moonies" in America: Cult, Church and Crusade* (Beverly Hills, Calif.: Sage, 1979); McAdam, "Recruitment to High-Risk Activism"; Toch, *The Social Psychology of Social Movements* (Indianapolis, Ind.: Bobbs-Merrill, 1975).

14. Snow, Rochford, Worden, and Benford, "Frame Alignment Processes," 464; Stoecker, "Community, Movement, Organization."

15. Stoecker, "Community, Movement, Organization," 113.

16. Stoecker, "Community, Movement, Organization," 115.

17. D. A. Snow, *The Nichiren Shoshu Movement in America: A Sociological Examination of Its Value Orientation, Recruitment Efforts, and Spread,* Ph.D. diss., University of California at Los Angeles, 1976.

18. Staggenborg, "Life-style Preferences."

19. E. B. Rochford, "Recruitment Strategies, Ideology, and Organization in the Hare Krishna Movement," *Social Problems* 29 (1982): 402.

20. E. B. Rochford, *Hare Krishna in America* (New Brunswick, N.J.: Rutgers University Press, 1985), 150.

21. D. McAdam and R. Paulsen, "Specifying the Relationship between Social Ties and Activism," *American Journal of Sociology* 99 (1993): 665.

22. I conducted participant observations and interviews between September 6, 1988, and January 4, 1990, with two PMOs, chapters of SANE/Freeze and Physicians for Social Responsibility (PSR), and their participants. The data consist of field notes of twenty-one meetings and events of SANE/Freeze and two meetings of PSR at which I was a participant observer; interview notes and transcripts of twenty-eight interviews I conducted with people who participated in those organizations during that period; and journal entries in a diary I kept of miscellaneous events and conversations that bear upon recruitment and participation in SANE/Freeze and PSR.

23. G. Marwell and P. Oliver, "Collective Action Theory and Social Movements Research," in *Research in Social Movements, Conflicts, and Change,* vol. 7, ed. L. Kriesberg (Greenwich, Conn.: JAI Press, 1984), 18.

24. Both SANE/Freeze and PSR participants have created a number of different projects designed to put them in touch with other organizations from which they hoped to develop adherents or win new participants. For example, PSR participants attempted to have a Comprehensive Test Ban resolution endorsed by the local medical society and the faculty of a medical school and they advocated for making a nearby village into a nuclear free zone. SANE/Freeze participants joined Earth Day activities in 1990 (the twentieth anniversary of the event) to develop ties to environmental organizations and they organized a War Toys workshop and began an annual fall holiday Peace Toys sale.

PSR was not engaged in project work at the time I was doing my research. However, many PSR projects were mentioned in interviews with PSR participants. The project mentioned most often was an attempt to influence emergency evacuation plans in Syracuse. A PSR cadre participant summed up the experience: "The group here did meet with people on the . . . county level who were supposedly going to be involved with this kind of planning associated with the [Federal Emergency Management Agency] and demonstrated to the county legislature that this is not a practical way to go, it's wasteful, and won't accomplish anything."

25. The following discussion is based on data drawn from observations of SANE/Freeze meetings and interviews with SANE/Freeze participants. PSR participants did not talk about their projects as vehicles for mobilizing participants, although it was clear from their descriptions of their activities that their projects had that effect.

26. McAdam and Paulsen, "Specifying the Relationship," 647.

27. Snow, Rochford, Worden, and Benford, "Frame Alignment Processes," 467, 472.

28. Snow, Rochford, Worden, and Benford, "Frame Alignment Processes," 467-76.

29. McAdam and Paulsen, "Specifying the Relationship."

30. Lofland, *Polite Protestors: The American Peace Movement of the 1980s* (Syracuse, N.Y.: Syracuse University Press, 1993), 52.

31. C. Boll, "Children of Peace," *Syracuse Post-Standard*, 5 August 1989, 1(B); "'Peace Child': Artistic Exercise in U.S.-Soviet Understanding," *Syracuse Post-Standard*, 11 August 1989, 3(D); L. McGinn, "Heartfelt Performances and Sincerity Carry 'Peace Child'" *Syracuse Post-Standard*, 14 August 1989, 12(C); C. Monk, "Peace Child," *Syracuse Post-Standard*, 10 August 1989, 7(CITY).

32. A. James, "Coffin Leads Community Activists toward a 'Grass-roots' Coalition," *Syracuse Post-Standard*, 23 October 1989, 1(B); J. Knauss, "Ed Swift Has Broad View of His Role as a Healer," *Syracuse Post-Standard,* 21 October 1989, 1(C).

33. "Food Arsenal Update," *Voice for Peace*, October 1988, 2.

34. "Food Arsenal Makes News," *Voice for Peace*, September 1988, 4.

35. "Peace Child Comes to Syracuse," *Voice for Peace*, August 1989, 1; "Peace Child a Tremendous Success," *Voice for Peace*, September 1989, 4.

36."Peace Child Creates a Stir," *Voice for Peace*, May 1989, 9; "Peace Child Chorus Selected," *Voice for Peace*, June 1989, 2.

37. "Peace Child: Creative Response," *Voice for Peace,* July 1992, 3.

38. I analyzed the biographical sketches of nominees to the board which were published in the SANE/Freeze newsletter, *The Voice for Peace* from January 1989 through October 1994.

39. Stoecker, "Community, Movement, Organization," 113.

40. S. A. Hunt and R. D. Benford, "Identity Talk in the Peace and Justice Movement," *Journal of Contemporary Ethnography* 22 (1994): 489.

41. Hunt and Benford, "Identity Talk," 49.

Index

About the Contributors

Sean Byrne is an assistant professor and director of doctoral studies in the Department of Dispute Resolution at Nova Southeastern University. He was the 1994–1995 Theodore Lentz Post-Doctoral Research Fellow at the University of Missouri-St. Louis. He has published in the journals *Ethnos-Nation, International Journal of Group Tensions, International Peacekeeping,* and *Journal of Intergroup Relations,* among others. His books include: *Growing Up in a Divided Society: The Influence of Conflict on Belfast Schoolchildren* (Cranbury, NJ.: Associated University Presses, 1997); *The Politics and Practice of External Economic Assistance in Resolving Protracted Ethnic Conflicts: Lessons from Northern Ireland* (Byrne and Irvin, Washington, D.C.: USIP Press, 2000) and (co-edited) *Conflict and Peaceful Change in Divided Societies: Theories and Applications* (West Hartford, Conn.: Kumarian Press, 2000). Byrne is a native of Ireland.

Verna M. Cavey has spent the last two years in Colorado as a volunteer researcher for AmeriCorps VISTA. She currently teaches, continuing to introduce older students returning to college to the practical, problem-solving nature of the social and behavioral sciences. She received her Ph.D. from Syracuse University.

Celia Cook-Huffman is an educator and training consultant specializing in designing and analyzing conflict resolution systems concerning ethnicity, culture, and gender. She is an associate professor of peace and conflict studies and sociology, the associate director of the Baker Institute at Juniata College, and the director of Baker Mediation Services. She has worked as a mediator for more than twelve years to resolve disputes and train new mediators. She has presented papers and seminars on "Gender Identity and Conflict" and "Social Identity in Intra- and Inter-group Conflict." Cook-Huffman has worked with several area school districts to create peer mediation programs.

Patrick G. Coy is an assistant professor at the Center for Applied Conflict Management and the Department of Political Science at Kent State University. Coy is the editor of and a contributor to *A Revolution of the Heart: Essays on the*

Catholic Worker (Philadelphia: Temple University Press, 1988, and New Society Publishers, 1992). He is the series co-editor and the volume editor of the annual series *Research in Social Movements, Conflicts and Change*. Articles by Coy have appeared in *Sociological Spectrum*, *Peace and Change*, and *Mediation Quarterly*. Chapters by Coy have appeared in *Transnational Social Movements and Global Politics*; *American Catholic Pacifism*; and *Nonviolence: Social and Psychological Issues*. He was formerly the executive director of the Lentz Peace Research Laboratory, the national chairperson of the Fellowship of Reconciliation (FOR), and a fellow of the Albert Einstein Institution.

Bruce W. Dayton is an assistant professor in the Department of Political Science at Syracuse University, where he specializes in both domestic and international environmental affairs, political psychology, and public policy dispute resolution. His doctoral thesis focused on the policy-framing differences found among various stakeholder groups participating in international climate change negotiations. Dayton has been active in community-based environmental advocacy work as well as environmental dispute resolution at the national level as a practitioner with the Center for Policy Negotiation, Boston. His current research examines the ways that environmental discourse can be modeled as an aid to off-the-record policy dialogue initiatives.

Nora Femenia received her Ph.D. in social science at Syracuse University in 1993. In 1994-1995, she was a visiting scholar in Latin American studies at the School of Advanced International Studies, Johns Hopkins University, and also worked with the Interamerican Development Bank designing alternative dispute resolution systems for justice system reform projects in Latin America. She is involved in a mediation project between Argentine decision-makers and Falkland Islanders, through a forum at her website <www.falklands-malvinas.com> Her publications include *National Identity in Times of Crisis: Argentina and the United Kingdom in the Falklands War* (New York: Nova Science Publishers, 1996). She has taught at American University and Nova Southeastern University. She is currently associate faculty at Florida International University.

Timothy Hedeen is a doctoral candidate at Syracuse University and serves on the Board of Directors of the National Association for Community Mediation. He has served as the executive director of community dispute resolution programs in New York and Minnesota and works as a trainer and consultant in conflict resolution. The author of numerous book chapters, journal articles, and training materials, he is an adjunct faculty member of the University of Minnesota's Carlson School of Management and of Metropolitan State University He is an active member of the Society of Professionals in Dispute Resolution, the Conflict Resolution Education Network, the Minnesota Association of Mediators, and the New York State Dispute Resolution Association.

Michael W. Hovey is coordinator of peace and justice education at Iona College in New Rochelle, NY. His dissertation examined the role played by non-governmental organizations (NGOs) at the United Nations in gaining recognition of the human right of conscientious objection. His publications include "Interceding at the United Nations: The Human Right of Conscientious Objection," in *Transnational Social Movements and Global Politics: Sovereignty beyond the State*, edited by Jackie Smith, Ron Pagnucco, and Charles Chatfield (Syracuse, N.Y.: Syracuse University Press, 1997), and "Ethics of Conscientious Objection," coauthored with Gordon C. Zahn, in *Encyclopedia of Violence, Peace and Conflict* (San Diego, Calif.: Academic Press, 1999).

Richard Kendrick is associate professor of sociology and anthropology at the State University of New York (SUNY) at Cortland. He received a Ph.D. in social science at Syracuse University in 1990. He teaches Introduction to Sociology, research methods courses, and courses on social and interpersonal conflict. His research interests include recruitment and participation in social movements, service learning, and the integration of academics and activism. His most recent publication is "Building Campus Community Connections: Using Service-Learning in Sociology Courses," in *Cultivating the Sociological Imagination: Concepts and Models for Service-Learning in Sociology* (Washington, DC: American Association for Higher Education), and he is currently working on an introduction to a statistics textbook.

Ross A. Klein is an associate professor at the School of Social Work, Memorial University of Newfoundland. In addition to completing research on disputes over fishing rights, he has served as an on-camera analyst for CBC and CTV in their coverage of Canada's fishery disputes with the United States and with the Spain and Portugal, has developed Anger Management Programs for use in correctional institutions, and has served as associate editor of the *Canadian Review of Sociology and Anthropology*. His current work includes an interest in building nonviolent communities and in integrating nonviolence in social work policies and programs.

Gina Petonito received a Ph.D. in sociology in 1992 from Syracuse University. She is currently on the faculty at Western Illinois University in the Department of Sociology and Anthropology. Previously, she was in the Sociology Department at Alma College in Alma, Michigan, where she was co-director of the Peacemaking in Conflict Resolution Program. Her chapter in much earlier incarnations provided the basis for chapter 4 of her dissertation, "Constructing the Enemy: Justifying Japanese Internment during World War II" (1992) and was presented at the meetings of the American Sociological Association in 1991.

Brian Polkinghorn is associate professor of conflict resolution in the Department of Dispute Resolution at Nova Southeastern University. He is the director of practicum and field research for the masters and doctoral programs and is an advisor to the U.S. Commission on National Security. As an environmental mediator Brian works on cases in North and South America, Africa, the Middle East and Europe. He publishes applied research on peace intervention, environmental policy, geology, and oceanography. Currently Brian is associate professor of conflict analysis and dispute resolution and the executive director of the Center for Conflict Resolution at Salisbury State University.

Anna Snyder teaches conflict resolution at the University of Winnipeg, Canada, through Menno Simons College, an institute that offers an undergraduate degree in conflict resolution. During 1998-1999, she taught at the University of Missouri-St. Louis as the Theodore Lentz Peace and Conflict Resolution Research Post-Doctoral Fellow. She has worked for many years as a peace activist and has three degrees in peace studies: a B.A. in peace studies from Manchester College in Indiana; an M.A. in international peace studies from the University of Notre Dame, South Bend, Ind.; and a Ph.D. in social science in affiliation with the Program on the Analysis and Resolution of Conflicts at Syracuse University, N.Y. Her current research focuses on women's peace movements.

Christine Wagner is the justice and peace coordinator for the Sisters of St. Joseph of Rochester, N.Y. She received a Ph.D. in social science from Syracuse University in 1993. She serves as the president of the Board of the Judicial Process Commission of Rochester, providing conflict resolution training in schools and the community. She also serves on the board of St. Joseph's Neighborhood Center in downtown Rochester, providing mediation services to the community. She teaches sociology part-time at Nazareth College.

Lynne M. Woehrle is an assistant professor of sociology and coordinator of the Peace and Conflict Studies minor at Wilson College in south-central Pennsylvania. She has published articles in *Women's Studies Quarterly, Sociological Spectrum, AssesmentUPdate,* and *Peace Review.* Book chapters by Woehrle have appeared in *Nonviolence: Social and Psychological Issues,* and *The Women and War Reader.* She contributed to *The Encyclopedia of Violence, Peace and Conflict,* and the *Encyclopedia of Sociology* (2d ed). She was the principal investigator in an evaluation of conflict resolution programs in the local schools. She serves as chair of the Peace Studies Association (2000-2001), an international organization for academics in the fields of peace and conflict studies.